A Million Miles Ago

Neale Shilton

Haynes®

Foulis

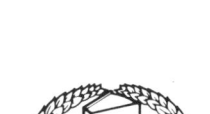

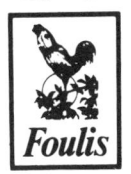

ISBN 0 85429 313 2

© Neale Shilton

First published October 1982

All rights reserved. No part of this book may be reproduced or transmitted in any form or by any means, electronic or mechanical, including photocopying, recording or by any information storage or retrieval system, without permission in writing from the copyright holder.

A FOULIS Motorcycling book

Printed in England by the publishers
Haynes Publishing Group
Sparkford, Yeovil, Somerset BA22 7JJ, England

Distributed in North America by
Haynes Publications Inc
861 Lawrence Drive, Newbury Park, California 91320 USA

Editor: **Jeff Clew**
Cover design: **Phill Jennings**

Contents

Chapter One	As it was in the Beginning	9
Chapter Two	The New Triumph Representative	23
Chapter Three	The Grand Prix Triumph	45
Chapter Four	My Third Meriden Year	53
Chapter Five	The Montlhéry Story	63
Chapter Six	The Shape of Things to Come	79
Chapter Seven	The 1956 Triumph World Speed Record	95
Chapter Eight	Birth of the Bonneville and the Saint	105
Chapter Nine	Never a dull moment	119
Chapter Ten	The Turning Point	133
Chapter Eleven	The Beginning of the End	147
Chapter Twelve	Farewell to Meriden	163
Chapter Thirteen	The Interpol Story	181
Chapter Fourteen	The Circuit Des Pyrenees	197
Chapter Fifteen	The End of the Commando and Trident	221
Chapter Sixteen	Per Ardua ad BMW	241
Chapter Seventeen	The Chiswick Chapter	253
Chapter Eighteen	The Sussex Police Saga	267
Chapter Nineteen	The Last Lap	277
Epilogue		290
Index		294

Dedication

This book is dedicated to the thousands of men and women who worked in the BSA, Norton and Triumph factories and took pride in the machines they built.

I believe, for the reasons set out in this book, that one of the causes of the collapse of the Industry was bad decisions by Management who failed to appreciate the pride and interest in the machines, both of their owners and the people who made them.

Acknowledgements

To the numerous friends I have been privileged to make in many countries throughout my life with motorcycles, I am grateful for all the kindness and help they have given to me. Their friendships have enriched these pages.

For the encouragement which made this book possible and for many of its photographs, I owe special thanks to:

Sgt. John Baker, West Midlands Police
Bob Burnie
Jeff Clew
Roy Cope
Ivor Davies
Capt. D.J. Elson, Royal Signals
Freddie Frith O.B.E.
Cliff Halsall, Assistant Chief Constable, Cheshire Constabulary
Mike Jackson
Tony Jefferies
Jock Hitchcock
Jack Mercer
Metropolitan Police 'B' and 'P' Departments
Kim Reinhardt
Bill Slocombe
Min Squirrel
Jonathan Vickers
Jack Williams

Chapter One

The 1930 500 cc Rudge Special, as good looking as the rider, Jack Williams of Cheltenham. He made his debut in the Island the following year and finished 11th in the Senior TT on a Rudge. He later became a member of the Norton racing team. [Cheltenham Newspaper Co. Ltd.]

Chapter One

As it was in the Beginning

THE FIRST of more than a million motorcycling miles is still quite clear in my memory, although it happened more than fifty years ago. On that day began a life-time which became more and more involved with motorcycles, and a few months ago I made what I felt was a pilgrimage to the place where I first experienced the excitement of a schoolboy — opening the throttle lever of a motorcycle and thrilling at the response of the engine to my command. The road along which the 350 cc Matchless took me that day was the private one which runs through Arbury Park, near my home town in Warwickshire. On the Arbury estate is Mill Farm, the Mill on the Floss of authoress George Eliot, who lived at South Farm nearby. The happiest times of my school years were those I spent at Mill Farm with the Pountney family, whose son George taught me the functions of camshafts, big ends, pushrods, clutch plates, and all the other components which riders in those days needed to understand. George had a 350 cc Matchless of the latest type and in the early morning we would ride it down the farm track to South Lodge, where I would open the park gates and climb back on the pillion seat for the exhilarating two twisty miles to North Lodge. Inevitably the early morning exercise was reported to the owner of the park, Sir Francis Newdigate,

Chapter One

once Governor General of Tasmania. Having risen early from his bed at the stately hall, his black cloaked figure under the oak trees was enough to put George off his racing line through the bends. It was also enough to put an end to Arbury Park Grand Prix practice, but not before I had been permitted to make my first solo on the Matchless. The traditional events in a young man's life, his first kiss, the first love affair and the first awakening of sexual desires, meant nothing, and were insignificant in comparison with the first solo. Perhaps it can be claimed that the same pulse rate and sense of achievement follow the first parachute drop or the first aircraft solo, but by that time, efficient training and preparations have dulled the feeling of individual adventure.

My nostalgic pilgrimage back to Arbury Park and Mill Farm was tinged with sadness, as most pilgrimages often are. The road from North Lodge had not been repaired for many years and Arbury Hall, now taken over by the National Trust, was empty and deserted. The autumn leaves were falling from the centuries old oak trees under which Sir Francis had stood to watch the Matchless go by, an old gentleman observing and perhaps envying two boys in the spring of their youth. Now as I went on to cross the moss-covered stone bridge which led to Mill Farm, I realised why I had felt compelled to go back to Arbury in the autumn of my life. Here where my love of motorcycling had begun, I would start the long journey I had planned through England, Scotland and Wales, retracing the roads I had ridden so many times on Triumphs, Nortons and BMW and making my farewell visits to some of the many friends I had made throughout the world during my long years in the motorcycle industry.

At Mill Farm, I found my old friend George was still alive, but too ill to see me. His sons had heard him speak of the days when we shared our affection for motorcycles and they took me to the barn where lay what remained of the Matchless. I would like to have told George what he and that machine had meant to me and of the adventures I had experienced in Africa on another Matchless, years later. I looked again at the long silent mill wheel and the stream where I had many times fished for pike. I closed my eyes for a few moments, looking back to those boyhood years then, with a last look at the Mill on the Floss, I began my nostalgic journey.

On leaving Bablake school in Coventry it was inevitable that I began work at the Rudge Whitworth factory, despite the wish of my father that I should become a parson. I became junior member of the Service Department in 1929, the year in which Tyrell Smith and Ernie Nott were third and fifth respectively in the Senior TT. Tyrell had broken three ribs in a crash at Glen Helen and against all the rules had restarted the wrong way of the course. He and Ernie were at once my idols and were to become my close friends at Triumph Meriden after the war. Frequently I found some reason to visit the Rudge Experimental Department when a racing engine was being run on the test bed. After becoming a nuisance in

As it was in the Beginning

the Repair Shop, I was finally permitted by the foreman, Doug Lamb, to ride machines down to the Road Test Department and my employment nearly came to an early end when the throttle slide jammed on one of the famous 500 cc Ulster models. I was impatient to ride on the open road but it would be a long time before I could afford to buy even a second hand machine. Then one day I met another of my idols, the great Walter Handley, who had a motorcycle business in Birmingham. I was able to be of some small assistance to him with a Rudge which needed attention and when I visited his premises at Holloway Head to see the Rudge on which he had won the 1930 Senior TT, he offered to loan me a machine for the journey home. It was a TT Replica Triumph and I could keep it for a whole week. That week will never be forgotten. Very early each morning I was a TT rider along the lanes between Nuneaton, Fillongley and Meriden, and I was sad when I rode the Triumph back to Birmingham. Walter, who incidentally taught the first Mrs. Edward Turner to fly, was killed during the war when his aircraft caught fire.

I had saved a few pounds and was a little nearer to buying my first machine when one day looking around a corner of the Repair Shop, I discovered the Rudge of my dreams. Dusty and with dulled plating, it was a genuine racer, with special petrol tank, quick-action Doherty twistgrip, racing Dunlops and open exhaust pipes. Surely not for sale I thought, but I enquired, or to be more accurate, I pleaded. A few days later the dream came true and I was the proud possessor of the machine which Frank Longman had ridden in the 1927 Senior TT. The crankcase casting was Elektron alloy but it was also porous, which is why he retired in the race with diminishing oil pressure. The porosity did not bother me although the consumption of Castrol R damaged my pocket money. I raced the Rudge at the old Syston Park and Gopsall tracks, but it deserved more than the moderate success I achieved. It had no lighting system, of course, and on the occasions when I rode after dark I used a couple of cycle lamps, which were only slightly legal and of no use for navigation. One dark wet night I did not see the pedal cycle the Police Officer was pushing, and the resultant court fine and costs meant a sad parting with the Rudge. Paradoxically it went to Percy Blamire, who had lost a leg testing a sister machine for the 1927 Senior Race. Years later he became a fine pilot and won the King's Cup Air Race.

Like all other employees at the Crow Lane factory, I was proud to be with Rudge in 1930, which was the great year of racing success. Three of the new radial head 350 cc models were ridden by Tyrell Smith, Ernie Nott and Graham Walker, and they took the first three places in that order. In the Senior, Walter Handley scored another first place for the marque, with Walker second, and Tyrell and Ernie in sixth and seventh places. The new 350 cc had a dream debut but disastrous commercial consequences. The design and development team was led by the brilliant George Hack, who later was to do fine work for the Bristol Air-

Chapter One

Jack Williams on a 1934 camshaft-engined works Norton. Judging by the tyres, it was probably prepared for one of the Red Marley hill climbs, where Jack had many successes.

craft Company. The Managing Director was very anxious to get a TT win and George Hack had enough confidence in the new engine to be certain it was a potential winner. However, he warned that it was essentially designed for racing and was not a viable proposition for commercial manufacture. In particular, the radially-disposed four valves involved a complicated transverse rocker arm arrangement with sixteen wearing points which could not be adequately lubricated. They would last the race but the wear rate would probibit any thought of putting a catalogue version of the machine on the market. Whether to achieve racing success with machines which could not pay commercial dividends is a question which has confronted more than one factory. As Edward Turner once

As it was in the Beginning

said, prestige is all very well if you can afford it. In the Rudge case, the factory needed it, but certainly could not afford it. Hack and his team achieved complete success in the Island and other classic events on the Continent, but in 1931 Norton took command. Despite the advice of George Hack, the radial 350 went into production and quickly proved to be an expensive mistake. The insoluble problem of rocker gear lubrication was compounded by wholesale failure of the dynamo drive. The driving sprocket was riveted to the engine crankshaft sprocket and when the rivets became loose, which was inevitable, they, with their sprocket fell into the primary drive chain case with disastrous consequences. Winning the TT cost the company a great deal of money and the factory struggled on into a future of declining fortunes.

I stayed at Rudge for five years and learned a great deal, which was to prove very valuable later on. Those were the days when dirt track speedway racing became a colourful attraction and began to produce such famous names as Squib Burton, Art Pechar, Tommy Farndon, Jack and Norman Parker, Ginger Lees, Syd Jackson and Sprouts Elder. The dirt Douglas, as we called it, was predominant, and with its flat twin engine and long wheelbase it was spectacular as it showered the fencing with cinders. The Americans brought over their shorter wheelbase Harley Peashooters as they called them, not as quick as the Douglas but able to stay nearer the inside line. Rudge got into the business with an Ulster-engined model, but it did not handle well enough. Syd Jackson from Kenilworth bought one and came to Rudge one day with the answer to the problem. A Coventry engineer friend had worked on the Rudge frame and moved the engine mounting backwards several inches. Syd left the new frame with me for a couple of hours whilst he made other calls, and by the time he came back, the Design Department had the measurements. New frames went into production quickly and were a great success. They marked the end of the Douglas era but they also removed much of the colourful speedway spectacle, now that riders could stay close to the inside line. One morning, one of the great American riders, Sprouts Elder, came to the factory and bought a couple of the new Rudges to use the same evening at Brandon Speedway, near Coventry. For some reason, maybe because I counted the fivers, I remember that they cost £85 each. I went along to Brandon with him and earned my first money as a mechanic. Soon afterwards I began a short career as a speedway rider, when I shared a Rudge in partnership with a home town friend Wilf Buckley, who later became a senior Police Officer. After I had won a novice semi-final race, Wilf took over for the final and was leading on the very last bend when he tangled with the second man. The Rudge was very distorted and a valve had dropped when the engine revs went way beyond the red line. My dreams of a speedway future ended that evening, and I had to be content with the less spectacular grass tracks.

For several years before the war I was out of the motorcycle business, but

Chapter One

Williams and the Norton in full flight at Red Marley.

still very much involved with Rudge machines, putting to profitable use the knowledge and experience I had gained at the factory. My workshop always had some model or other for overhaul or tuning and the roads around Nuneaton became my test tracks. My 500 Ulster, with its copper extension exhaust pipes, was my pride and joy, but it attracted the attention of the Warwickshire Police, who added to my running costs with a couple of fines.

On Thursday 31 August 1939, the 6 pm news announced the call up of all military reservists — and I had signed to become T 74677 only one month before. The following morning I gave the Rudge a coating of preservative grease and put it away for what proved to be the last time, for I never saw it again. I went to Feltham, and a week later to France, to begin the six years of my life in uniform.

As it was in the Beginning

However there were to be plenty of opportunities to continue enjoying my love of motorcycling.

In the Loire valley there is the village of La Chapelle sur Erdre and at the end of the tree-lined road which leaves the square and passes by the church, there is the Château de Sevilly, in beautiful grounds sloping down to the river. I called there a year or two ago on my way to ride in the Circuit des Pyrenees, and I talked to the Count de Sevilly about the time I had spent there in 1939/40. The park was then crowded with large tents, full of vehicle equipment, spare parts and tyres, enough to maintain the trucks, cars and motorcycles of several Army Divisions. For weeks I unpacked and stored parts for Nortons, Enfields, Triumphs, Matchlesses, Ariels and Humber cars, most of which finished up in the river when we left in June. In the severe winter conditions I slept in a packing case which had contained a Humber front axle, but I had to move for a while to a hospital bed after collecting broken ribs playing rugby football for the Army against a French university.

One of the machines used by the regiment's despatch riders was a 1939 Tiger 100 on which I took a ride whenever I could. I well remember the day when an inspecting Major came from Command HQ and asked for a ride on the Tiger. The Sergeant Major was very reluctant either to risk the machine with an officer, or vice-versa, and he advised great caution as the visitor started the engine. He need not have been worried for the Major was none other than the legendary Jimmy Simpson, with 24 TT rides to his credit, numerous record laps and finally his first win when he rode a Rudge on his last Island appearance. After the war I was proud to number Jimmy amongst my friends.

My last ride in France was particularly memorable and to my fondness for motorcycling I almost certainly owe my life. The evacuation from Dunkirk was all over by the time my unit moved out and headed for the Atlantic coast, hoping to get to St Nazaire before the German columns cut the roads. I was in the first truck, having foolishly mentioned that I knew the route. When we finally arrived at St Nazaire airfield it was full of vehicles of all kinds and bombers were busy dropping their loads on evacuation ships, having already mined the harbour exit. There seemed little point in joining the exodus along the road which led down to the jetty from which the Royal Navy was running a hazardous ferry service out to the Cunard liner Lancastria. With me was my good friend Len Langhorn, who had been a member of the Army Team which rode in the suddenly-abandoned 1939 International Six Days Trial in Germany. We soon discovered a couple of Triumphs and spent an hour or so racing around what was left of the airfield perimeter until the petrol tanks were empty. Then we joined the few stragglers making their way to the harbour and as we neared the jetty there were two loud explosions. The Lancastria had taken two direct hits and she went down very quickly, taking thousands with her. Two Staff Sergeants had good reason to

Chapter One

This 1938 photograph of Jack Williams was taken at the Wroughton, Wiltshire Mountain Grass Track, the type of event which was the forerunner of motocross. There is little evidence of motorcyclists amongst the spectators.

As it was in the Beginning

thank their enthusiasm for motorcycling. We got back to England on the Ulster Prince, and were later sent for to answer a charge of using WD vehicles without permission. Rather like Drake making the Spanish Armada wait whilst he finished his game of bowls, the German invasion had to wait whilst the British Army disciplined two Staff Sergeants. Of course we had the complete answer. We disliked leaving motorcycles behind for the enemy so we had drained the oil tanks and ridden until the engines were wrecked. The Colonel smiled, but dismissed the charge. After defending Bognor Regis with one Bren gun and one drum of ammunition, the rest of the war years added thousands of motorcycling miles to my log book, starting when I was sent to the Officer Training Unit at Southend. Many of the nights during the course were spent on convoy training, and with most of my colleagues preferring the front seat of a Bedford truck, I had no problem in satisfying my preference for a 350 G3/L Matchless. I became very fond of this Woolwich-made machine and with masked headlamp I led convoys through many dark Essex lanes, night after night. Months later, I was to ride Matchlesses in very different conditions, thousands of miles away.

At the beginning of 1942, I watched the Scottish coast fall astern as the convoy headed into the rough and dark Atlantic. A week later my ship made its slow way back down the Clyde, after an unpleasant affair which was classed as justifying survivors' leave. After being patched up in dry dock she made another attempt, and a month later arrived in Capetown. Every day of the month I lectured on motorcycles, dismantling and re-assembling Rudge engines and gearboxes on the blackboard. Most of the 10,000 passengers must have attended, but perhaps this was because the alternative lectures were on subjects such as politics and accountancy. However, as I have since confirmed, most men are or have been, interested in motorcycles, the most notable exceptions being some of the board room directors of the post-war British industry who have later places in this book.

After Capetown, the new convoy separated somewhere in the Indian Ocean, and my Dutch ship put us ashore at Mombasa, which I thought curious because my draft had been kitted out for Burma. However, at journey's end 300 miles further on, we arrived at the Command Training Depot, Mbgathi, where we were to help train the 11th East Africa Division being formed for service in Burma. We were to transform bush natives into soldiers, drivers, cooks, mechanics, nursing orderlies, and all the other experts required to help the 14th Army defeat the Japanese. I thus became a driving instructor, but suggested that I might usefully add despatch rider training to my duties. The Adjutant agreed, but recommended me to take a look at the only machines in the camp. They were a couple of Harley-Davidsons which, to say the least, had not been given tender care, and to my amazement a 1936 Rudge Special which looked in reasonable condition from a few yards away. A closer look revealed a sad deficiency. The front fork coil

Chapter One

Williams and the Norton on which he finished 10th in the 1937 Junior TT. He finished in the same position in the Senior that year, also on a Norton. [S.R. Keig Ltd.]

spring was no longer there and had been replaced by a solid ten inch bolt, which meant no front suspension. Rear suspension had not arrived at the time the Rudge was manufactured and so to ride this machine was going to be an unpleasant experience which could not be inflicted upon a trainee DR of the King's African Rifles.

There was a fourth machine which, when removed from its protective covers, made life suddenly more promising. It was a 350 Matchless in excellent condition and this had to be mine. I reported to the Adjutant that I had two Harleys for DR training and a Matchless for personal supervision use. He gently but firmly corrected me. The Matchless was solely and exclusively for the use of the Brigadier. I was surprised that such a senior officer should need a motorcycle when he could use a Humber Hawk staff car and I said so. Then the Adjutant warned that the Brigadier was the famous Bill Bennett, known in the Army as 'Bicycle Bill' because of his enthusiasm for motorcycling. It was the only Matchless in the Command and the Brigadier had a habit of collecting it at any time. I had heard of this legendary motorcycling Brigadier and wondered how an ordinary Lieutenant could persuade him to loan the Matchless occasionally. The Adjutant said it would be much easier to borrow his staff car! The problem was solved

As it was in the Beginning

253268 Lieutenant, Kings African Rifles. On the road to Abyssinia 1943.

when the Brigadier left the Command and was unable to take the Matchless with him.

One of my favourite rides was to the top of the Ngong Hills, which are the Sheba's Breasts in Rider Haggard's classic, King Solomon's Mines. From the summit of 10,000 feet there is a breathtaking view of the Great Rift Valley, one of the wonders of the world, and formed millions of years ago when the earth's crust cooled down. The Great Rift begins in the south of the African Continent and runs northwards for thousands of miles into the Middle East. Looking down through binoculars from Ngong, the bare surface of the Rift, devoid of any trees or vegetation, looked firm enough, and the temptation to attempt a motorcycle crossing began. It would have been too risky to go alone across miles of burning desert as a machine failure could have fatal consequences. Even a successful crossing could meet problems in finding a way up the steep hills the other side, so far away that the binoculars could not penetrate the heat haze and judge the distance. There was also the initial difficulty of finding a way down from the Ngong Hills to the floor of the Rift. As I looked down at this barren and forbidding vastness, I thought that the lines by Lord Tennyson, 'Where no one comes or hath come since the making of the world', fitted the scene very well.

Chapter One

Certainly nobody ever crossed this desolate waste, which seemed a good reason why I should suggest to my friend Bing Bingham that he and I should attempt it. He could take a Harley and I would use the Rudge with its solid front forks. Our official reason would be to find a route difficult enough for advanced despatch rider training but we would only say so afterwards, if necessary.

Bing was friend enough to join me, and on a Sunday dawn we rode away, climbing to Ngong where we paused to look south to the glory of Kilimanjaro mountain, its snow cap coloured pink by the rising sun, and northwards to the peaks of Mount Kenya, glorious in the clear sky. Then on downwards towards the still dark bed of the Rift. We followed rhino tracks until they ended where vegetation no longer existed and we had passed the point of no return. It took a long time to reach the bottom and brake drums became as hot as the engines. The surface, which had looked firm thorough binoculars, was very different, as I should have known. The old volcanoes which I had seen from the Ngong summit had been dead for more than a thousand years, but the dust of their eruptions still lay deep on the bed of the Rift. There was no way back and we started towards the far away hills. It was bottom gear, plus leg power and frequent stops when the machines found particularly deep dust. The distant hills seemed as far away as ever as the hours went by, and the heat soon resembled that of oven temperature. The Harley needed frequent clutch adjustment and we praised the designer who had made it possible to restore clutch grip time after time. As the sun descended behind the hills, now only several miles away, with less than an hour of daylight remaining, the last turn of adjustment was made and the Harley gave up just short of the foothills. There it was abandoned and unless someone has used a helicopter, it is still there. Bing walked to the foothills and led the way out of the Rift. Four hours later we reached camp, just too late to wash the volcanic dust from our throats in the mess bar. The Rudge was of little use afterwards. Rift dust is very abrasive and the lack of compression told what it had done to the engine internals, as well as to wear out the rear chain and sprocket. However the Rift had been crossed and a decayed Harley remains a monument to what was really a foolhardy idea.

A few months later I left Mbgathi with a Transport Company, and took along the Matchless, on which I was to cover thousands of miles on convoys between Eritrea to the north and Rhodesia to the south. The thick clouds of dust throughout most of the year extended the distance between vehicles to several hundred yards and, from nose to tail, the convoy often stretched for five miles. Any village where there was an Indian trader shop, and there were very few without, meant beer and temptation for the tail end African drivers to stop. There had been all too many instances of wrecked trucks caused by a combination of beer and the hurry to catch up with the convoy. I decided that with the help of the Matchless, this was not going to happen to any convoy of mine.

As it was in the Beginning

My NCO would use the lead truck and I would have a roving commission on two wheels. The main routes ran north and south and any wind was usually east or west, so I made sure that drivers would leave me enough room to pass on the windward side, where there was less dust. The tactic was completely successful as far as I was concerned but there was an outcome which displeased other people. Somewhere on the ten day northward journey to Marsabit, the thirty-two vehicle convoy was passed by a southbound staff car, flying the pennant of a General. I was riding on the inside and so did not see the car and knew nothing of it until returning to base two weeks later, when I was sent for by my Colonel. He had been asked the name of the Convoy Commander and told to compliment him on the most orderly convoy the General had ever encountered. The Colonel, in his pleasure, explained the motorcycle control and its prevention of straggler crashes.

Bob Burnie at the 1946 Shelsley Walsh hill climb, who served with the Author in France during the war. A successful sand racer at Pendine and Southport, he was 2nd fastest in the 350 cc. class. Fastest of the day was Triumph-mounted Ernie Lyons, who beat the entire entry in this first event to combine racing cars and motorcycles. [Guy Griffith].

Chapter One

A Command order followed and did not please those who preferred sitting in the front vehicle away from the dust. All convoy commanders would in future use motorcycles.

From my thousands of motorcycling miles in Africa I have many memories and one in particular has always pleased me. African askaris always delighted in identifying an Officer with some individual feature. For example, there was a Major Somen who wore a monocle and was known as the Bwana ya Darisha Moja — the Bwana with the one window. I had the title, Bwana ya Pik-Piki — the man of the motorcycle. So many years later that was to be the name of the film made of my exploits by the Government Central Office of Information.

Chapter Two

The New Triumph Representative

ON LEAVING the Army in 1946, I was keen to find a place in the motorcycle industry, but the weeks went by without result until I was invited to an interview at Watsonian Sidecars in Greet, Birmingham. There I talked with the Works Director, Cliff Bennett, who wanted an assistant, and I have always been grateful to him for offering me my first post-war employment. Cliff and I became good friends and in later years I was able to show my appreciation by giving him substantial export orders. I had a couple of weeks to consider joining Watsonian and with only several days to go I became aware of a vacancy at Meriden, for what was described as an area representative. This was what I wanted and I wrote a letter which I thought would convince Triumphs that they need look no further. So did many other applicants, as I discovered later, but at least I was told that I was on the short list for interview. Wearing uniform for the last time, I presented myself a week later to the great man Edward Turner himself, and left his office with only a reasonable hope that I would enter it again. The next day came a letter instructing me to report for duty on April 1st, and thus began my twenty-two Triumph years. They were to be momentous years in which I was privileged to make a substantial contribution to the world-wide success of Triumph business,

Chapter Two

but they were to end in heartbreaking sadness.

My first few days were spent in the factory, and for my fifty miles daily ride I borrowed a Tiger 100. Any hope I had of a permanent loan was soon destroyed, when I was told that the Company did not provide transport, and to cover my territory I would have to buy my own, and quickly. The other two representatives had cars, but they had not been to the wars and come back with a gratuity of only £100. I went to Charles Parker, the Financial Director, and asked two questions. First, could I be permitted to do my travelling on a motorcycle, and if so could I buy it with payments from my monthly salary. Parker obtained the approval of Edward Turner and I became the proud owner of a new Speed Twin, MNX 673, which cost me a little more than the price to a dealer as I was not paying cash. During the twelve months and 50,000 miles I rode this machine, it was used for test development of experimental components — and so were all the others I bought afterwards. The Speed Twin was finally sold at a profit to Mike Hailwood's father Stanley, and he made a profit also. Triumphs were rare and in keen demand those days.

My area of operations was designated the South West territory, although it included such places as Peterborough and Stamford, which would not claim to be in the South West. It was a large territory compared with present day standards, when zone managers, as they are now called, stay dry in their motor cars. No motorcycling clothing was on the market for a long time after the war and I used my army greatcoat, stained saltwater grey by an Atlantic gale when I made my life-line way across the deck of the troopship Antenor, damaged and waiting for a torpedo. The snows of the Welsh mountains and the gales of Dartmoor never did restore the coat to its original khaki green. I divided the territory into eight runs of five days each, which meant a thousand miles each week. Seven years later, when I moved to a Meriden desk I handed over my territory on the day that my friend Les Graham was killed in the Senior TT. I learned of his death on my arrival at Exeter. Only several weeks earlier, Les and I had discussed his interest in a Triumph dealership at Swindon, where he had been stationed as a fighter pilot.

In my seven years on the road I had many adventures and made many friends, all of whom deserve a place in this book for the pleasure their friendships gave to me. Those were the days of severe petrol rationing and there were always a couple of gallons without coupons for the Triumph representative who was, in fact, not only the first from Meriden but the first since the Company was formed in 1936 by Jack Sangster at the old Priory Street factory in Coventry. There were only a few established Triumph dealers in the territory and my task was to create an efficient sales and service organisation for the future. Like other manufacturers, production was limited and far below the early post-war demand. The new Turner-designed Tiger 100 and Speed Twin were way ahead of other makes and

The New Triumph Representative

Three famous riders at the 35th anniversary of the Williams' Cheltenham business in 1939. Ten times TT winner Stanley Woods [left] talks to Rem Fowler, who won the first TT [twin cylinder class] in 1907. In the centre is Graham Walker, who won the 1931 Lightweight TT and who became Editor of Motor Cycling, as well as an outstanding TT commentator. [Motor Cycling]

Harold Daniell [centre], three times Senior TT winner on Nortons, listens to Rem Fowler at the Williams' party.

Chapter Two

A happy 1939 group of personalities. Left to right: Peter Bradley of Sunbeam fame, TT and speedway rider Wilmot Evans, A-CU chief Sam Huggett and Andy Anderson of Castrol [known to his many friends as Castrol Andy]. Looking over Huggett's shoulder is Arthur Bourne [Torrens], for many years Editor of The Motor Cycle. [Motor Cycling]

No party was ever complete without Allan Jefferies, seen here with Peter and Mrs. Bradley.

The New Triumph Representative

This memorable photograph recalls the famous riders and personalities who attended the Williams' party. Standing, L to R, Peter Bradley, Vic Brittain [trials expert and rider in 9 TTs], Harry Perry [Sales Manager of the old Triumph company who once crossed the Channel on an Ariel equipped with skis], Graham Walker [who rode Nortons, Sunbeams and Rudges in 23 TTs], Bill Mewis [who prepared all the Norton racing machines], Stanley Woods who created an all-time record with 37 TT rides], Frank Varey [a great speedway rider in his day], J.H. 'Crasher' White [Norton works rider with 10 TT rides to his credit], Ginger Wood [two second places in 15 TT rides], Wilmot Evans [who rode in 10 TTs and was a successful speedway rider too], Charlie Rogers [top class trials rider on Royal Enfields], Harold Daniell, and Alfred Williams [founder of the Cheltenham company in 1904]. Seated, L to R, Ernie Nott [rider in 13 TTs and the first man to cover 200 miles in 2 hours], Dennis Mansell [a Norton Director from 1938 to 1947], Jack Williams, Bert Perrigo [Trials star and BSA technician for many years], George Rowley [19 TT rides and long standing member of the AJS staff] and Allan Jefferies.
[Cheltenham Newspaper Co., Ltd.]

my problem was not to appoint Dealers but to eliminate those who were interested only in making money whilst the demand lasted and not building up a specialised Triumph business. I found a simple and effective solution. With no advance notice of my visit to the dealer applicant, I would walk into the premises as an ordinary motorcyclist and ask to see whoever was in charge of the Motorcycle Service Department. The Speed Twin had been parked out of sight. Frequently I was told that no motorcycle repairs were undertaken and that was all I needed to know.

Chapter Two

My first journey was to South Wales by way of Gloucester, Ross on Wye and Beaufort, at the top of the Ebbw Vale. It was late April and a cold wet evening as I rode down the valley in search of a room for the night. John Elson at Beaufort had suggested the Station Hotel at Ebbw, but the doors were locked and it seemed deserted. Further down the dark valley I called at the Travellers Rest and St. David's Inns, with no success, and eventually stopped at the Hanbury Arms in the village of Aberbeeg. The landlord was an old motorcyclist and, although there was no accommodation for guests, he made an exception. We talked motorcycles long after closing time and I was to stay at Aberbeeg on all of my future journeys to South Wales. Occasionally, I played the piano in the Assembly Rooms and one evening the landlord asked if I would play at a party being given for the retiring village policeman. With thoughts of free ale in between a few Rugby songs and the Land of My Fathers I agreed, and at 8 pm I went into the Assembly Room. It was crowded, with the entire village dressed as for Sunday chapel, and silent, as I was introduced as a visitor from England who would give a piano recital. Two hundred music loving Welsh people awaited a virtuoso performance. I did my best with the Warsaw Concerto and Dream of Olwen, but must admit that the applause was more polite than overwhelming.

From Aberbeeg my route took me via Pontypool and Newport to Cardiff, where the Triumph agency was shared by Robert Bevan and Alex Thom. Robert, who was Winston Churchill's double, later became Mayor of Cardiff, and invited me to his inauguration ceremony. I was to use the journey from Meriden to check the petrol consumption of my Thunderbird fitted with the first SU carburettor. I remembered the occcasion even more as undoubtedly the only time when motorcycle clothing hung in the Mayor's robing room. The memory of Alex Thom is a sad one. He had raced at Pendine Sands and one Sunday afternoon he sat in his Rolls Royce on the sands, probably recalling his racing days. The car was still there long after dark and when someone investigated, they found that Alex was dead.

From Cardiff I rode via Bridgend, where I was snowed-in for three days the following year, to Ystrad Rhondda, Neath, Swansea and Pontadulais, where Thomas Griffiths owned Forest Garage on the steep hill out of town. Thomas always insisted on filling the petrol tank until it was difficult to replace the cap and however carefully I accelerated away, the over-flow always washed away the wax polish of the tank. His young son took over the business on his father's death and is still a good friend of mine. It was from Forest Garage that I collected one of the very first BSA twins on instructions from Edward Turner, who wanted to test it.

On from Pontadulais to Carmarthen, where I always arranged to arrive in time for an excellent Welsh tea in the home of Eddie Stephens. Eddie was a keen yachtsman and one autumn, when he took his boat out of the water at Tenby and

The New Triumph Representative

Jack Williams with the 250 cc Rudge on which he finished 5th in the 1935 Lightweight TT. The Rudges of Tyrell Smith [2nd], Ernie Nott [3rd] and Williams won the Team Prize. The Williams machine was a standard model bought from Whalleys, the Bristol Rudge dealers, for £42 10s. Centre in the photograph is Alfred Williams, Jack's father. Third man is Bob McGregor, ISDT rider on Rudges and TT rider on Raleighs. He is the McGregor of Killin, who has a special story in this book.

brought the aluminium mast back to Carmarthen, it touched the overhead power lines outside his garage. Most of the country was plunged into darkness, but Eddie survived the shock, which threw him through the showroom window. From Carmarthen I rode further westwards to Haverfordwest, where the boss of Greens Motors always convened a board meeting to which I had to report the lastest news from the Midlands. Invariably the meeting ended when I had no time left for lunch, as there were many more miles to go before my night stop at Brecon, via Aberystwyth and Builth Wells. They were hungry miles.

There was no point in arriving at Builth Wells before late afternoon, as Archie Colcombe opened his premises after spending most of the day on farms, repairing tractors, then repairing motorcycles until midnight. Rarely was it possible to get inside the old premises as they were full of mechanical rubbish accumulated over the years, but Archie was the only motorcycle man for many miles and gave the kind of service which, to me, was more important than a showroom. He was the only dealer to sign his Triumph agency agreement on the petrol tank of my machine, and it was often a rain soaked document. To Archie I owed the top award I was later to win in a National Rally, which had a midnight control point at Llanberis. Archie had shown me the quickest way from Builth to Brecon

Chapter Two

over the mountain track, and with all the other riders going the long way round back through Newport, I became the only one to reach Llanberis on time.

Brecon was another evening call after I had checked in at the old Red Lion hotel and visited the dealer on his return from Thursday night chapel choir practice. I was homeward bound the following morning via Abergavenny and Monmouth, where Len Hunt sold petrol, cycles, and Triumphs. I always left Monmouth, not only with a full tank, but with butter, bacon and eggs, so strictly rationed on the English side of the Monnow bridge across the river Wye. So ended my five-day journey through my Welsh territory, back to Coventry to prepare for the even longer one through the western counties to Penzance and back.

Of all the roads I travelled in those years, my favourite was the old Roman Fosse Way which, after I had left Meriden, I would join at Halford, beyond Warwick, then follow through Moreton in Marsh and Stow on the Wold to my first stop at Cirencester. There was little traffic around in the early post-war years and on several occasions, when I was riding Thunderbirds, I have left Meriden after 9 am and kept a lunch appointment at Exeter. I enjoyed checking my progress against the clocks at Moreton, Tetbury, Bath and Ilminster, and arrived one day at Honiton some minutes quicker than my best time. As I entered the town I was stopped by a Police Officer, who was endeavouring to assist an elderly gentleman reverse from his parking spot. Evidently the motorist was someone of local importance, but he was getting into a hopeless situation as my hard earned minutes ticked away. I became impatient and suggested that the policeman let me through. He too was impatient, and having finally waved the motorist on his way, took his time in examining my license and expressing his views on a motorcyclist who interfered with the duties of the law. On my arrival at Exeter, I mentioned the incident to my friend Jack Eddy, the Managing Director of Pikes, who were Triumph distributors for Devon and Cornwall. Not until Jack reached for the telephone and asked for the Superintendent of Honiton Police did I remember that he was the Chief of Devonshire Special Constabulary. I wondered how the policeman felt when he was rebuked by his boss for his attitude to a motorcyclist.

My last stop before Exeter, on my way to Cornwall, was at Taunton to see Frank Jarman, one of the real characters of the motorcycle trade. Each year, in January, he organised the Taunton Motor Club ball, and it was a point of honour for every motorcycle factory representative to be present. None were permitted to go to bed before 3 am but it was compulsory to have breakfasted and be on parade in time to join the 10.30 am convoy to an inn several miles away. There at 11 am began the annual skittles tournament between the locals and the trade visitors. This was a serious affair which lasted four hours, and the losing team had to pay a large bill for drinks and food. The rumour that the locals went into serious training a month before the tournament was probably true, for the

The New Triumph Representative

visitors never won. We came very close on one occasion, when we needed only four skittles down from the last man, who was that famous character Dickie Davies, Competitions Manager of Dunlops. Dickie was not much taller than a Somerset skittle, and after much advice from his team mates, all was silent as he prepared to hurl the wood down the alley. Upon him rested the honour of the visitors and the payment of the bill. The wood was heavy, the Somerset ale was strong, and Dickie made an Olympic effort as he took aim and sent the wood on its way. At the moment of release, he fell flat on his back, his head hit the alley floor and the wood smashed the overhead lights. He recovered in time to pay his share of a bill, which included new lamps.

Dickie's services to riders in the Island and Continental classics were legendary and he deserved better than to die suddenly, soon after his retirement. I shall long remember one evening in a Douglas hotel after the Senior TT when, with my piano accompaniment, he went through the repertoire which had entertained guests at many a trade party. The hotel lounge filled rapidly with holiday makers clamouring for encores, and the management offered us engagements for the season.

My ride back to the Midlands in the January of our near win at Taunton was one of the worst of many I have had in conditions of driving snow and freezing temperatures. I had stopped near Bath at a café, empty except for one lorry driver, who asked which way I was going. When I told him I was heading over the Cotswolds to Cirencester and Cheltenham, he was quite certain I would never get as far as Tetbury. He had been turned back by snow drifts on the hills around Bath. I should have taken his advice and found a room in the town, but instead I 'phoned my hotel near Evesham to expect me very late. My feet were rarely on the footrests for the sixty miles of second gear slow progress, during which the only other vehicles I saw were those which had been abandoned. Finally I arrived at the Beckford Arms hotel, numb with the cold, and ordered a hot rum which I poured into an icy mouth. It was a bad mistake to expose the nerve ends of a frozen jaw to hot rum and I was at Cheltenham in the morning waiting for the dental surgery to open.

Another memory of the Beckford hotel is not so unpleasant. I was riding back from Cornwall one March evening and had stopped for a meal at a café on the Bridgwater side of Bristol. It was misty as I parked the Triumph and an hour later it took me some time to find it. A dense fog had come down over the Severn Valley and I suspected that it might extend to the Avon as far as Tewkesbury, which was near my destination. I 'phoned my hotel and my fears were confirmed. It was the week of the Cheltenham Gold Cup and racegoers who had stayed in the town for dinner had all 'phoned the hotel to say that it was impossible to get back. The fog had stopped all traffic and so I reckoned that all I had to do was to stay on the white line in the centre of the road. The theory proved justified and I

Chapter Two

Few riders continue road racing when in their fifties, but Frank Cope of Birmingham must surely have been the only one to have started at that time of life. From 1950 to 1953 he rode in eight TT races and finished in each of them. This photograph shows him enjoying his second youth in the 1956 Ulster Grand Prix. [W.N.C. Salmond]

The New Triumph Representative

A determined Frank Cope in the 1956 Skerries 100. Son Roy, now Managing Director of the motorcycle company founded by Frank in 1919, inherited his father's love of riding and became a successful competitor in sidecar trials. [*W.N.C. Salmond*]

did not see even one moving vehicle during the journey of sixty miles. In Cheltenham I did two laps of the bus station before finding the way out.

It was midnight when I arrived at the Beckford Hotel. There was a glow of light through the fog as the door opened and before I had time to put the Triumph on its stand, I was greeted by a voice with a broad Scots accent, and handed a very large whisky. In the bar of the hotel I learned that my benefactor was a pre-war motorcyclist, and the owner of a Glasgow transport company. With a friend, he was down for the Cheltenham race week, and they had both had a profitable day. He talked of his motorcycling days and asked if I had ever heard of his old friend Bob McGregor, from Killin, who had been an International Six Days rider. I remembered that Bob was a medal winner on Rudges when I was at the Coventry factory. My Scots friend insisted that his McGregor never rode Rudges and would wager five pounds that I was wrong. I knew I was right but since there was no way of proving it, I declined the bet. It was by now an hour

Chapter Two

after midnight and I could well imagine the annoyance of the village telephone operator when she had to leave her bed, and find the number of Bob McGregor, the wholesale fish merchant at Killin. Bob must have been even more upset to have a call asking him what machine he rode in the 1929 and 1930 International Six Days. My friend insisted that I accepted his Scottish five pound note and I learned the reason the next morning. He had wagered an even ten pounds with his companion that I would make the journey through the fog from Bristol, having been assured by the landlord that I had promised to do so. The McGregor bet was his way of sharing the winnings. Last year I stayed the night at the Bridge Hotel at Killin and I enquired about McGregor. He would have enjoyed the story, but he had died a few weeks before.

My five-day journeys through Somerset, Devon, Cornwall and back demanded a high speed schedule in between calls and overnight stops, the first of which was at Chudleigh, near Exeter. I was fortunate that the landlord of the Clifford Arms had been a keen motorcyclist and did not mind the wet trail I sometimes made up to my room, or drying my clothes in the kitchen. How different from the four star Devon hotel, of which Edward Turner told an interesting story. Riding Triumphs, Edward, with Arthur Bourne, the Editor of *The Motor Cycle* for many years, and a third companion, parked their machines and entered the hotel to order lunch. The Head Waiter beckoned to the Manager, who suggested that they might prefer a snack at the bar. Asked for a reason, he inferred not too diplomatically that the standard of the hotel and its clientele was hardly suitable for motorcyclists. He had made a bad mistake. The third member of the trio was a top executive of the Royal Automobile Club and from that moment, the hotel was no longer RAC approved. The outside sign was taken away the next day.

From Chudleigh I made calls at Newton Abbot, Torquay, Kingsbridge and Plymouth, then across the Tamar to Truro, where old Bill Hicks never once failed to tell me of the days when he drove the first Humber to Cornwall from Coventry more than thirty years before. After Truro, Falmouth, Helston and Penzance, I turned to join the A30 and ride back eastwards to Camborne, Redruth and across Bodmin Moor to Launceston. Many times in the winter months my headlamp has probed the swirling mists across the moor past the Jamaica Inn of Daphne du Maurier's novel. More than once a south west Atlantic gale has soaked through the back of my coat, whilst the front remained nearly dry. At Launceston, my last call was on A.J.Wooldridge, who often stayed late until I arrived, and filled the tank for my long ride back to the Midlands. Each of my Triumphs, Speed Twins, Tigers and Thunderbirds, would make the journey on the Launceston petrol which was reassuring, because very few garages were open after dark in the winters of those fuel-rationed days. I have often thought back to those late night rides from Cornwall to Worcestershire, which left me with predominant impressions of my early years with Triumph and of the machines I rode. Those were the

The New Triumph Representative

years of quality manufacture and of Meriden workers who were proud of the products. They were the years of a company directed by a man who made certain that the excellence of his designs was matched by the standard of workmanship from foundry to final test department. Turner would have stopped production rather than risk any customer problem with a suspect component. In my 300,000 UK miles as a factory representative I was proud of the machines I rode, and which served me with complete reliability.

Only once in that time did I have a technical problem, and it was a very unpleasant experience. Turner had achieved something which other engineers in UK and other countries had tried unsuccessfully to do. He had designed and built the first internally sprung wheel in 1946, when conventional rear suspension had not yet arrived. The sprung hub, as it was called, was ingenious, and although it necessarily had a limited travel of some three inches, it was enough to make a big improvement in rider comfort and machine stability. Technically, the device was excellent, but it demanded adequate lubrication of wheel bearings which had to be of substantial dimensions to carry the load of a heavy hub. None of the major bearing manufacturers such as Hoffman, Ransome and Marles or Skefco could offer journal bearings without a long delay, and so Turner went ahead with ball bearings in an open cage. On his instructions the production prototype sprung hub was installed in the Shilton Tiger 100 and I left the factory one Monday morning, looking forward to a more comfortable ride through Wales. The brilliant conception of rear springing had fascinated all the dealers, and homeward bound on the Friday evening I was looking forward to giving Turner a 1000 miles first class test report. Then it happened. At around 70 mph on the Ross to Gloucester road, the rear wheel locked suddenly and before the Tiger had come to a stop, the tyre had been torn from the wheel rim. The black streak of rubber on the road was still visible a year later. When the hub was dismantled at the factory on Monday morning, the bearings had disintegrated through loss of grease, and Turner, who presided over the inquest, said that it was exactly what he had expected. I wish he had told me when I set out for Wales. Later, the sprung hub went into production with journal bearings, but only 20,000 were fitted before it was made obsolete by the introduction of swinging arm suspension.

After covering Wales and the West country, there remained twelve more counties on the territory and I established an itinerary timetable from which every Dealer knew not only the day of my visit, but the hour. I well remember the comments made to Edward Turner by Mike Hailwood's father Stanley, in 1947, when he was head of Laytons of Oxford. 'Although I can get only a few of the machines I want, Shilton calls regularly to explain why, and he can be sure of my support whenever the factory needs it'. Stanley, who became a close friend of mine, kept his word in later years, when the USA market recession affected Meriden. Before then I had the privilege of arranging with Stanley for Mike to spend some

Chapter Two

months at the factory. I was also to be involved in Mike's debut in the racing field, when he and my friend Dan Shorey, of Banbury, won the Thruxton 500 miles race of 1958 on a Tiger 110. Stanley, who was an ex-racing driver himself, was in the Triumph pit that day and did a marvellous job of organisation which added miles to the margin by which the race was won.

The character of motorcycle dealerships and their personalities have changed completely in recent years and I was fortunate to be a factory representative in the days when most of them retained the keen interest in motorcycles on which their businesses had been founded. I remember them well and have been proud of their friendships. At Cheltenham, Alf Williams opened his cycle and motorcycle shop early in this century, and in due course was joined by his son Jack, who rode in thirteen TT races from 1931 to 1938. Alf promised himself that if he was still around when the business reached its fiftieth anniversary, he would celebrate in a big way at Cheltenham town hall. He achieved his ambition, and personalities from the entire industry filled the ballroom. Alf personally greeted each one of his guests as they arrived, and I was proud to be one of them. Son Jack, with whom I have had a lasting friendship, was given control of the business soon afterwards, and now, many years later, continues to be involved, although he has handed over operations to his son, Andrew. The loyal support which the Williams company gave to the British industry was unsurpassed but, one by one, Velocette, AJS, HRD, Norton and Triumph disappeared from the scene and finally left their showrooms to BMW and motorcars. I wonder what grandfather Alf would think of the new look of his old premises in Portland Place.

My next call beyond Cheltenham, on my ride to the south, was at Stroud, where the H and L Motors business was built up on Triumph spares by Jack Lewis, who raced in the Clubmans events in the Island. Jack was a provocative character and as the industry declined in later years, he would upset us on his weekly visits to Meriden, with his severe criticisms of the BSA Group management, despite our protests that we at Triumph were making the same criticisms. He would then come to my Stratford upon Avon home on his way back to Stroud, and stimulated by his favourite brandy, would lecture me for two hours on the same theme. On a visit to Stroud in 1947, when I was still searching for weather-proof riding gear, I was excited to find a genuine and new Stormguard one-piece riding suit. This was the thing I had never expected to find, and I did not argue about the price. At last I could get rid of my army greatcoat and face all the elements. For a week or two my miles were in dry weather and then one evening, as I left Weymouth to travel back to the Midlands, the rain began. At first it was only a drizzle, until I left my last call at Fifehead Neville on my way to Warminster, Chippenham, Cirencester, and over the Cotswolds. Then the rain started to fall heavier and I was grateful for the Stormguard as I followed the dark Fosse Way to Stow in the Wold. There I stopped and, as every long distance

The New Triumph Representative

motorcyclist knows, there is an all too-brief warning from the bladder that it is necessary to stop. Especially in the middle of a town, as I can testify from painful experience. At Stow, on that dark wet night, I dismounted from the Tiger 100 and, as I did so, the rain water ran down my thighs from the pool of water which had collected in my lap. I learned that the Stormguard had been in stock from pre-war days and was no longer waterproof in its most important area. Not until the Barbour company marketed the motorcycling version of their submarine suit did I remain dry on my long distance journeys. Even this suit had its problems. The oil proofing necessarily attracted heat, so that in the summer it became too warm, and on cold days it drew heat from the body. I have spent many hours in front of an open fire, re-proofing a Barbour with linseed oil, which kept out the rain but spoiled any lounge suit I was wearing. After all my motorcycling years I have yet to find truly reliable weather-proof clothing and although some friends, especially Police riders, have recommended certain brands, I remain unconvinced that there is any suit which one can remove after a 300 mile wet ride, and walk comfortably into an hotel dining room. I decided long ago that the only answer was a fibre glass protective fairing, which is why I became involved in the design and manufacture of what was to become known as the Avon fairing. My own Triumphs were the first to be fitted with this equipment, and it was an important factor in the development of Police motorcycle business, as will be told later.

From Stroud, my itinerary took me via Chippenham to Melksham where, late in 1946, I had a big problem with my Speed Twin. My dealer friends Ventons had kindly filled my tank with two gallons of coupon-free fuel, and I was very grateful. Five miles later, when I called at Trowbridge, the engine was overheated and by the time I arrived at my Frome overnight stop, the exhaust pipes were glowing red. In Arthur Starr's garage I checked everything to find the cause, without result, and the next morning I rode on to Warminster, Salisbury and Parkstone with frequent stops to cool the hot engine. At Homestead Garages, Parkstone, managed by my good friend and TT rider Reg Marsh, it was a routine arrangement for enough workshop space to be reserved for the Triumph representative to service his machine. This time the service was essential and I was helped by Tiny Camfield, a fine mechanic who did remarkable things with the Marsh and Fry Excelsior Manxman racers. Tiny and I stripped the Triumph down to the main bearings and could find no reason for the obviously excessive heat. At around midnight, when we were both completely baffled, Tiny walked around the workshop and commented on the strange smell which had puzzled him all evening. With a sudden inspiration he removed the petrol tank filler cap, smelt the contents and discovered the trouble. My friends at Melksham had diluted my four star petrol with two gallons of TVO tractor fuel, and my Speed Twin had brought me to Parkstone on a mixture which should have stopped it before Warminster. At 26,000 miles this was the only one of my Triumphs which

Chapter Two

The New Triumph Representative

Inches away from the 'Section Ends' card, Bill Slocombe fights for wheel grip in the 1962 Colmore Cup Trial. [B.R. Nicholls]

Left: One of Britain's best-known motorcycle dealers, Bill Slocombe of Neasden, London, had a fine record of victories in the National trials of the fifties and sixties with a 500 cc BSA sidecar outfit. Here he is climbing Upper Preeces Hill, in the 1962 British Experts. The studious spectator in the sporting jacket is Ralph Venables, who still writes for the motorcycling press. Next to him, wearing the beret, is Bernal Osborne, who for many years was the Midlands Editor of Motor Cycling. [Motor Cycling]

had to have major attention before more than double that mileage. A year or so after this episode, the Melksham premises of Ventons were completely destroyed by fire, and I was told that a paraffin stove had mistakenly been filled with petrol.

Parkstone became a very strong Triumph area with Homestead Garages at one end, Huxhams at the other, and later on, Bob (Fearless) Foster opened a business between the two. I became very fond of Joe Huxham, a true gentleman

Chapter Two

and ardent motorcyclist, whose partner was Morgan racer Tom Bryant. I was amongst many trade guests at the fiftieth anniversary of the business, and was a sad mourner at Joe's funeral only several years ago. His son Peter was the Vicar of St. Peter's church, where Joe was buried, and he conducted the service of farewell to his father. Afterwards, he also conducted a second and brighter farewell affair at the inn where Joe had been a regular patron, and this great character would have been proud of the way in which his son ensured that the drinking was up to his father's standard.

Bob Foster had chosen to open his motorcycle business in the Bournemouth area because his doctor had said that the climate would be good for his asthma, after he retired from racing. His choice gave me a problem when he applied for a Triumph agency, as I already had two good dealerships. However, he had the BSA agency, and I was always ready to compete with Small Heath, a personal policy which was to make me very unpopular when Meriden business became part of the BSA Group. Besides, Bob was a friend who I admired greatly as a fine rider. Born at Stow on the Wold, he had worked at nearby Shipston on Stour for Arthur Taylor, who encouraged his racing ambitions and set him on course for his future brilliance. In his second appearance in the Island, Bob won the 1936 Lightweight TT on a Taylor-entered New Imperial. In 1947 he won the Junior on a Velocette, and was second in the 1948 Junior on the same make. His style of riding, especially on certain machines which scared everybody but Foster, earned him the title of 'Fearless' and this was certainly justified when, in 1949, he battled on a Grand Prix Triumph against Les Graham on the AJS Porcupine at Blandford. Every spectator, and especially myself, will never forget that race. The highly dangerous Blandford course was the narrow road of an Army camp. Graham and Foster quickly left everyone behind and fought out a battle with never more than half a front wheel between them. Neither would give way, with handlebars touching lap after lap and, as they screamed over the finishing line, the AJS won by a fraction which the timekeeper's clock could not measure.

The years in which I served Meriden as a representative gave me the finest possible training for my future progress. The thousands of miles I rode were to prove the most valuable experience in preparation for the long distance demonstration rides I was to undertake later on, and which were to continue until the longest one of all in 1980. Above all, those early Meriden years are remembered for the many friendships they created. The list of names is very long but all too frequently I have had to draw a line through those to whom the last farewell has been said. At my Stratford on Avon home I started a book of guests, and it contains many famous names. Next to the signature of John Surtees is the name of Rem Fowler, who won the twin cylinder class of the first TT in 1907. Rem was a frequent visitor, and so was John. When John became World Champion, I gave a party to which I invited Rem and many friends, also the press boys. Rem was the

The New Triumph Representative

centre of attraction, with everyone wanting to know about the early TT races, whether it was true that cattle strayed on the course, whether stops were made to open gates, and so on. Rem and I appeared on BBC television in 1957, the week before the fiftieth anniversary of the TT races, and I was seen sitting on one of the Triumphs we provided for the Travelling Marshals, and equipped for the first time with radio. The following morning I was sent for by Edward Turner, who was delighted with the Triumph publicity. 'Did you realise', said Turner, 'that the cameras were on the Triumph for eight minutes? That would have cost thousands of pounds on commercial television.' 'Thank you sir' I replied, 'will you approve my expenses for the three pounds I spent on entertaining in the BBC bar?' Turner grudgingly gave his approval after some consideration. He suspected I had made a small profit, and he was right. Dear old Rem died at a great age when he was still working as a skilled pattern maker in Birmingham. I treasure the memento he gave to me of our friendship. It is an old woodworking plane on which he had burnt his initials HRF.

This chapter would not be complete without resurrecting the remarkable character who represented Triumph in Scotland and the northern half of England. His name was Harry Goodby and when I joined the company he was already well past the normal retirement age although he was to continue for a few more years. Harry was a Wolverhampton man and from early in the century he sold bicycles made by his father until moving to the old Triumph cycle company in the days of its founder, Siegfried Bettmann. When he was finally persuaded to retire, he could rightly claim to have attended every London motorcycle show since the very first one. Many stories could be told about Harry Gooby, but if he was alive to choose, I am sure he would want to hear again the tale of his last journey to Scotland. There were several reasons why his final journey for Triumph had to be to the country of Robbie Burns, all of whose poetry Harry could recite to perfection as he had demonstrated at many a Burns night. In the post-war years, when Triumph motorcycles were in short supply, the same applied to whisky, and so it was a natural sequence for his Scottish dealers to show their appreciation of the efforts he made to send more Speed Twins and Tigers north of the border. On his return from his twice yearly tours, the benevolent bottles left little room to spare in the car boot, and they were duly delivered to those Triumph dealers in the Midlands who had placed standing orders in 1945. Any temptation to keep a bottle for himself was not hard to resist, for although he enjoyed a dram as much as any of his customers, Harry was very stong willed about one rule. He never drank his own.

On the farewell tour, the driving was done by his successor, John Hickson, who was to become the Ariel Sales Manager in later years, and the car had a generous boot space to accommodate what was sure to be a heavy load of auld lang syne for auld Harry. The goodbye drams were drunk at Edinburgh, Glas-

Chapter Two

gow, Dundee, Brechin and at his favourite City of Aberdeen, where late at night he was put to bed by a very worried Hickson. The emotional farewells and Scottish hospitality had proved too much for the old man, and a doctor was called. After examining the patient and learning that his home was in Wolverhampton, the doctor advised Hickson to drive there as gently as possible, with Harry wrapped in blankets on the back seat. Wolverhampton was reached the next evening and the passenger carried to his bed. As Hickson quietly was leaving the bedroom

The Edward Turner design dictum insisted that the engine and petrol tank must look beautiful. This was his first 'Tiger' tank creation of 1936. The disappearance of tank knee grips is something the Author has always regretted.

he heard the weak words from the blue lips, 'Don't forget the bottles John'. Hickson made four journeys up the two flights of stairs, carrying five bottles each time, and put them under the bed as instructed. As he put down the twentieth bottle he held Harry's hand and looked down at the pale face on the pillow for what was likely to be a final farewell. He leaned over the bed to hear the words Harry was trying to say. The words of an old man who, after sixty years of travelling had made his last journey. 'There are four more bottles to come, John'.

Not only did Harry recover and deliver the scotch to his old customers, but he survived a few more years, and he arrived one day in my office at Meriden. He talked of his travels, of the friends he missed and especially those north of the

The New Triumph Representative

border. I understood what he meant and poured him a whisky. A large one.

Amongst my other friends in the Midlands was Frank Cope who, with his brother Arthur, founded the now very large motorcycle and car business of C.E.Cope. Frank once told me the story of how he finally started racing. In his early years, when he was eager to race, his brother insisted that the business could not afford the time for such personal enjoyment. As the company progressed, Frank's family responsibilities had to come before his racing desires, but as the years went by his desires remained. Came the time when the business was doing well, his son Roy and Arthur's son Douglas had been given responsibility, and Frank felt himself free at last to start racing, well beyond the time when riders put away their leathers. Frank entered the 1950 TT races, on AJS machines, finished 8th in the Lightweight and also got a Replica in the Junior. He achieved the remarkable record of finishing in all of the eight TT races in which he rode, the last being the 1953 Junior, which was the last year he could obtain an International license within the age limit regulations. This did not stop Frank from racing, for he continued to ride in South Africa, where the FIM regulations did not apply, and he added more trophies to his collection. He ultimately died after a Japanese two-stroke seized at a rev counter reading which defies anyone to de-clutch before crashing. I was particularly sad to add Frank to the number of my rider friends who who were given their last chequered flag, Les Graham, David Whitworth, John Hartle, Bob McIntyre, Artie Bell, Alec Bennett, George Boudin, Dickie Dale, Harold Daniell, Howard Davies, Geoff Davidson, Freddie Dixon, Frank Fry, Walter Handley, Mike Hailwood, Stan Hailwood, Jim Harrison, Victor Horsman, Allan Jefferies, Ernie Nott, Tyrell Smith and Graham Walker. I was privileged to know them and each has a special place in my memory book.

Chapter Three

The Manx Grand Prix celebratory dinner for Ernie Lyons, held in Leamington Spa on 5th October 1946. Ernie, still clad in leathers from his Shelsley Walsh win, heads the table with Edward Turner. The Author leans forward on the left-hand side, fifth from the front.

Chapter Three

The Grand Prix Triumph

ON MY visits to the factory in between my 1946 travels, I heard rumours of a racing machine being built in the Experimental Department by a team led by Freddie Clarke. Freddie was a rare combination of brilliant rider and 1st class engineer, who had many successes at Brooklands including the all time 350 cc lap record at 105 mph on a Tiger 80. The experimental shop was the holy of holies and I did not get a look at the machine until September, in the Isle of Man. Meanwhile, I learned that it was being prepared for the Ulster Grand Prix over the Clady Circuit and that it would be ridden by Irish farmer Ernie Lyons. Basically a Tiger 100, the engine was Clarke's brain child and he had cleverly adapted the light alloy cylinder head and block used on the wartime airborne generator set. The still experimental sprung rear wheel was used, and no doubt with some improvements after the failure of the prototype on my Tiger 100. The machine had carburation problems in the Ulster, but promised such great potential when these were sorted out that it was decided that Lyons should ride it in the Manx Grand Prix in September. He had ridden a Triumph in the 1938 race, but had crashed spectacularly, near Ramsey. However, his Triumph successes in Irish road and grass track events, plus his Irish charm, persuaded Turner to relax his

Chapter Three

views about racing involvement and Clarke was told to help. If the Lyons charm was not enough, he had three able supporters who visited Turner to make sure of the Manx machine. The legendary Stanley Woods, winner of ten TT races, Rex McCandless, creator of the Norton 'featherbed' frame and Freddie Dixon, sidecar and solo TT winner, who went on to racing car fame. Freddie once put a front wheel of a racing Riley over the edge of the Montlhéry banking, and got it back again. These three remarkable characters were the formidable Lyons support group in the Island and they were joined by Freddie Clarke, who did not arrive until the afternoon boat the day before the race. They told me afterwards that Edward Turner did not know he had come, and this seems to bear out the story that Clarke had been told to prepare a machine without spending much time away from more important things.

I was in the Island with my Advertising Manager colleague Ivor Davies, as he mentions in his excellent and well illustrated book *It's a Triumph*. Like Clarke, we were not there officially, but as new boys at Meriden we wanted to see the lone Triumph do battle against 64 Nortons, and to enoy the first race week since 1939. As soon as Clarke arrived, the team took the Triumph to the mountain for final test runs, and Lyons did some high speed descents from the 33rd milestone to Creg-ny-Baa. Plug checks at the Creg revealed a speck of aluminium on one electrode and back went the team to their Douglas workshop. Race officials extended the weighing-in time to the following morning and the engine was taken apart. Work went on most of the night and when I spoke to McCandless early the next day, he was quite confident that Lyons would win, provided it rained. The three fastest Nortons of Londoner Ken Bills, Midlander Albert Moule and Manxman Bertie Rowell probably had the edge on the Triumph and they had much more experience in the Island, but Lyons was superb in wet conditions. The Irish prayers for rain were answered by 9 am but two hours later, when the race was due to start, wet mist covered most of the course and blanked out the mountain from the Gooseneck to Brandish. The start was postponed to noon, by which time Ivor and I were having aperitifs at the Railway Hotel on the right sweep at Union Mills. The radio reported mist still on the mountain and rain over the entire course.

At noon we heard the maroon signal the start of the race. Albert Moule was first away and as he raced past us I started my stop watch to check the interval before Lyons, number 12, arrived. Five more riders went through and then amazingly we heard the sound of the only twin in the race. Even my friend, double TT winner Eric Williams, could hardly believe it when Lyons flashed through in the misty rain, having passed half a dozen riders in the first few miles. He made his own line through the right and left curves, narrowly missing the Post Office which still showed the marks of the Freddie Hicks' Velocette and the Syd Lawton Norton. Race favourite Ken Bills went through fast, but slower than Lyons, and

The Grand Prix Triumph

Ivor and I went back to the bar with some doubt as to whether Lyons would come through again. We had chosen to spectate at Union Mills for two reasons. We could get back to the Grandstand quickly if Lyons should win and we would swallow our disappointment in the bar if he didn't. Back outside in the rain we waited to check Moule on his second lap and as he became due, we heard the scream of the twin as Lyons changed down to third gear. It was incredible that he could have passed Moule and now be first man on the road. Moule followed more than two minutes later and told me afterwards that Lyons had gone past at Windy Corner. 'I was braking hard for the misty blur of the corner when I was passed' he said, 'and I knew it could only be Lyons.'

Freddie Frith jumps Ballaugh Bridge with his front wheel high in the air, during the 1948 Senior TT. [W.N.C. Salmond.]

Chapter Three

By the time the Triumph was due to arrive on the third lap, Ivor and I no longer had any doubts that it would, but perhaps the bar had helped our confidence. We started the crowd cheering as we heard the twin and the bar did more business as Lyons raced away to Ballacraine. As he came and went for the last time, we found our Speed Twins and made our way back to Douglas. As we parked them behind the Grandstand, Freddie Clarke came from the Paddock in a hurry to get the boat to Liverpool. After our warm congratulations he told us that the front down tube of the Tiger frame had fractured and the Press had taken photographs. We pushed our way through the crowd to find the ever smiling but thoroughly soaked Lyons, but we had to wait until the evening to talk to him as he was completely deaf after his amazing ride. We asked first if he knew when the frame broke and he gave a reply which should go into any book of Irish humour. 'I think it must have been when the bicycle suddenly began to steer much better'. Actually he never could be sure when it broke but it could not have been far from the finish, otherwise it would certainly have meant retirement. In the evening edition of what was to become the 'TT Special' newspaper published by TT winner Geoff Davison, the story of the Lyons win reported the scare when a dog ran across the road in front of the Triumph. I asked Lyons where this was and whether it had worried him. More Irish humour as he tried to recall the incident and remembered 'Yes it was at Hillberry on the first lap, but it was only a small dog'.

In October, Lyons and the Triumph competed at the mixed car and motorcycle hill climb at Shelsley Walsh and against the top class racing car experts. He made the fastest climb of the day, the first and only time a motorcycle had beaten the four wheelers. A dinner had been planned that evening to honour Lyons for his Manx victory and it seemed appropriate that he sat down still in his leathers, having arrived from Shelsley too late to change. The dinner proved not only to be a celebration but his farewell, for he never rode a Triumph again. That great character Gilbert Smith, the Norton chief, wanted him to join his Harold Daniell, Artie Bell first team, and Turner had no plans for a serious racing programme although many people pressed him, especially the distributors in overseas countries. I went to Belfast some weeks later to recover the racing engine, which Rex McCandless had borrowed from Meriden to fit into his prototype 'featherbed' frame. He and Artie Bell told me how Gilbert Smith had talked to Lyons for a whole afternoon before he was able to sign up his new rider. Why he did not ride in the 1947 Senior TT I do not know, but his Junior Norton did not finish. In the 1948 Junior, won by Freddie Frith on Velocette, Lyons rode an AJS into sixteenth place, but his career nearly came to an end in the Senior when he rode a works Guzzi. I was at the Bungalow to see this race which, on paper, was the Guzzi versus the Nortons and the Triumphs of Frith, Foster and Bills, these three having been entered by Nigel Spring, who had somehow persuaded Edward Turner to change his policy against building pure racing machinery. In all, six

The Grand Prix Triumph

Triumphs started in the 1948 Senior and all blew up, as explained later, but now back to the Bungalow and the excitement as the first machine was heard coming fast up the mountain. It was number 2, Lyons, who had already overtaken the man who had started a minute ahead of him. He came into the left-hander before the mountain railway crossing faster than anyone before, hit the grass bank and narrowly missed the deep drain culvert. The Guzzi was completely out of control but Lyons fought it and might have stayed aboard but the Bungalow café was in the way. He was unhurt but a Marshal, unaccustomed to Guzzi exhaust systems, tried to get the machine off the road by pulling the exhaust pipe and sustained a badly burnt hand. Lyons rode twice more in the Island, being placed second in the 1949 Junior on a Velocette behind Frith, and third in the Senior on a Velocette behind the Nortons of Daniell and Lockett. We all missed the charm of this remarkable Irishman when he put away his leathers and I for one will always remember his great Manx ride.

So goodbye to Lyons, but what happened to Freddie Clarke, the architect of the Manx success? This brilliant engineer and rider was Edward Turner's problem child. Like his boss, Freddie was essentially a strong willed individual, and ran his Experimental Department on his own lines. When Turner wanted him urgently, Clarke did not hurry to finish what he was doing and he was the only member of the Triumph staff who was not in Turner's office within a minute of being sent for. I held the record with twenty seconds. When Turner made his 1948 visit to America, he instructed Works Manager Alf Camwell to bring Clarke into the discipline line and Camwell took the instruction seriously. Turner returned from America to find Clarke gone, which upset him, but he was even more upset when he found that the brilliant engineer, for whom he had the greatest respect, had joined AJS at Woolwich. Within two years, Freddie Clarke was dead, killed on the prototype AJS twin which he had developed, and paradoxically the accident happened within a mile of Meriden. He was riding the twin with wife Barbara as passenger on the Stonebridge to Kenilworth road, late at night, when he touched the grass verge and was thrown. Freddie's death was the second tragedy for Barbara, whose first husband Henry Laird, a distinguished journalist of the motorcycling press and Morgan racer, had also been killed in a road accident.

What happened to the Grand Prix Triumph project which Edward Turner had been persuaded to pursue in 1948? It was much against his policy to permit his technical staff to divert their work away from production machine development and give any attention to special racers. However, he had been under external pressure to manufacture some replicas of the Manx winner, and finally he decided to produce 100 and no more. They had a fair amount of success in minor International races overseas, in National events at home, and Manxman Don Crossley repeated the Lyons performance in winning the 1948 Manx Grand Prix. The 1949 Senior TT heard the swan song of the GP, with fifth and seventh places,

Chapter Three

Sid Jensen and Edward Turner outside the Meriden Works with the machine on which the former finished 5th in the 1949 Senior TT. This was the machine given to Jensen by Turner in acknowledgement of his epic ride.

and I well remember that when I was in New Zealander Syd Jensen's pit, Turner came and asked me where I estimated he would finish. It was the fifth lap and I said that if the Triumph had no trouble, it would be in the first six, as it was then lying seventh and two of the Nortons ahead of him sounded rough and were slowing. 'If you are right' said the boss, 'I will give the machine to Jensen as a present'. He kept his word, but was a little upset when Jensen came to Meriden to collect it, to see that the New Zealander had one of the new AJS twins which he had bought to take home also.

The history of subsequent years proved that Turner was quite right in withdrawing from the racing scene and concentrating upon commercial production success. As the Meriden factory enjoyed supremacy in all of its markets, Nortons, with their sweeping victories in the racing field, were not having the same success

The Grand Prix Triumph

with sales, which after all have to keep a factory going. Turner took a more favourable view of racing where standard production machines were concerned, and his promises to support this class of competition were later kept, and adequately rewarded, by Triumph successes. It was, however, sad to realize that little need have been done to make the GP Triumphs equal to anything in those first post-war years. Each of the Nigel Spring entries in the 1948 TT went out with big end failure and I saw the last one go. Ken Bills was accelerating away from the Bungalow when suddenly there was silence. The main problem was undoubtedly the plunger-type oil pump, which could not cope positively with the higher engine revolutions of the racing engine. It may well be that but for the bad weather which helped Lyons to win the 1946 Grand Prix, the GP Triumphs would never have been made and the 1948 ignominy of 6 started, none finished, would not have happened. Even so, the model which Turner was reluctant to build died hard and the 100 maximum he agreed to produce became nearer 200. Improvements brought 7 across the finish line in the 1949 Senior and 6 the following year. Race speeds went higher and in the next three years only one GP finished. That was the end of the unsuccessful chapter of Triumph history which was soon to be forgotten in the great years that followed.

Chapter Four

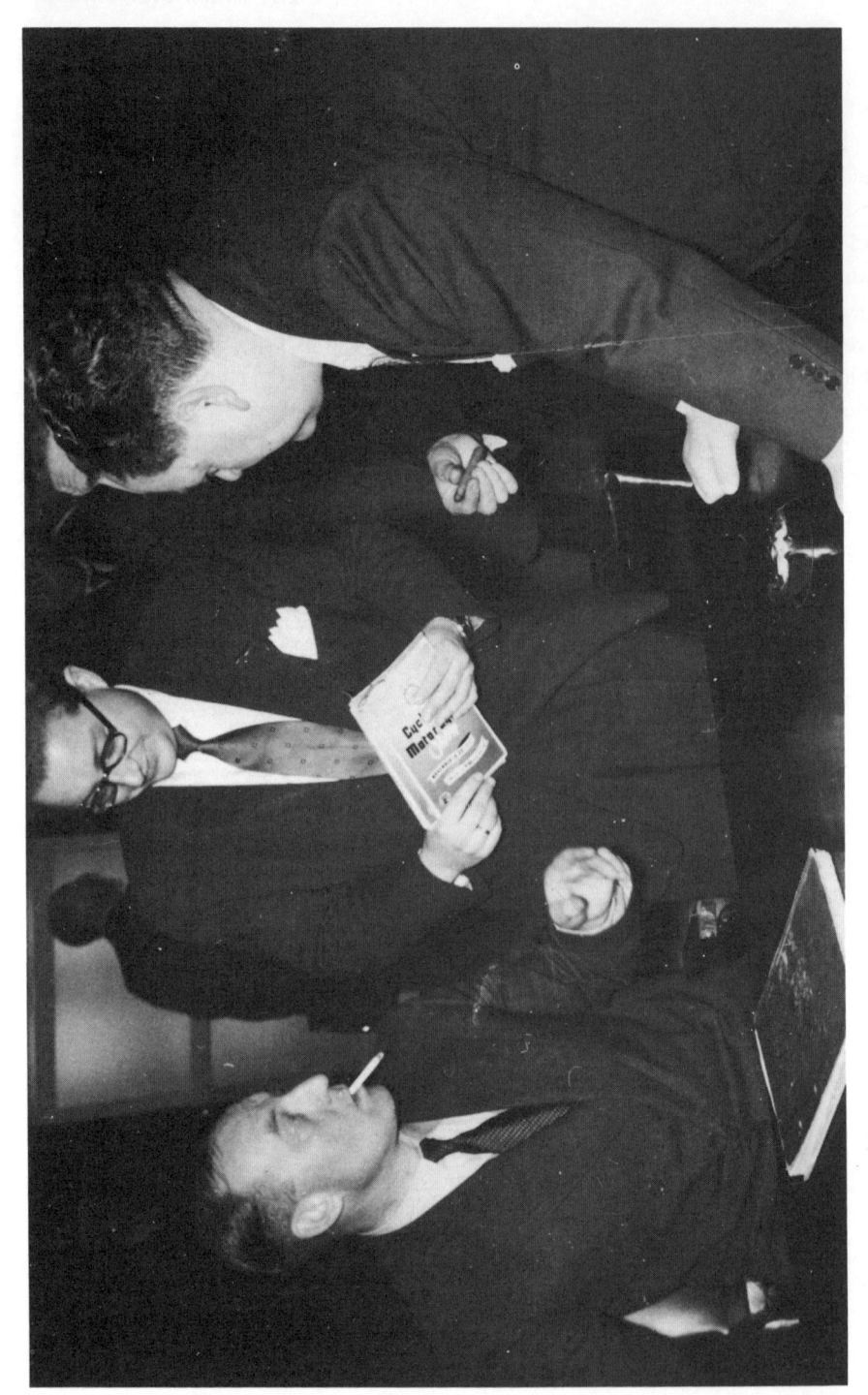

At Earls Court in 1949 with the Danish Triumph importers. I was probably telling them the story of the bacon!

Chapter Four

My Third Meriden Year

IN 1948 I was sent for by Edward Turner and given an assignment which, as I realised later, would decide whether I was to remain a UK market representative indefinitely, or move into wider areas of Triumph business developments. Turner briefed me on the mission, which was to go to Copenhagen where the British Trade Week was taking place, to have discussions with the recently-appointed Triumph importers and to report back to him my recommendations as to whether they were the right people. The pre-war importers were not yet back in business and I was to make discreet enquiries in certain quarters as to their prospects. They had been very successful Triumph people in the difficult years before 1938 and the Meriden Export Manager might have been premature in appointing another company. In his inimitable way, Turner ended the briefing by saying that he would act on my recommendations — provided he agreed with them.

I rode my Tiger 100 to Northolt Airport, having first fitted a pair of panniers in the hope of bringing back some Danish produce in those still food rationed days. From Northolt I flew to Copenhagen in a twin engined Viking aircraft, which took more than twice the time of the modern jet. Since then I have flown many times to Copenhagen by Trident, DC9 and Airbus, and the time from

Chapter Four

home to hotel is only a little quicker than in 1948, thanks to road trafic congestion and airport delays. Such is progress.

The mission was entirely successful, mainly due to the information I obtained from Axel Petersen, the head of the Danish Castrol organisation, whose stand at the trade exhibition did as much for English tea as for Castrol oil. His wife was reputed to have dispensed as much tea as all other exhibitors supplied Carlsberg beer. All these years later, I find myself writing these words in the Danish house where Axel and his wife lived. I flew back to Northolt with enough Danish bacon to fill the panniers of the Tiger and as I packed the kilogram packages after landing in mid-afternoon, I wondered whether to have a gentle ride home or a quicker one to get to Meriden by 5 pm and report to Turner. Then I remembered it was Friday and it would be nice to give a few packages to my friends before they departed for the weekend. So I used all the performance Turner had designed for the Tiger and arrived at Meriden in good time, via Aylesbury and Banbury. I parked the machine outside the office entrance, removed my riding gear and before I went to the chief, I mentioned to a colleague that there was bacon in my panniers for him and one or two others. Half an hour later I returned to the Tiger to make the distribution, but I was too late. My friends had helped themselves and bacon was on my shopping list that weekend. However, there were to be many more visits to Denmark as Turner accepted my recommendations, the original distributors were reinstated and the country became the best Triumph market in Europe. The wheels of my Triumphs, Nortons and finally BMWs, were later to follow the roads to Copenhagen from Esbjerg, Cologne and Bremerhaven. For all of those pleasant rides I had to thank Edward Turner and the mission he gave me in 1948.

Meanwhile, after my brief taste of export affairs, I went back to my UK market duties and my 1000 miles per week, and on my next ride to Cornwall I had an experience which I still remember as though it happened yesterday. Approaching Ilchester along the straight Fosse Way I saw a line of Army trucks ahead parked on my side of the road. A driver training unit from Yeovil camp, there were around thirty Bedfords, twenty-five or so yards apart, with their drivers lying on the grass the opposite side of the road having the morning break. I slowed down from very fast to fast, the half road past the trucks was clear and I was waved through by the soldier acting as traffic controller at my end of the parked convoy. At the distant end his colleague did the same. This was where I would put on a Triumph speed show for the Army. As I flashed past the first truck, one in the middle pulled out, having evidently thought that my all clear signal was for him. To say that I used both brakes is an understatement, especially as the rear one did nothing at all to help. The back end of the Bedford loomed up fast and I took to the grass. Soldiers scattered in all directions, mainly into the ditch, but I had other problems. Drain channels had been cut into the grass verge at twenty yard

My Third Meriden Year

intervals, and neither the Triumph nor I liked them. The machine touched the ground briefly in between channels, and I was out of the saddle just as briefly. We somehow got back on the road at the end of the performance and I took a quick look back at a lot of angry soldiers, waving their arms, which I thought was rather unfair. I went more slowly into Ilchester and stopped to examine the rear brake. I did not have to look very hard to see that the rear wheel and tyre were soaked with oil. Neither did I have to look for the reason. Before leaving the factory that morning I had routed a rubber tube from the oil tank breather pipe to the rear chain, thinking that the oil mist should be put to good use and help the chain which otherwise had no lubrication. At the same time I had filled the oil tank and thus I learned the lesson that the pressure scavenge side of a Triumph oil pump was more powerful than the feed side. Consequently at high speed a full oil tank lost half a pint through the breather pipe.

I have been fortunate in my million miles to have had only several accidents but it was unfortunate that one should happen only one week before the Earls Court Show in November 1948. It is worth recalling, if only to show what can happen when claiming against the insurance company of the other driver. I was returning on a Speed Twin after demonstrating it to the Somerset Police, and was approaching the Warwickshire village of Loxley where I was to spend the weekend. In the narrow lane a car approached round the bend on his wrong side of the road and as I stopped with my footrest hard against the grass bank, the protruding hinges of the driver's door hit my shoulder and leg. The Triumph was also damaged and I was quite sure that my leg was broken. The butler from the nearby Loxley Hall came out when he heard the crash, and I asked him to phone for the Stratford upon Avon Police. The worried and very apologetic car driver asked what he could do and I told him to leave the car where it was, on my side of the road, until the Police arrived. It was the day of the Stratford races and it was an hour before a Police Officer arrived. Meanwhile, the once-a-week bus came along the lane and the car had to be moved, but its brake marks were black lines on the wrong side of the road and so I had no objections. The driver made and signed a statement to the Police admitting full responsibility and explaining that he had swerved to avoid a dip in the road by a field gate. Quite true, and I had done the same myself, more than once. The Police Officer then asked me if I wished to make a statement and I said merely that having heard what the driver had stated, I confirmed it. He wrote this down and I added my signature. That proved to be a bad mistake. I wrote to the car driver's insurance company informing them that I should be making a claim in due course, and my solicitors did so.

My leg was not broken but badly injured internally and each day before I went on duty at Earls Court on crutches, I had pain-killing injections at the hospital. It was a difficult show week but I was consoled by the anticipation of a

Chapter Four

Edward Turner in Denmark, with alloy Tiger and Steib sidecar.

useful cash recompense for injuries, plus repairs to the machine. My solicitors had received no response and I asked them to press for settlement. Weeks later they asked me to call and see the reply. With it was a statement from their client flatly denying responsibility and describing how he had been unable to avoid the motorcyclist who was travelling fast on the wrong side of the road. I rushed to the Stratford Police station and asked for a copy of the statement signed by the driver. Not possible, I was told, but I could have a copy of my own which was, of course, useless, as it merely agreed with the driver. My appeals were in vain and the Police explained that the fault was theirs in not being able to prosecute because they had omitted to give statutory notice to the driver of possible

My Third Meriden Year

prosecution. His insurance company took full advantage of this and knew that there was no independent witness whereas the driver had a passenger friend. For many months afterwards I carried a camera in my pannier but never had cause to use it.

At the end of 1948 I was told to hand over my Speed Twin to the Experimental Department for some modification or other, and I am sure that Edward Turner did not know, or had forgotten, that I had to buy each of my machines. However, it felt good to be doing something more than ride 200 miles daily for the main purpose of maintaining dealer goodwill, with only a few deliveries for their many customers. Meriden production was, in fact, getting well past the 250 per week mark and America wanted them all, but Turner ensured that the UK market received at least one third of the output. My machine came back to me and I could not see what had been done to it, but when I rode away from the factory that evening, I felt a big difference before I had even changed up to second gear. I learned the next day that I had a prototype of the 649 cc engine. Basically a bored-out Speed Twin motor, the same cylinder block casting was used and the stroke was only a couple of millimetres longer. However, there were another 7 bhp to push the maximum speed up from 85 to a genuine 100 mph, as was to be most effectively demonstrated a few months later. My Advertising Manager colleague, Ivor Davies, had the other prototype engine fitted to his Speed Twin, and we both had great enjoyment showing our rear number plates to riders of quick Nortons, Velocettes and even Tigers, who were not accustomed to being passed by Speed Twins. Ivor and I rode down to the Blandford circuit one bank holiday to see the Foster Triumph versus Graham AJS battle. We were a few miles apart on the road and on the way we had no problem in passing all the many riders bound for Blandford. To add to the undoubted surprise of the quicker ones, Ivor had his wife Doreen on the pillion. The two machines were parked near to each other at Blandford and it was amusing to see riders examinng the engines closely, especially the engine prefix letters and numbers stamped on the crankcase. No clue there because they had the original Speed Twin prefix identity 5T. I rode some 20,000 enjoyable miles on my machine before the secret of its performance was disclosed by the dramatic debut at the Montlhéry circuit of the new 650, to which Turner gave the name Thunderbird. A strange name for a motorcycle we all thought, but as always the boss knew best. The new model was to be a great success in America especially, and the name had a North American Indian origin. There had been Indian Chiefs whose name Thunderbird, from the mythology of the tribe, had been handed down over the centuries by their ancestors. Now the Meriden Chief was to create a Thunderbird which was to become a legend in the motorcycling world.

A very important section of the Meriden factory was a small area adjoining the engine assembly line and known as Baker's corner. It was inhabited by two

Chapter Four

A Daytona Tiger 100 attracts female interest at a Copenhagen Show. The price ticket is 8898 Kroner [£500] and the price of a Bonneville in Denmark now would be six times as much - one reason why none are sold.

My Third Meriden Year

highly skilled men, Frank Baker and Stan Truslove, whose duties were not specifically defined but could best be described as product development, though that was a loose term for some of the work which went on in the corner. Frank was a brilliant engine tuner and in the same class as men like Joe Craig, Freddie Clarke, Harold Willis and Doug Hele for producing a few more bhp out of a motor which was not supposed to give any more. Truslove learned the Baker skills efficiently and the pair stayed together until Frank took over as Head of the Experimental Department. Meanwhile a strange machine was born in the corner and the illicit birth was a well kept secret. The new child was undoubtedly the most attractive Triumph ever built in the factory before or since, but it was to have an unfortunate christening in the Isle of Man. Edward Turner frowned heavily on anyone who played around with his products and had he visited Baker's corner during the gestation period of the embryo baby, it would have been aborted.

Built around a very quick Tiger 100 engine which outwardly looked standard but internally was very different, the machine was low, lighter even than a GP Triumph, and with an appearance which was sheer poetry in metal. The entire factory would have been proud of it but it disappeared quietly in a van on the evening when its two parents went on holiday. It was late May and they went to the Isle of Man. On the first morning of TT practice the Triumph appeared at the grandstand and a New Zealand rider, Maurice Lowe, eagerly agreed to give it an outing on his second lap after having done the first one on his BSA Gold Star. The Triumph lap time pleased Baker and so delighted the New Zealander that he wanted to change machines for the race. The temptation was strong but Frank resisted it, not wanting the machine to attract any publicity. His purpose in bringing it to the Island had been achieved and that was enough. It had been tested over the most demanding of all circuits, handling and braking had proved excellent and it had lapped quicker than the GP Triumphs, so back it went to the hotel garage. If that had been the end of the story there would be no point in writing about the machine from Baker's corner, Frank and Stan would have enjoyed their visit to the Island and there would have been no repercussions at Meriden.

On the day before practice ended the New Zealander was on the fast descent from Kate's cottage to the Creg when his Gold Star engine made expensive noises of the most terminal kind, and there was no way it would recover for the race day. Baker's breakfast was duly interrupted by an anxious young man who had made a very long journey from his home to ride in the TT and whose appeal for help was difficult to resist. The appeal was granted, the stewards approved the change of machine and the racing number plates were moved from the BSA to the Triumph. Blissfully unaware that Edward Turner had decided to make a very rare visit to the Island, Truslove proudly wheeled the attractive machine towards the scrutineers. It caused much interest amongst the spectators and one of them

Chapter Four

My Third Meriden Year

Above: Rem Fowler, winner of the first TT [twin cylinder class] in 1907, talks to Hans Baumer, President of the Triumph Owners Club of Austria, at the Vienna to Meriden Rally.

Top Left: On 20th April 1950, Works Director Alf Camwell retired from Meriden. A packed works dining room heard Edward Turner's tribute to a man who had served the company for more than 40 years, from Bettman days well into the Turner era. On his shoulders rested the responsibility for the manufacturing and assembly quality for which Triumph was world famous.

Bottom Left: The Automobile Association sidecar outfit had long been a familiar and welcome sight on British roads [particularly if you had broken down!]. In May 1951 the AA took its first post-war delivery of outfits. Triumph twins, here seen lined up outside the works with Edward Turner doing the honours.

Chapter Four

spoke to him. 'A good looking machine Truslove' said Edward Turner, 'who does it belong to?' Had Stan simply given the name of the New Zealander he and Frank might well have got away with it but unfortunately, like others who had experienced the laser beam penetration of a Turner question, he answered more or less truthfully. 'It's ours sir'. An explanation was demanded and the well-kept secret of Baker's corner was revealed. Back at Meriden a few days later a note from Turner's office made it very clear that there would be no repetition.

In the race the New Zealander and Triumph performed extremely well. By the fourth lap they were in eighth place and with a couple of slowing machines about to disappear from the leader board there was every hope of equalling, if not bettering, the 5th place which another New Zealander, Syd Jensen, achieved on a GP Triumph in 1949. That had pleased Turner and a repeat might even have relaxed his veto on racing involvement but it was not to be. Climbing out of Ramsey on the 5th lap the engine cut out on one cylinder and limped to the pits where Baker retired it without looking for the trouble. In fact all that was wrong was a blocked jet in one carburetter.

Chapter Five

The Montlhéry Story

I WAS proud to be given the responsibility of organising the administrative arrangements for launching the new Thunderbird model in September 1949. The motorcycling journals gave full reports of the event at that time and it has been recalled more recently in two books of Triumph history, especially by the Davies' 'It's a Triumph' with its fine pictures. However, there are stories behind the Thunderbird debut which have never been told and which are well worth the telling. The target for the Montlhéry introduction was 500 miles at 90 mph and Turner decided that, as there would not be enough impact publicity if only one machine was used, or even two, he would go for the grand slam and have three. They were prepared, plus one spare, by a team led by Tyrell Smith and Ernie Nott, who also did the test riding on the straight mile of road near Meriden village. By the second week of September all was ready, the circuit and the Cheval Blanc hotel had been booked, the Dunlop tyre technician alerted, and the press given news of the project. I collected travellers cheques to pay all the bills in France and on 15 September the four machines left the factory and headed for Dover. Photographs remind me that I was riding number four, with Alex Scobie leading the way and Tyrell Smith and Len Bayliss between us. Watching Tyrell's

Chapter Five

great performances in the Island when I had not long left school, I never could have dreamed that one day I would be riding with him to Montlhéry. Len Bayliss was a member of the Triumph test staff and a fine grass track rider on his Elbee specials. Alex Scobie was number one test development rider, who covered hundreds of miles between dawn and dusk every week day, and enjoyed every one of them. The tales of his riding adventures were legion and not always believed. Especially the one about giving a lift to an Indian who had lost his elephant. Alex vividly described the happy reunion of elephant and Indian in a field off the A5 near Daventry, with tears of relief from the Asian gentleman and joyful trumpeting from his large friend. There were roars of laughter from the Experimental Department staff and Alex protested in vain that the story was true. That evening the *Coventry Telegraph* reported that a circus truck carrying an elephant had run away down the steep Weedon hill, turned over at the bottom, and catapulted its passenger into a field. The annoyed animal had departed hurriedly across the Northamptonshire countryside in the general direction of Oxford. Alex accepted humble apologies the next morning. He was to have another adventure on our way to Montlhéry, which created problems for the three of us behind him.

We had left Meriden very early as I had been instructed by Turner to report to him in Paris at an address in Rue Pershing, where he was visiting friends. The four machines made fast time to Paris and we halted in the Place de la Concorde, which I knew was somewhere near the rue we wanted. The first people I asked for directions were inevitably tourists and it was some time before I found a native who knew the area. He poured out the gauches and the droites and pointed his finger. I took the lead and followed the line he had pointed. Four Thunderbirds accelerated away, but the wrong way round the traffic system of the Place de la Concorde. To upset one French car driver is an unpleasant experience but to throw a stream of cars and taxis into chaos causes a fair amount of unpopularity. We hurried away from the scene of bent bumpers and smiled when Turner asked if we had found him without much trouble. Soon we were on our way south to Montléry and Alex took the lead. Some miles out of Paris, travelling quickly and fairly close together, we approached a cross roads with a Gendarme standing in the centre. He had his back to us, the Thunderbirds were quiet, and maybe we were travelling up wind. As Alex arrived, the Gendarme turned round suddenly and took an unfortunate step to his right. Alex touched his foot and the close formation team had much difficulty in avoiding a Gendarme who was literally hopping mad. It became very desirable to reach the Cheval Blanc as quickly as possible and get the machines out of sight.

The next day was spent at the circuit on test runs and making everything ready in the pits. The surface of the track was not so good, especially on the bankings, and the rear tyres would need to be checked carefully during their 500 miles of hard work. For the riders it was to be no pleasure trip, as there were

The Montlhéry Story

many bumps which could only be avoided by taking a higher line on the banking, which would mean losing time, and this was out of the question. One or two seconds a lap adrift would upset the whole schedule. As the machines came in from their test runs, Tyrell and Ernie went to work to find the cause of some misfiring at maximum speeds. Plug colour indicated too weak a mixture on each engine and jet sizes were increased. Misfiring continued and the plug colours remained the same. The experience which Tyrell and Ernie had when preparing Rudge TT engines on the test bed in Coventry gave them a clue, and a machine was sent out to lap at 80 mph. It came in, the plugs were checked, and found to be the perfect shade of brown. The trouble was inadequate fuel flow at more than 80 mph. The bore of the single petrol tap was large enough for the Speed Twins on which it was used as standard, but the Thunderbirds needed a larger one to feed them at sustained high speed. The taps were reamered out and the problem was solved. At the end of the day each machine was given a thorough service, new tyres were fitted, and we returned to the hotel to await the arrival the next evening of the rest of the rider team, the motorcycling press boys, and Harold Taylor, who was the ACU official observer. Dear old Harold was a fine sidecar driver in

Return of the Thunderbirds to Meriden from Montlhéry, September 1949. Left to right: The Author, Bob Manns, Len Bayliss, Tyrell Smith and Alex Scobie.

Chapter Five

trials events despite having only one leg, and he became manager of Britain's international motocross team. I always regretted that Harold used a crutch instead of an artificial leg, for when he appeared occasionally on TV at motocross events, he was not very good visual publicity for motorcycling.

Far away in Wales at Llandrindod Wells, the 1949 International Six Days Trial had ended its fifth day as we locked the Thunderbirds away for the night. The Triumph team riders Allan Jefferies, Jim Alves and Bob Manns were on the Gold Medal standard and after the speed tests which would end the final day, they were to travel fast to Birmingham airport, accompanied by Harold Taylor. Waiting to take them to France was the DH Rapide owned by the Dunlop Company, which had generously made the aircraft available to us at no cost.

Its passenger list merits a personal commentary. Allan Jefferies was, in my opinion and that of many other people, the finest all-round motorcycle rider ever known. He was Captain of the British team in International Six Days events, a brilliant competitor in the trials classics and winner of the Experts, the speedway exponent who partnered the famous Frank Varey in the Argentine and, as he demonstrated in June 1949, a road racer of the highest ability. Spectators in the Island that year will always remember his great ride on a Triumph Tiger, when he finished second to the rising star Geoff Duke on a faster Norton in the Senior Clubmans. Incidentally, the day before that race, having watched Geoff in practice I introduced him to Courtenay Edwards of the *Daily Mail* as the future World Champion and Courtenay printed the prophesy. Allan was one of the greatest personalities the motorcycling world has ever known and stories of his experiences would make a fascinating biography. One of my favourites goes back to the International Six Days in Italy in 1948 when the British team, captained by Allan, won the Trophy. The celebrations at a San Marino hotel finished up on the roof garden and, bidding a very late goodnight to those who had survived the party, Allan removed a large sunshade umbrella from a table, walked to the edge of the roof and stepped into space with his improvised parachute. It was a fair drop down to the street but Allan walked away happily singing the song of Ilkley Moor.

Jim Alves is best remembered as the man who destroyed the supremacy of the single cylinder in the classic trials. Having won the 350 cc class in the 1946 Colmore on a Velocette, and the same class on an Enfield in the Victory the same year, he was signed by Triumph and switched to the 350 twin. A hopeless trials machine, said the pundits, far too smooth and with the power band in the wrong place. Alves promptly proved them wrong by winning three of his first National events. He went on to become a regular member of the British International Six Days teams. Montlhéry was his first experience of long distance, high-speed circuit riding, but if he was at all apprehensive, he did not show it. To taciturn Alves, the Montlhéry speed saucer had advantages over such trials sections as

The Montlhéry Story

Camp in the Colmore and Nailsworth Ladder in the Experts. There were no rocks or mud.

At the 1950 Swedish show in Gothenburg, Triumph Distributor Uno Ranch [on the right] introduces the Thunderbird to Police Chief Fontell [in uniform], and a member of the Swedish Government. The Swedish Police standardised on Triumphs for many years.

Chapter Five

The Triumph stand at the 1951 Brussels Show. The machines on display comprise the Speed Twin and Thunderbird on plinths, the Trophy and Tiger 100 with their die-cast alloy engines, and a Thunderbird/Steib outfit. Also shown is a sectioned example of the internally sprung rear wheel.

The Montlhéry Story

The versatile Bob Manns was a Triumph development rider based in the Competition Shop, where all the trials and ISDT machines, and later on the scramblers, were prepared. Trials, motocross and circuit racing all had Manns in the entry lists and later on, when he left Meriden for Woolwich, he was a successful performer in the Thruxton 500 miles race on AJS twins.

On the Saturday afternoon I left Montlhéry in a large Citröen to collect our Welsh contingent from Le Bourget airport. I calculated they would leave Birmingham in the Rapide around 4 pm and should arrive less than three hours later, after going into Lydd for customs clearance. By 7 pm I was still waiting and when they had not arrived an hour later I asked Le Bourget control to check with Lydd. The radio report was worrying: the Rapide had left Lydd two hours earlier and was now seriously overdue. I had visions of good friends down in the Channel, until control learned that the aircraft had landed at some airfield near Versailles. It took a long time before I found the airfield and drove up to the dark and apparently deserted war-time control tower. I thought I was at the wrong place and was about to drive away when I saw a light coming from underneath the control tower. I descended the steps towards the light and as I emerged into what had once been an air raid shelter and was now a flying club bar, I was greeted rudely by the Yorkshire voice of Allan Jefferies. Where had I been, why was I late and did I have plenty of francs to pay a large bill for drinks? I ordered another round for the British and French flyers and heard the story of how Jefferies, on his very first flight, had enabled the Rapide pilot to clear the trees on the take-off from Lydd. The Rapide, with its load of heavy passengers, luggage and fuel, was at maximum weight for a grass field and took a long run to become airborne. As it lifted towards the boundary trees, the pilot yelled for a couple of passengers to rush towards the tail. Jefferies beat Alves by two seconds into the luggage section, the nose lifted, the trees were cleared. It was late when we arrived at the Cheval Blanc but, like all French bars, closing time was determined by the customers.

Early on Monday morning 20 September, preparations were made for a 9 am start and the weather forecast was for a cloudy but dry day. Edward Turner arrived and set me thinking when he asked what I would do if any machine had trouble. I could only answer that we were lapping at close to 100 mph, which would give us enough bonus time to take care of anything short of major problems, and we were hoping the rear tyres would last. As start time approached, the machines went away on their warming up laps and at 9 am the stop watches clicked and sent Scobie on his way, followed by Manns and Alves. Such was the consistency of their lap times that the distances on the circuit between the riders varied only by a few yards and the only signals necessary were to bring a rider in at the end of his period. Hour after hour the machines flashed past the pits with precise regularity, until number 3 made an unscheduled stop

Chapter Five

This unique photograph of Allan Jefferies was taken nineteen years before he rode in the Triumph team which launched the Thunderbird at Montlhéry. Taken in 1930 at Esholt Park, near Bradford, it portrays one of the road race events for which Esholt was famous. Even more famous was the exhaust note of the two-stroke, two cylinder Scott, manufactured nearby and which always thrilled spectators in the Isle of Man. Here at Esholt, Jefferies and his Scott accelerate away from Gatepost Corner. [C.H. Wood]

The Montlhéry Story

The competent riding style of comprehensive craftsman Allan Jefferies is well illustrated by this photograph of him on a Triumph during the 1948 ISDT in Italy. As always, he was on Gold Medal standard. [Motor Cycling]

71

Chapter Five

Again the unmistakable A.J., this time in the John Douglas Trial. The machine is a single cylinder Triumph, probably a Tiger 80. [Motor Cycling]

The Montlhéry Story

Famous son of a famous father, Tony Jefferies rides a Triumph Trident in the 1973 Anglo-American Match Races at Oulton Park.

Chapter Five

Few riders could get past short circuit ace John [Mooneyes] Cooper on the Scarborough circuit. One of them was Tony Jefferies, seen here going around the outside of Cooper during the Gold Cup Race of 1971.

The Montlhéry Story

Continuing the remarkable tradition of father Allan and brother Tony, Nick Jefferies has become a very fine trials rider and road racer. Here he is seen on a works Honda in the Scott Trial, an event which Allan enjoyed on so many occasions.

Chapter Five

with a leaking fuel tank. It was away again in less than five minutes with a replacement from the spare machine, and we crossed our fingers against needing another tank. At the end of the fourth hour the Dunlop technician made his final checks on tyre conditions and tread depth, with the pronouncement that they would all last the distance. The last hour became tense and we listened even more intently to the exhaust note of each machine as it passed the pits. As Tyrell and Ernie double-checked the lap scoring and the 500 miles target figure came nearer, I prepared the final signal board. Numbers 1 and 2 went across the final line within seconds of each other and continued at reduced speed whilst the third machine completed the distance. The trio then closed up and were timed on a final flying lap at over 100 mph. There were congratulations and handshakes from Edward Turner to the whole team as the speeds of each machine were calculated and ACU-checked by Harold Taylor. A jubilant celebration began in the Cheval Blanc as I telephoned the figures to Ivor Davies in the anxious factory at Meriden. Each machine had averaged over 92 mph and had covered the final lap at more than 101 mph. The details of the Thunderbird debut were put on the news media wire service by a reporter from Paris, who we had assumed was a member of the Montlhéry circuit staff, and BBC radio made it a news item in the evening.

After I had finished 'phoning the good news to Ivor Davies, he gave me the bad news. Whilst we had been busy at the circuit, the Government had announced the devaluation of the pound, and I had a problem with my travellers cheques. The Bank of England had allowed only £300 for all expenses and this had suddenly been reduced to £270. Even worse news awaited our return to Paris the next morning, when I found that French banks had suspended dealings in Sterling. We had to ride back to England early the next day, but urgently needed francs to pay bills. Then I remembered an old friend and Triumph enthusiast Fred Payne, who owned the Artists' Club in the Rue Pigalle. Fred visited England each year and amongst other things he bought a new Triumph with Sterling currency which he had changed into francs for British visitors. The severe Bank of England restrictions on foreign currency did not permit much enjoyment of the pleasures of Paris. I telephoned Fred, whose morning paper had delighted him with the Montlhéry news, and there was a warm welcome to his club, which opened at 10 pm. We borrowed enough francs from our hotel to take the Metro to Montmartre and Fred greeted us in his bar, where stood his latest Tiger 100. The first drinks were on the house and I earned a few more by playing the piano. It proved to be a delightful night, which ended with a high-speed tour of Paris and the Bois de Bologne in a fast Delage driven by a French Air Force officer. I was very sad to learn of Fred's death several years later. His sister wrote to give me the news that he died, after falling down the cellar steps of his club. He had done this before but this time he was sober, otherwise she was sure he would not

The Montlhéry Story

have been hurt.

Someone had aranged for a Police escort to lead us out of Paris the next morning and we made good time to Boulogne. At Folkestone we made a quick visit to Jock Hitchcock, the most loyal dealer Triumph ever had. His service became legendary and on his weekly visits to collect spares from Meriden, he was always at the factory by 8 am. I phoned Ivor Davies to give him our arrival time estimate, so that he could inform the press and BBC boys. As we rode along the Coventry by-pass there were many employees having their lunch break outside several factories, and as they spotted the machines with their Montlhéry numbers on the headlamps, they cheered us on our way to Meriden a couple of miles further. Line astern, we entered the factory gates to be greeted by the entire Triumph workforce. The day when the first Thunderbirds returned home was an important milestone on the road along which Edward Turner led his company for many successful years. Inside the factory the production line was full of the new blue machines and in the Despatch Department were hundreds of them in packing cases, labelled for America.

There was a pleasant surprise in the mail the next morning. On instructions from the Bank of England, Barclays wrote with congratulations to say that we could not possibly have paid all expenses with a devalued £300 and they would be happy to authorise more, to repay any loan we had obtained in France. A nice gesture, as contravening exchange regulations always meant a heavy fine. The end of my Montlhéry story is that I bought number 2 machine and rode it for another 50,000 miles. To the headlamp nacelle I attached a brass plate engraved with the words 'This is one of the three Thunderbirds which covered 500 miles at 92 mph and a final lap of 101 mph at Montlhéry. September 1949.'

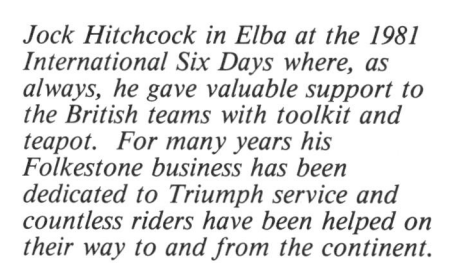

Jock Hitchcock in Elba at the 1981 International Six Days where, as always, he gave valuable support to the British teams with toolkit and teapot. For many years his Folkestone business has been dedicated to Triumph service and countless riders have been helped on their way to and from the continent.

Chapter Six

A photograph for 1950 Speed Twin publicity. In those days models wore clothes.

Chapter Six

The Shape of Things to Come

1950 PROVED to be an important turning point for my future Triumph years. I was directed by Turner to spend as much time as possible assisting the Export Manager in developing new markets. Production was increasing, and was well below demand for America and the UK alone but, as always, Turner was planning for the future. Accordingly, I gave half of my time to export business and I rode further and faster to maintain the Dealer relationship on my home territory. My Export Manager friend was Harry Holland, who had moved to Meriden after years of loyal service to BSA, whose internal policies he finally found intolerable. Although Turner did not say so, my move was to understudy Holland and take over when he was due to retire several years later. Our business association led to a warm friendship throughout the many years until Harry died when he was 90 years old in the Motor Trades retirement home at Sunninghill, the week when I left BMW at nearby Bracknell. I was the last of his friends to see him and, on the Sunday evening before his death only a few hours later, we talked of our good Meriden days. Harry had so enjoyed our weekly chats and there were tears in his eyes because this would be my last visit until I returned to England. I promised him a copy of my book, but now he will never read my tribute to one of

Chapter Six

the finest gentlemen to serve the motorcycle industry.

My work in the export field was the beginning of specialised activities in Military and Police business. There were a number of countries overseas which could not afford to import machines for private use, but they did need them for official duties. The 500 cc side valve twin TRW, which was introduced in 1949, had been developed for the British Services to meet a War Office formula of performance and specification. The basis of the formula was for a machine which was capable of withstanding any kind of treatment given to it by service riders. The programme of proving tests to which the TRW was subjected at the Fighting Vehicles Research Establishment at Chobham in Surrey, was similar to that used for Crusader tanks. I spent many days at Chobham with the TRW and in later years with the Military Cub and ohv twins. Even the slightest modification involved much paper work and starting the test programme all over again. The final outcome, as far as the British Services were concerned, was a few TRWs for the Navy and RAF, but none for the Army. However, our time and efforts had not been wasted, for large numbers were sold overseas, notably to Canada, South Africa, Burma and Pakistan. Having ridden the TRW on test I can affirm that it achieved the original specification aim of being rider proof. The maximum speed was 60 mph but, with no rear suspension and a hard saddle, no rider would want to do that speed.

The standard Police machine in those days was the Speed Twin, to catalogue specification, even to the colour. Except for the Metropolitan Force, no large fleets were used, and I set to work to change this. Overseas, the standard machine was quite suitable and good fleet orders were obtained, but for the UK changes were desirable to make it more specialised for Police duty. One important requirement was for weather protection, and I certainly needed this myself for my long distance rides, which invariably ended at hotels with no way of drying clothes for the next morning. I went along to Wiltshire to talk to my friend Doug Mitchenall, whose family business later produced the well-known Avon range of equipment. We discussed the idea of a fairing which would give substantial protection and, with his flair for design and expert knowledge of glass fibre, Doug soon had a prototype which was fitted to my machine. From then onwards my weather problems were minimal and, looking back now, I like to believe that the fairing was a major factor in widening the Police use of patrol motorcycles.

Another important Police requirement was for radio equipment on machines and I took the view that a Police rider who could be in radio contact with his control room would be a much more valuable unit. Police car radio was much too cumbersome to be mounted on a motorcycle, but was there a company prepared to make a suitable set? I found one which was interested, British Communications Corporation at Wembley, and they were very helpful. The result was the type 88 BCC and I had one fitted to my machine for demonstrating to Police

The Shape of Things to Come

Trying out an early Mitchenall fairing. The Author has often wondered why it took years for fairings to become popular, and then probably because of racing practise.

Forces. I talked to Frank Nurdin of the BCC about the idea I had of publicising the development by using radio on the TT Marshals' machines and he was in favour. Then I faced the more difficult problem of persuading Edward Turner to make six Triumphs available for the Marshals, and I well remember the words of his first reaction. 'As we are not taking part in the play, we should keep off the stage'. Finally he agreed that it was worth while to help Police business prospects. Nurdin and I went to the Island in March to test radio reception around the course and I remember riding to Liverpool through sleet and fog. When we

Chapter Six

The Tiger 110 pictured in a pleasant location near the Meriden factory. The rear styling and the deep front mudguard, so popular on the 350 cc. 3TA model, were not so liked by Tiger 110 owners, and the attempted breakaway from the normal mudguards of a high performance machine was soon abandoned. [Richard C. Bailey]

The Shape of Things to Come

The 200cc Tiger Cub had its own assembly line at Meriden, and this baby of the family made a big contribution to Triumph business for some years. Its removal to the BSA factory was a serious mistake. It quickly lost its Triumph identity and never recovered from the transplant.

Chapter Six

reached Douglas, the Island was bathed in warm sunshine. The next day Nurdin set up the control set at the Grandstand and I did a lap of the course, stopping at intervals to call him on the radio telephone. As far as Glen Helen signals were good, but then they began to deteriorate and before Ramsey they had disappeared. They did not appear again until the Guthrie Memorial, and it was evident that Snaefell mountain blanked out the far side of the course. The problem was overcome by putting a relay set on the top of the mountain.

The ACU and race organisers, especially the Medical Officers, were delighted with the offer of radio-equipped machines. Subsequently in the Junior, when a New Zealand rider crashed beyond Ballacraine, his life was probably saved by the instructions given to the first aid men through the Marshal's radio by the Chief Medical Officer at the Grandstand control. The week before the races I had apperared on a live BBC TV programme with my radio-equipped Speed Twin, and acting as a Marshal I used the radio with Ivor Davies elsewhere in the studio in the role of controller. Good publicity for the BCC, for Triumph and for the TT races. Regrettably, although Graham Walker in his TT commentaries for BBC praised the innovation of radio-equipped Marshals' machines, he could not mention the name of the radio manufacturer. Nurdin was upset and refused to help next year. As for the machines, I did not have to ask Edward Turner, as Stan Hailwood bought six new Triumphs the following year for the Marshals to use. He was that kind of man.

In 1951, when I was still combining my export and territorial duties, Chairman Jack Sangster called a meeting of the Triumph senior staff and gave us the news that he had sold the company to the BSA Group. The reason he gave was the vulnerability of the company to death duties and the tax man, but paradoxically it was not the tax man but BSA who liquidated Triumph many years later. The story is probably true that BSA also had to buy a concern called ET Developments for nearly a quarter of a million pounds, in addition to the 2.5 millions they paid Sangster. There certainly was such a concern and, as the initials imply, it protected the designs of Edward Turner. The story deserves to be true and I like to believe it. The Sangster news shocked us all that morning as there was keen commercial and personal rivalry between the two companies, but we were relieved to be assured that Turner was not part of the deal. He would remain Managing Director at Meriden and we knew that as long as he did so, Triumph would continue to lead the industry. The Sangster sale also gave him a seat on the BSA Board, of which Sir Bernard Docker was the Chairman, and I was wrong for many years in suspecting that Sangster was ambitious to take over from Sir Bernard. When he did so five years later I was sure I had been right. It was Edward Turner who revealed the true story to me when I spent a day at his home only a few months before he died. Sangster was one of the guests attending a London function of leading industrialists and financiers, not long after the BSA

The Shape of Things to Come

Some Meriden personalities of the 1950s. On the left, holding a glass, is Percy Tait, and next to him is Ernie Nott who, as long ago as 1928, covered 200 miles in 2 hours, on a Rudge. The other glass holder is Alex Scobie, and on his left is Ivor Davies. Left front is TT rider of the 30s, Ginger Wood. Also in the photograph are Stan Truslove, John Nelson, Jack Wickes and Steve Tilley.

deal. He heard a group discussing his appointment to the Board and some disparaging remarks were made about his motorcycle background. It was then that he decided to plan his way to the Chairman's seat and once Jack Sangster made a decision, he would carry it out. The BSA Group certainly needed a new architect and after less than four years of Sangster's direction, it achieved a record profit of more than 3 million pounds. This brilliant but unassuming man always retained his fondness for motorcycles and whenever we met he would chat as one rider to another and challenge me to continue motorcycling as long as he would.

Having reached the top of the complex BSA Group empire of factories from Durham to the Midlands, producing machine tools, steel, metal powders, guns, motorcars, buses and motorcycles, Sangster appointed a Vice-Chairman within two years. Later in his life he was reported to have admitted that this was his second major mistake, the first being to sell Triumph to BSA.

The newcomer was introduced to the Motorcycle Division executives in a

Chapter Six

The Triumph team in Italy for the 1951 International Six Days Trial. Left to right: Jim Alves [659], Bert Gaymer and Peter Hammond [500s]

The Shape of Things to Come

Edward Turner chats to B.J. Hargreaves after his 1952 Clubmans TT win on a Tiger 100. Turner believed this was the formula of racing which most benefited production development and provided opportunities for enthusiasts who could not afford special machinery.

Chapter Six

most unusual way. I had been instructed to report with my colleagues to the Mallory Park circuit and I was to wait at the entrance for Sangster. We were to have the range of Triumph models with us and they would be joined by the BSA and Ariel machines. Nobody knew the reason for the strange arrangements and the Meriden contingent thought it very odd that whatever was afoot should be happening in the absence of Edward Turner, who was on his way to Australia. On a cold wet morning I sat on a Tiger 110 at the Mallory gates, waiting for the Chairman's Continental Bentley to arrive. It drew in with Sangster driving, and his passenger told me to lead the way, before the Chairman, with his usual charm, apologised for keeping me waiting in the rain. We joined the assembly and within a few minutes Sangster had put on his riding kit and was enjoying himself round the circuit on my Tiger. Afterwards, everyone adjourned to the clubhouse where the collection of machines was paraded. During aperitif time the as yet unknown visitor asked me if I had served with his regiment, whose tie I was wearing, and in which he mentioned he had been a Brigadier. The enquiry could have been made more diplomatically and the ex-Captain was not favourably impressed by his first meeting with the ex-Brigadier.

After lunch Sangster addressed the assembly and explained why it had been arranged. First, he wished to introduce the new Vice-Chairman, Eric Turner and, second, to invite him to give his impressions of the Group machines. The new second in command gave a reply which, to say the least, did not make a favourable impression on his listeners. He did not like motorcycles and having come from the aircraft industry, he could not understand why three factories should be making different types of machines. He would have expected rationalised models, using a standardised range of engines, many common parts and differing only by colours and tank badges. We made our various ways back to Meriden, Small Heath and Selly Oak, with apprehensive feelings. The Triumph contingent wondered whether Edward Turner had been made aware of the new appointment before he left for Australia and whether he would be able to preserve the proud individuality of the Meriden models.

On his return he was appointed Managing Director of the Automotive Division of the Group, which gave him the added responsibility for Small Heath, Selly Oak and Daimler. We at Meriden who admired him so much all felt that he should have had the Vice-Chairmanship but, for all we knew, he did not want it. He gave me a hint of his feelings one evening when we were having a personal talk. He was not prepared, he said, to attempt the impossible task of making the Small Heath factory viable. It was too late for anyone to do that but he would be bound to ensure that Triumph progress did not leave BSA too far behind. His immediate task was to get the Daimler plant back into profitable business after years of losses. He did so very quickly and soon produced the sports SP 250, using his design of a 2.5 litre V8 engine having a cylinder head with a distinct rela-

The Shape of Things to Come

tionship to the Thunderbird arrangement. The Daimler Majestic saloon was given a larger capacity engine of the same type and the revitalised factory, restored to its old prestige and profitable production, was sold to Jaguar.

Here is the proof, in a Keppel Gate photograph, that the Author once rode as a Marshal on the TT course, though only for a day in March 1951. He was testing the radio equipment which was used on the Marshals' Triumphs in June and again the following year.

Meanwhile, Turner had added to the Triumph range the Tiger 100 on which the young Hailwood was to have his first success, and the unit-construction 350 cc model Twenty One, so named to commemorate the twenty first anniversary of the company. A lot of the development work on this model was done by Charles Grandfield, who came to Triumph from Rolls-Royce, and who was best known for his contribution to the design of the Jowett Javelin. The Twenty One was a well-kept secret mainly because the prototype grew up in Grandfield's home at Lichfield.

Meriden output was now keeping the factory busy round the clock, with a short break from 6 to 8 pm for machine tool maintenance. I was having to give

Chapter Six

The Triumph stand at the 1953 Earls Court Show. NWD198 is a Gold Medal winning Trophy model. In those years, a despatch rider left the Triumph factory at 8 a.m. on most mornings, with parts to replace those stolen on the previous day. When the first Tiger 100 die-cast alloy engire unit was exhibited, the magneto, carburetter and manifold were removed during the night before the show opened.

The Shape of Things to Come

Sir Harold Scott, the Commissioner of Police, inspects the new Beat System Crime Squad Motorcycle Patrols at Scotland Yard. The 500cc Triumph Speed Twins are fitted with a two-way radio telephone which has a radius that covers the Metropolitan area.

Chapter Six

Above: The Triumph-mounted Beat System Crime Squad lined up for inspection at Scotland Yard.

At the 'Whitehall 1212' Exhibition, Mr. J. Barnett, the Chief Constable of Leeds, and Mr. C.P. Fox, O.B.E., M.A., the Chief Constable of Oxford, examine a Triumph Speed Twin Police patrol motorcycle.

The Shape of Things to Come

most of my time to export affairs and in 1953, after covering my UK territory for the last time, I handed it over to a new representative. I was due to take up my appointment as Export Manager when, to my surprise, I was sent for by Edward Turner and offered the position of UK Sales Manager. I was reluctant to accept as I was enjoying the development of new export markets, but I agreed and Turner was good enough to promise that in due time he would create the new position of UK and International Sales Manager and it would be given to me. He kept his promise in October 1960. As I write these lines I am looking at the Turner letter of September 1953, confirming my UK appointment, and it covers just about every aspect of Triumph business. I would still give every assistance to the promotion of export business, I would be directly concerned with publicity, competitions, production, product quality and service. I particularly liked the instruction 'to conduct yourself in a manner which will lend prestige to yourself and the Company'. Also the admonition at the end of the letter that I would be in a position to make a substantial contribution to the company prosperity upon which depended the annual bonus payments to the senior staff. I am sure I did but, in later years, pressure from Small Heath, where no such benefit was enjoyed, steadily reduced the bonus at Meriden, and finally killed it. I remember that in one of my traditional addresses to Turner and his co-directors at the Meriden Christmas Luncheon, I asked them to note that the staff were all wearing their small check suits. I remember also that no car went with my new appointment, but in effect I joined the Final Test Department and rode new machines on my 78 miles per day to and from home. I had to make regular reports to Turner on quality and as he prided himself on using the minimum of metal for the maximum work, I particularly enjoyed reporting to him after my ride on the first 150 cc Terrier. This lively lightweight certainly supported his axiom, I told him. Admittedly it was a very dark night, but when I arrived home I could see the piston. Turner, himself a great humorist, was only slightly amused.

I was to have the special pleasure of arranging for Mike Hailwood to spend some months in the Triumph factory at the request of his father, Stanley. Not long out of his Pangbourne school, where he had been boxing champion, he kept fit at a Coventry gymnasium run by a Triumph worker who had been in the professional ring. He was very impressed with Mike and told me that he had all the qualities of a top class fighter. Some of those qualities were to be evident in his brilliant racing career. Mike was extremely popular at Meriden, even when he scattered the strolling lunch break workers on the Tiger 110 he soon acquired. His victory in the 1958 Thruxton 500 partnered by Dan Shorey gave immense pleasure to his friends at Meriden. Only a few hours after writing this paragraph I learned of the tragic death of Mike and his daughter. I spent an evening with him some while ago and we talked of times more than twenty years ago. He smiled as I recalled one Monday morning at the motorcycle premises of Laytons, owned by

Chapter Six

his father, in New Road, Oxford. The floor of the large showroom had just been polished when 17 years old Mike rode in from the Oxford canal tow path and performed an intricate but very muddy pattern of wheel marks. Many tributes will have been paid to S.M.B. Hailwood and great riders will honour him as the greatest. I am proud to have been one of his many friends.

Ahead of me in 1953 lay many exciting experiences and developments in which I was to be involved: The Johnny Allen World Record and the subsequent battle with the FIM. The machine which I persuaded Edward Turner to introduce and which I named the Bonneville. The specialised Police 650 of which I sold thousands around the world and to which I gave the name Saint as an abbreviation of the description Stop Anything In No Time. Above all, during my remaining years at Meriden I enjoyed most the many thousands of UK and Continental miles demonstrating and publicising the Saint.

Chapter Seven

The 1956 Triumph World Speed Record

IN SEPTEMBER 1955 three Americans arrived at the Bonneville Salt Flats in Utah, bringing with them a strange-looking machine: a long and narrow streamlined shell with the Texas stars painted on the nose and Triumph painted on the tail. The shell had been constructed from the drop tank of a Mustang fighter plane and so its aerodynamic shape had been wind tunnel designed. Behind the small cockpit was a 650 cc Triumph Thunderbird engine and gearbox. The Texan who thought up the drop tank idea was a veteran airline pilot, Stormy Mangham, who had many times flown aircraft in conditions which today would demand radar and navigation beacons. The Texan who had built the machine and prepared the engine was Jack Wilson, whose hairstyle evidenced the Indian ancestry of which he was justly proud. He had given the engine more power than the Meriden Factory had ever dreamed of, though outwardly it looked standard except for twin carburettors. The third Texan was the driver, slim, dark eyed Johnny Allen, also of proud Indian origin, who was to need all the courage of his forefathers when he piloted the yet untried machine towards the distant mountains beyond the salt flats. Either it stayed on a straight line or Johnny would have to be pulled from the wreckage. The very short stub of a handlebar was of

Chapter Seven

little use in correcting any deviation from the black line across the white salt, and any deviation at the targeted 200 mph would mean disaster.

This was the dedicated team which journeyed from Fort Worth to Utah to probe the problems of achieving the new World Record which they hoped to secure the following year when the salt would again be suitable for high speeds. Only in late August and the early days of September is this possible, and only then in the early morning. For the rest of the year the surface is waterlogged and only for a few days does it dry out in the hot sun. High speed runs must then be made soon after dawn as several hours later the temperature and the salt are too hot.

The Texan trio worked hard in the hours available to them and the final results were promising. The Texan Cigar, as the machine later came to be known, flashed across the white expanse at the highest speeds permitted by the standard tyres. For maximum effort, very special tyres would be needed, and they would have to be manufactured to the finest precision perfection, using a rubber compound which would be capable of withstanding the combination of abrasive salt and speeds beyond 200 mph. The team made the long journey home reasonably confident that, with few modifications, they had developed a machine capable of achieving their target the following year. Meanwhile, they took home with them a new American two-way record of 193 mph.

Thousands of miles away in Germany, another and much more powerful team was planning its own visit to the Bonneville salt in 1956. The NSU factory was developing a streamliner aimed at setting a new World Record and bringing it back as the highlight of the International Motorcycle Show at Cologne in September. The Texan trio with their hand-built Triumph-powered Cigar, and the NSU factory with its modern techniques and resources, were to create the most remarkable controversy in the entire history of the motorcycle world.

In the months that followed, the Triumph importers, Johnson Motors of California, became keenly interested in the Texan project and the possibility of boosting further the already big sales of Triumphs in the States. New American Motorcycle Association records would be of tremendous publicity value. America was not then a member of the FIM, the International Federation of Motorcycle Sport, and as far as the American sport was concerned, the FIM meant nothing. The FIM authorities had not been able to attract American membership and many years were to pass before they did so. American National records were all that concerned the States, but Edward Turner at the Triumph Meriden factory wisely took a broader view. He and Johnson Motors offered full support to the Texans and it was my privilege to be entrusted with the factory aspects of that support. As the first months of 1956 went by, I became more and more involved in important developments and from its simple beginning as an American record attempt, unimportant outside the States, the project became of major signifi-

The 1956 Triumph World Speed Record

cance to the Triumph Company in a much wider field.

Manufacturers such as Dunlop tyres, Amal carburettors, Lucas magnetos, Renold chains and Lodge plugs could only give support to a record which would have International recognition, in other words, FIM confirmation, otherwise under the strict rules which governed their advertising conduct, they could not publicise the use of their products. I had been instructed by Turner to obtain technical and financial support from such manufacturers and nobody argued with him. He once told me that he had no time for anyone who always agreed with him but admired a man who would challenge his views. However, he added that such a man would be unlikely to stay with the Company very long.

Seeking support from the component manufacturers quickly convinced me that I had to do something about FIM recognition and approval of the American attempt. This had never been done before and to make the problem worse, the FIM President, Piet Nortier, was already aware of the official attempt by NSU under FIM supervision. In fact, I understood he was to go to Utah to supervise it.

I found a most helpful friend and adviser in the person of Major Tom Loughborough, the Secretary General of the FIM, whose office was in Kent. Tom had done fine work over many years for the Federation and indeed did more than anyone else to preserve its remaining authority. He advised me on all the formalities and regulations necessary to obtain FIM recognition, should a record be achieved.

There were two major problems: first, approved timing apparatus and second an FIM-appointed official to supervise the attempt. These obstacles appeared formidable, but Loughborough provided the answer to both. An Austin Healey team would be at Bonneville during late August attempting long distance records, supervised by an official on behalf of the FIA, the International Federation of Automobile Sport which was affiliated to the FIM. The official was Philip Mayne, whose home was in Worcestershire. The questions were: would he be able to check and approve the timing apparatus to be used for the Triumph project, and could he either supervise the attempt or appoint a qualified official? I contacted Mayne and he was most ready to help. Loughborough issued official approval of the record attempt and all that remained was for Philip Mayne to check and confirm the accuracy of the timing apparatus. He was not only to confirm the accuracy but to be most impressed by its ability to record a time within decimal points of a second. It had been perfected by the Californian Institute of Technology and was the most sophisticated in the world. Mayne reported back to Loughborough, appointed a highly qualified American timekeeper, and world recognition had been secured for a successful attempt by the Texans. Meanwhile, the UK component firms confirmed their financial support and the Dunlop company went to work on ultra-special tyres. The standards of perfection they set themselves were so high that one hundred tyres were specially

Chapter Seven

The Triumph stand at the 1955 Earls Court Show with Johnny Allen's 'Thunderbird' streamliner in the foreground. Two months before it had clocked 193 M.P.H. at Bonneville Salt flats. The following year it achieved 214 M.P.H.

The 1956 Triumph World Speed Record

manufactured and tested, to produce the six to be flown to America. It was very satisfying to know that the Texans had complete faith in Dunlop to produce tyres capable of withstanding speeds and conditions never before attempted by a motorcycle.

As the Texan Cigar arrived at the Salt Flats at the end of August 1956, the NSU team was celebrating its success. The German streamliner had set a new World Motorcycle Speed Record of 211 miles per hour. The Germans must have smiled benevolently at the garage-built Cigar as they went home to proclaim their achievement and proudly exhibit the World's fastest machine at the Cologne Exhibition.

On 6 September the Salt Flats awaited the dawn challenge of Johnny Allen in his Triumph-powered fighter drop tank. The black strip he saw from his low cockpit aimed him at the distant hills, shimmering in the haze as the early morning sun evaporated the night moisture from the salt. The timekeeeper crew was ready, the rescue vehicles were positioned at intervals down the course, and Stormy Mangham, with Jack Wilson, held the red machine as the engine growled its warming up note. The seconds ticked by to the moment when the machine would flash across the electronic starting beam and either fulfil or destroy the faith of the men who had built it and their friend who was driving it.

The Cigar was pushed away and gathered speed over the mile approach to the timing strip. Wilson had expertly calculated the gear ratios and the timing beam was broken at close to maximum velocity. Stormy Mangham had equally expertly calculated the aerodynamics of his drop tank and the machine stayed precisely on the black line as it flashed past the end timing mark.

The timekeeper signalled a speed of 213 mph for the measured distance and all now depended upon the return run from which the average speed would be determined. A quick check and the run up to the timing mark began. The machine became a red blur against the shimmering white salt as it flashed towards the distant timing beam. It left behind the full power sound of the Triumph twin cylinder engine, without the slightest variation in the high note of more than 7500 revolutions per minute, until the salt flats became quiet once more as Allen closed the throttle at the end of his journey into the record book. The average speed was confirmed at 214 mph. The sun had risen higher over Bonneville and so had the satisfaction of the three Texans, whose hand-built machine had gone faster than any motorcycle had travelled before. It is worth recalling that at the end of his runs in a machine which would either go straight or destroy him, Johnny Allen was as calm as a man after a morning stroll. It has been stated by a Doctor who was present that his pulse rate remained perfectly normal and knowing Johnny very well I can believe this. Having had the privilege of looking after his welfare when he later came to England, I can also believe the legendary story that his pulse only quickened when he met a pretty girl. Certainly I can testify that the

Chapter Seven

pulse of pretty girls quickened when they met Johnny. He was that kind of man.

The Cigar was loaded ready for the long journey back to Fort Worth, the Officials dispersed and the course plough was then taken away for another year when the Bonneville speed week would again disturb the now silent expanse of salt. Philip Mayne cabled the timing figures and speed to Tom Loughborough in his FIM office at the Old Forge in Hawkinge and Tom telegraphed news of the record, with his congratulations, to the Triumph factory. The NSU organisation halted its Cologne Exhibition preparations and FIM President Piet Nortier halted recognition of the Triumph record. Then began the extraordinary sequence of events which were to end many months later in a London Court of Law.

I was convinced there was no way in which the record could be questioned, for I had meticulously ensured that the FIM rules and conditions governing record attempts had been observed. Secretary General Loughborough had done the same and had no hesitation in sending his congratulatory telegram. It was impossible to understand how President Nortier could, and for the first time, overrule Loughborough and the authority of his position. The history of the FIM since then has more than once been clouded by controversy and there have often been harsh words about its attitude to motorcycle sport. The death of Tom Loughborough marked the end of a much more pleasant era.

Official recognition of the Triumph record was refused on the grounds that the timing apparatus was not approved. When, at a later meeting in Paris, I pointed out that we had an approval document signed by Loughborough, the remarkable answer from Nortier was that the Secretary General should not have issued it. The fact that FIM timekeeper Mayne had been satisfied with the accuracy of the apparatus made no difference.

In America, outside the jurisdiction of the FIM, the record was given world status in press publicity, but in Britain, it would only be advertised as an American National record. The editorial stories in the UK Press of the controversy provided much more publicity space than we could have paid for, and it was pointed out by more than one Editor that an approved record would have been news for only one issue of his journal. However, we at Meriden were not prepared to accept the FIM ruling and we demanded a meeting with the President. Meanwhile, we had the idea of bringing the record breaker to the Earls Court Show, also to invite Johnny Allen along. Our Pasadena friends, Johnson Motors, went ahead with arrangements to fly the machine from Texas to London and Johnny accepted our invitation, which meant his first trip outside the States. From Fort Worth he flew to New York and found his way to what is now Kennedy Airport. His open ticket was for no specified flight but he charmed a receptionist into finding him a seat on a crowded night flight and arrived at Heathrow the next morning. At Meriden, where we anxiously awaited in vain for news of his departure from America, I answered the telephone and found myself speaking to

The 1956 Triumph World Speed Record

a Post Office telegraph boy with whom was Johnny Allen. The boy had brought a telegram to the airport town terminal on his motorcycle and as a keen young rider he had read about the Triumph record and Johnny Allen. Johnny had asked him how to 'phone the Triumph factory and his Texan drawl was all the young man's imagination needed. He had a fine tale to tell his friends that evening.

The Cigar was not far behind as it crossed the Atlantic and arrived at Heathrow. There it was unloaded and transferred to a Dakota freight plane for the flight to Elmdon Airport, Birmingham, the next day. Reception arrangements made by my friend Ivor Davies, Triumph Publicity Manager, were worthy of the occasion. Coming home to the factory which had its name proudly inscribed on the streamlining, was a machine eagerly awaited by the workers, the thousands who would crowd around it at Earls Court and, at the airport, the press and TV Cameras. The Dakota touched down and taxied to its apron. The crate was unloaded and opened, and the machine wheeled into an English November sun so different from the one which rose over Utah as the crimson shell flashed across the white expanse of salt. The airport customs officials played their prescribed part in the reception. The engine number had to be checked against the document we had provided in evidence that the Meriden factory had once exported to America a Thunderbird with the same number. On my desk at the factory was a permit from customs authorities in London to import the machine on payment of a customs deposit which would be refunded provided the machine was only used for display at the Earls Court Show, which is all we had intended. That afternoon, however, BBC Television telephoned to ask if the machine could appear on the Sportsview, programme the following evening and would it be possible to have it do a demonstration run somewhere in the morning. The temptation of a National TV appearance was too great to resist, and so was the idea of seeing the streamliner in action. I would argue with HM Customs afterwards. The Commandant at the RAF Wellesbourne airfield, near Warwick, agreed to give us a runway and, after a few hours on proud display at the Triumph factory, the machine was taken to Wellsbourne. Johnny again entered the cockpit he had last vacated at Bonneville and did a bottom gear run at a speed which would have broken the law on a motorway. The BBC cameras took their pictures for the evening programme and the machine was transported to the Shepherds Bush studios to appear with Johnny on Sportsview, which surely would be seen by, or reported to, the customs official who would be upset at breaking of the conditions he had imposed.

Two days later came a letter, saying that we would forfeit the customs deposit we had paid. I replied informing the gentleman that I would pass his letter to the local MP, with details of the value of American orders we had received following the record achieved by the machine. A telephone call response announced that our deposit would be refunded and would I so advise the MP.

Chapter Seven

The Certificate of Appreciation presented to the Author for his part in helping Johnny Allen to raise the World's Motorcycle Speed Record to 214.40 m.p.h. at Bonneville, on 6th September, 1956.

The appearance of the machine and its driver at Earls Court was a tremendous success. My colleagues and I were wearing lapel badges which had been hurriedly made and which bore the legend 'Triumph 214'. Beneath each badge was suspended a tiny bag of salt from Bonneville, taken from the postcards sold there and thoughtfully brought to London by Johnson Motors. Johnny Allen was the guest at a number of receptions, the first being given by the motorcycle Press, where I had a problem when Johnny and the hat check girl were mutually attracted. Their conversation took preference over the impatiently waiting two hundred guests. She also was the cause of the alterations I had to make to the schedule of further receptions during the next few days.

In due course, the machine and Johnny went back to Texas, but in 1979 the streamliner came back to England, permanently. It will have a proud place in the new Motorcycle Museum to be built within sight of Elmdon Airport.

No World Speed Record has ever had so much and prolonged publicity. The Triumph company did not seek any more but an insistent Editor of a motorcycling journal asked Edward Turner whether he was prepared to take legal

The 1956 Triumph World Speed Record

action against the FIM. Such a course was unprecedented and undoubtedly Turner would never have considered it in his own mind. On the spur of the moment he gave an answer which was interpreted as affirmative unless a meeting with FIM President Nortier was productive. The Editor duly printed the story and Turner was committed.

A meeting was arranged with Nortier to take place at the FIM Headquarters, which were then in Paris, and I accompanied Turner. As Piet Nortier began the proceedings, he asked whether the discussion was to be off the record or otherwise. Looking back, I know that we made a mistake in opting for a meeting which would not be recorded, and therefore could not be communicated to the Press or used in any subsequent action. However, we had hoped for an honourable settlement, as we were entitled to do, and the meeting was off the record. Now, many years later I recall as though it was yesterday, the opening statement by President Nortier. He had no doubt whatsoever he said, that the Texan Triumph had established a new World Record. He did not doubt the accuracy of the timing apparatus, the qualifications of the officials and that the arrangements all fulfilled FIM regulations. However, the fact remained that the electronic timing apparatus had not been approved by the FIM. I emphasised that, in fact, approval had been issued by the Secretary General ... on the report by official FIM timekeeper Philip Mayne. The Secretary General had no right to do so, replied Nortier, and the meeting reached an impasse. Our visit to Paris had been a waste of time, although in retrospect it may have accelerated the approval which the FIM later gave to the American apparatus. It has since been used for many record attempts at Bonneville, including the officially recognised record of 224 mph by Bill Johnson in 1962, also on a Triumph.

After our return to England, my dossier was handed over to a QC and, after studying all the details, he advised the Company that a case against the FIM, requiring them to confirm the record, was bound to succeed. On his advice, we went ahead and the QC presented our case to a High Court Judge. The learned gentleman promptly asked whether we had been to an FIM Court of Appeal and the QC was unsure of his answer. Until we had done so, the judge was not prepared to give a ruling, and I realised that we should have given a different answer to the first Piet Nortier question in Paris. Edward Turner promptly decided to go no further and the full story of the 1956 achievement at Bonneville has waited until now to be told.

Chapter Eight

The partnership which continued for 100,000 miles. Leaving the Meriden factory gates on my first Saint 177 EUE, which I subsequently presented to the Metropolitan Police for permanent display at the Hendon Driving School. It was expertly sectioned by a Metro engineer, but its service as an instructional model must have ended now that riders and mechanics are trained on BMW. However, the Saint stays in its proud place at Hendon, with a plaque recording its history, and each time I have seen it, the memories of our many miles return.

Chapter Eight

Birth of the Bonneville and the Saint

FOR SOME time the thought had persisted in my mind that a Triumph named the Bonneville would be a natural outcome of the Utah record. However, the only time when anyone could make a major technical recommendation to Edward Turner was if they were told to do so. Perhaps there could be an exception in this case for, after all, my appointment letter to General Sales Manager made me responsible for most activities at Meriden. I decided to take a chance and so one morning I approached the top man very diplomatically, and I began by saying that no doubt he had already thought of the proposal I wished to make. I outlined the main features of a model to replace the Tiger 110, which was due for changes in any case. The Tiger was designed as a quiet, although fast, touring machine, and was not too popular in America. I recommended a more sporting appearance and a twin carburettor motor. The machine would be called the Bonneville with a two colour finish of Utah sky blue and salt flats white. There was a long pause, interrupted only by the tapping of the Turner pencil, which was usually an ominous sign. Of course he had considered the idea already, he finally said, but had rejected it because he did not like two carburettors, they were a difficult problem for an aircleaner. This I had expected him to say and in consequence I

Chapter Eight

had prepared my answer. I commented that I had bought a new Triumph every year for six years, each one had covered more than 50,000 miles, and none had an aircleaner. Besides, I added, the Americans would only remove them to get more power. As I left Turner's office a few minutes later, I knew we would have the Bonneville in September.

During the next six months, the prototype was built and tested with excellent results, and first production was scheduled for late August. For early September I planned a departure from the traditional way of announcing the new model programme to the motorcycling Press. Instead of the normal pre-Earls Court Press Release, we invited the technical journalists to a test weekend in the Welsh hills beyond Shrewsbury, during which they would each ride every model. Their reports would be published simultaneously and every journal would be predominantly Triumph. Turner approved the programme and said he would join the party.

Singly and severally, the journalists rode the machines away from Meriden on a Friday afternoon and headed for the A5 old Roman road towards the Welsh border. The Bonneville was claimed by old friend and Triumph enthusiast Barry Ryerson, whose regular mount was a 350 cc 3TA. A convivial dinner at the hotel was hosted by Turner and the forecasts both for the Saturday weather and a successful day were good. The following morning, as machines were wheeled from the garage, Turner wearing his famous bowler-type helmet announced that he would ride the Shilton Bonneville, and I felt proud of his description, but not for long. First, it refused to start and the impatient Managing Director changed over to my Thunderbird. With all other machines running I begged the Bonneville to start and ultimately it did — on one cylinder only. I was the target for very caustic remarks by Turner, including the assurance that never again would he listen to any ideas from me about motorcycle design. Bonneville production would be deferred, if not in fact abandoned. I rode my one cylinder dream machine back into the garage and, as the echoes of the others died away towards the distant hills, I searched for the trouble and found it. No compression on one cylinder.

In the evening, as the riders returned and Turner departed with a curt goodbye to me which foreshadowed a difficult Monday morning, I intercepted Barry Ryerson. Never had I appealed to anyone more earnestly than to him. Upon his answer depended the future of the Bonneville and perhaps my own. What had happened between Meriden and Wales? When did the engine become a single cylinder power unit? Our friendship had lasted a long time but now depended upon his true answer to my suspicions. Barry and I had been the founders of what became the Volunteer Emergency Service when, one Friday evening in response to his telephone appeal, I rounded up fifty riders to rush vaccine to the Birmingham smallpox outbreak the next morning. The Medical Officer for Birmingham announced to the Press that but for this action, the outbreak would have become

Birth of the Bonneville and the Saint

an epidemic.

Barry told the truth as I knew he would. On a long stretch of the A5 approaching Shrewsbury he had missed his gearchange from third to top and the engine revs went far beyond the red line, a valve touched a piston and bent its stem in the process. He was exceedingly sorry — and our friendship remains to this day.

On the Monday morning I had the cylinder head removed and I took it, together with the marked piston on a tray to the Head Man's office. My reception was unpleasant, to say the least. Rather like that given years later to the BSA Chief Accountant when he took the balance sheet to the Chairman. It was difficult to persuade Turner to look at the evidence of the missed gear change and to accept my assurances of the Ryerson explanation. Ultimately his engineer's interest prevailed and in the Churchillian manner for which he was renowned he pronounced his judgement on the future of the Bonneville. It was to go ahead with stronger valve springs. Go ahead it did, to become the most successful of all British motorcycles. Not until now has the story been told of its conception and how very nearly it came to being stillborn.

The other birth I attended in the Triumph family was that of the Saint, which was basically the Thunderbird with modifications to meet a performance formula laid down by the Metropolitan Police. The cylinder head had larger inlet valves and porting, the exhaust pipes were of smaller bore and the intermediate gear ratios were lower. A Police seat and handlebars were fitted, and a certified accurate speedometer was used. The result was a machine that was very docile in traffic, with an excellent acceleration and a top speed a shade over 100 mph. Vibration was non-existent and this was an important factor when a radio was fitted. When Edmund Majewski of Cossors came to talk to me about Police radio equipment, I urged him to design a set small enough to be accommodated in a recess in the petrol tank. The Cossor 108 type set was the result and my friends Homers of Birmingham, who supplied our tanks, produced a recessed version into which the radio fitted perfectly. For the first time Police riders would be able to transmit and receive without having to stop their machines.

In the Metropolitan Police Driving School at Hendon is permanently displayed the machine which was my demonstration model on which I covered 100,000 miles. It was the one for which I created the name Saint and which was used by the Metro when they did evaluation tests of machines submitted by all British manufacturers. At the end of its fine service in UK and Continental countries I presented Saint EUE 177 to Metro Hendon, where it has stood ever since above a plaque inscribed with its history. The Saint performance has never been surpassed by any other Police machine and I was very sad when its world-wide success came to an end as one of the results of BSA management interference with Meriden when Edward Turner was no longer around to prevent it.

Chapter Eight

With the Saint in front of the statue of the most famous of all story tellers, Hans Christian Andersen, in Copenhagen. We share the same birthday, but his was a little earlier.

Birth of the Bonneville and the Saint

The Saint and I with Danish Triumph Importer, Carl Reinhardt. The emblem on my helmet is that of the Volunteer Emergency Service, which I helped to form at the time of the Birmingham smallpox outbreak. Within twelve hours overnight, hundreds of motorcyclists were ready to rush vaccine to Birmingham from all parts of the country, and prevent an epidemic.

Chapter Eight

At the end of my first ride to the Cologne Exhibition on the Saint. Everyone, including the Burgomaster [on the right] appears to be enjoying the joke, except me. I wish I could remember what it was.

The name Saint became very popular but later it did involve me in a problem. My friend Leslie Nicholl of the *Daily Express* had talked to me about a Metro Police rider who had impressed him in a race at Brands Hatch and who was seeking a machine to ride in the Isle of Man Clubmans' TT. Leslie, who was later to give good publicity to my own long distance rides, promised a good story if his man could have a Saint, not only for the race but to ride to the Island and back. Of course it presumed a reasonable performance in the race and I emphasised that it would have to be a standard engine with a maximum speed of little more than 100 mph. So it came to pass that PC Graham Bailey rode a Saint to the Island, finished the race on the leader board and rode it back again, much to the delight of Nicholl and Shilton. Leslie wrote a fine story which occupied a half page of the *Express* the next day, and at the top of the page was the well known Saint symbol complete with halo. Before I had seen the paper my office telephone rang, the caller being the secretary to Leslie Charteris, the Author of the Saint books and creator of the world famous symbol. He had been instructed to obtain an explanation of its unauthorised use in connection with the Triumph motorcycle. I assured him that although I had not seen it, I was certain that it had

Birth of the Bonneville and the Saint

not been used in any way which would be to the disadvantage of Saint publicity. He did not suspect the double meaning of my answer. Our conversation was quite pleasant and he agreed that it was not a bad thing for the Saint symbol to be associated with a Police machine. I asked if there would be any objection if I painted the halo symbol on my helmet and he was happy about this. Many times afterwards, in various countries, the symbol was recognised by children and on one occasion, when I stopped in a Swiss village, a group of children thought I was the Saint and asked for autographs. It seemed a pity to disappoint them and so on Swiss school exercise books I scribbled my name in such a way that it looked more like Saint than Shilton. It was once one of my hopeless dreams that all motorcyclists should have the Saint symbol on their helmets and behave appropriately.

With the UK Police order book filling rapidly, EUE 177 and I turned our attention to export markets, beginning with the Continent. My targets were the BMW strongholds and first I rode to Denmark where the machine was demonstrated to the Politi in Copenhagen. My visit proved very successful but the Danes were apprehensive about the radio mounting on the tank. They explained their concern that in an accident the rider could be thrown forward and damage his vulnerable organs. I pointed out that if the machine was travelling fast the rider could be killed anyway. This it seemed was more acceptable than a live Dane with reproductive organ damage. I left the Police headquarters late and with barely enough time to cover the 185 miles to my ship at Esjberg, plus the one hour ferry crossing from Zealand to Funen. Some thirty miles before Esjberg I closed up on a fast travelling GB-plated Porsche and got past him on a twisty section. The Saint arrived alongside the Winston Churchill with twenty minutes to spare and, after cleaning up in my cabin, I made my way to the bar as we headed out into the North Sea. I called for a whisky to celebrate the promised Politi order and, hearing my English voice, a fellow traveller introduced himself and asked if I was familiar with the route from Harwich to York. He was driving to a school there to collect his daughter at the end of term and wanted to know how long the journey would take. I advised him the best route and estimated mileage but, as to the time, it would depend on what car he was driving. It was a 3-litre Porsche he said, whereupon I gave him a reasonably accurate journey time and commented on the capabilities of a Porsche to do the trip even more quickly. As he ordered two more drinks he praised the Porsche and revealed that until that evening nothing had got past it. The record had been spoiled by a British Police motorcyclist who, for some reason, was on the road to Esjberg and presumably was on the boat. I gave him another drink, revealed my identity, and piloted him in the right direction from Harwich the next morning.

With the Cologne International Motorcycle Exhibition approaching, I had the idea of a high speed publicity ride on the Saint from Coventry cathedral to the

Chapter Eight

President Kennedy and Metropolitan Police escort on his visit to London.

cathedral city of Cologne, which seemed an appropriate connection for a machine of that name. A journalist friend on the *Daily Mail* liked the project and promised a good story, with action pictures. In fact he used two editions. The BBC also liked the idea, and arranged to record an interview for the evening before I left. I prepared EUE 177, obtained a letter of greetings from the Lord Mayor of Coventry to the Burgomaster of Cologne, and recorded the BBC interview which I learned was to be included in the Jack Di Manio programme the next morning. It ended with the sound of the Saint accelerating away from the cathedral, which was to cause me considerable delay when I arrived at Liege in Belgium.

I left my Stratford upon Avon home at 5.30 am and an hour later was waved away from the centre of Coventry by Police friends. A few miles out on the London road, as I slowed down for the Dunchurch traffic island, two figures emerged from the darkness and a camera flashed to take the picture which was in the *Mail* the next morning. At Colney Hatch outside London my Metro Police friend, Len Farmer, was waiting on his Triumph to escort me to the Blackwall Tunnel. The Met boys gave me this service on a number of occasions and I was always impressed by the way in which they went through congested traffic as though the road was clear. I have ridden with the Police of many countries and none are so expert as those in Britain. Farmer waved farewell at Blackwall and I headed for

Birth of the Bonneville and the Saint

P.C. Finlayson and his public address-equipped Triumph on traffic control duty at the Festival of Britain in May 1951.

Chapter Eight

The Geneva-bound Saint at the gates of Fontainebleu Palace.

Maidstone and Lydd. A few miles before Maidstone my journey nearly ended, when an approaching car driver misjudged my speed and pulled across my lane, to turn into a side road. As I swerved to my right to miss him, he changed his mind, and turned back as though determined to have an accident. The reflex actions of motorcyclists must always be quicker than those of car drivers and my split second swerve back to my left kept me alive. I reached Lydd on time and there were more *Mail* photographers as the Saint went aboard the Bristol Freighter. On the aircraft en route to Liege I met an interesting character, who offered me a job. He was looking, he said, for an adventurous individual to assist him in his business selling guns to African countries in general and the Belgian Congo in particular. He was on his way to Brussels and a big deal in FN rifles which would reduce the population of whichever African country could afford them. He gave me his business card and I kept it in my office until several years later when I checked it against a newspaper report of a man on trial for illegal arms deals. It was the same man and he went to prison for a long time.

The Bristol landed at Liege and I had calculated that I would be in Cologne for the Press lunch reception, not that I was expected there, or so I thought. Unfortunately the Jack Di Manio broadcast upset my schedule for, as I wheeled the Saint from the aircraft, I saw my Belgian Triumph dealer friend Max Noe and a number of riders who had heard Jack's programme and the machine 'leaving'

Birth of the Bonneville and the Saint

Into the Police fairing era. A Lancashire Officer on motorway patrol with an Avon-faired Saint.

Chapter Eight

An M6 motorway photograph of Lancashire Police on a high-speed training run with Triumph Saints.

Opposite: Highly successful for many years and remembered with great affection by the Author, the 650cc Triumph Saint well merits its own Earls Court photograph. The year is 1956.

Coventry. Max had checked with the airport and verified that I was on the plane. The nearest bistro beckoned and as a result I was late leaving for Aachen and joining the autobahn for Cologne. Meanwhile, the show organisers had arranged for my official reception in the presence of the Burgomaster, not to mention Edward Turner, Jack Sangster, other dignitaries from Britain and the Press. Everyone had been informed except me, and aperitifs were being served even before I was on the autobahn. On arrival at Cologne I finally found which of the many Messe exhibition halls was housing the motorcycle show and I was met by an anxious Norman Aubury of the British Manufacturers Association, who rushed me to the reception with no time to remove my riding gear. I made a most embarrassed entry in my blue overalls and walked through the line of well-dressed guests, carrying my well-worn haversack, to be greeted by the Burgomaster and a diplomat from the British Embassy. From my haversack I extricated the letter from the Lord Mayor of Coventry and it must have been the first time the Burgomaster had seen a postman take a letter from his pyjamas. The photographers wanted to take pictures of the Saint and Turner told me to bring it to the balcony of the reception room. This meant riding it up two flights of steep steps and, as I

Birth of the Bonneville and the Saint

Chapter Eight

approached them, the gradient looked impossible. Surely I would ground the crankcase and do a loop, but Turner called down from his high level amongst the expectant group and ordered me to join them, one of the many occasions when he ordered the apparently impossible and had it done. Thanks to the *Mail*, the cathedral ride had much more publicity than it merited and it also got me a night out in Cologne with Turner and Sangster. The Saint was displayed on the British stand and it was the only Police machine in the show, which was very kind of BMW. I rode to a number of German shows in the following years but crossed the channel by ferry and there were no more pleasant delays at Liege. EUE 177 and I were to enjoy more and much longer rides than Cologne but in between them there were important things to be done at Meriden.

Chapter Nine

Never a dull moment

THE SIDE valve twin TRW having gone out of production, Meriden had no military model, and unhappily I had to decline invitations from our traditional markets to submit tenders for light or medium weight machines. Then along came the 200 cc T20 SH, which was a Tiger Cub with larger wheels and modified styling. It was not long before we had an official approach from our Ministry of Defence friends to submit the T20 SH for evaluation tests and, as with the TRW, we started the not so merry go round of modifications, test programmes, more modifications and paper work. The Cub engine was an eager to rev unit and one part of the test programme demanded maximum speed until either something broke or the relay of testers got tired of trying to break it. On the speed circuit at the Ministry establishment at Chobham, the standing starts on the severe gradients, the water troughs and the worse than French cobblestones, the Cubs did well. They also took their programmed punishment over the scramble course at Bagshot. However there was ultimately some big end trouble and at that point we should have broken off relations with the Ministry and been satisfied with our excellent commercial business which was keeping the Cub assembly line busy turning out 275 per week. However, we put more life into the big end and four

Chapter Nine

factory testers were detailed to ride Cubs at maximum speed nine hours each day from Meriden to Hendon and back. It was not long before the flying four attracted the attention of the Police and one of them was stopped for questioning. He had not been briefed on what to say in such circumstances and unfortunately, in his answer, he used the words 'destruction test'. Within the hour the Bedfordshire Police Traffic Chief rang me asking for the testing to stop and painting a dreadful picture of an exploding engine depositing debris and oil on the motorway, a pile up of vehicles and bodies all over the place. The exercise was called off, but when we stripped the engines, the big ends were perfect. However, we told the single cylinder minded Ministry that we would be interested only in supplying twins and that led to the very complex events which will be described later. Meanwhile, our time had not been unprofitable, for we supplied several thousands of Military Cubs to the French.

Incidentally, one of the flying four testers was the as yet unknown Percy Tait, of Slippery Sam fame. My good friend Percy, with whom I had many interesting duels on the Midlands roads, had three accidents in his tester days. The most severe was at walking pace on the Tina scooter, due to ice. The second was at moderate speed on a Cub. The third was in the Junior TT on a Manx Norton,

Enjoying a session with a band at the Dealer Convention dance in Pasadena, California.

Never a dull moment

which I had arranged for him to ride through Les Hallen, the Cambridge Triumph dealer. The impetuous Percy decided to pass the works Norton of Ken Kavanagh going into Hillberry at over 90 mph. The Norton left Percy and he went through the hedge and down the field like a shot rabbit, to finish rolling quite unhurt. Obviously he had been going too slowly on the Tina and Cub.

Having decided to discontinue the Military Cub after completing the French contract, we turned our attention to Army versions of the unit-construction 350 and 500 twins. Orders were obtained from the authorities of our traditional TRW markets and a promising enquiry came from Holland. A large order resulted and when I first drafted the story which was associated with this order, I gave it the title 'Cigars and the High Waterguard Officer'. He is an official whose title goes back to the days of muffled oars and midnight smugglers.

I have never met the High Waterguard Officer, but many times I have met his staff. They are called Customs Officers and they are reputed to be kind men whose high standard of training is designed to convince travellers that they are exactly the opposite. The Junior Officer who dealt with me one evening on my return from Amsterdam had been highly trained. I had in my brief case an order for 1100 Military Triumphs, handed to me a few hours earlier by the Chairman of the Triumph Importers, Stokvis of Rotterdam. In my bag I had a box engraved with the Stokvis crest and containing Corona cigars, a gift of appreciation from the Chairman. His secretary had commented that she hoped the Heathrow Customs would not spoil the gift and I replied that a sight of the impressive export order would surely be proof against any duty charge; she had her doubts.

The order from the Royal Netherlands Army had been the result of long-term personal effort, commencing with my ride on a prototype machine from Stratford upon Avon to the Hague and back. Departure 5 am, to the Hague via Rotterdam, a day of demonstrations, and the return journey which ended in the middle of the night. In due course came an order for two sample models, another visit to the Army and finally the big order and a box of cigars.

After take off from Amsterdam in a Viscount, the pilot reported poor visibility at Heathrow but expected we could land. The runway approach lights appeared out of the night mist and the plane taxied towards the dim outline of the terminal buildings. Conditions were obviously at minimum permitted visibility for a propellor aircraft and impossible for a jet. The baggage collection area was deserted and the Viscount passengers were the only arrivals. This, I was told by a fellow passenger was the time when Customs Officers are able to give more attention to baggage inspection, and when a Junior member will be gaining experience. I was selected for questioning by a young Officer, who was being supervised by a Senior. I declared the cigars, and began to explain that I had more than the duty free quantity because they were to be shared amongst the men who had helped me obtain a valuable order for motorcycles from the Dutch Army. As I took the

Chapter Nine

Receiving an award in Vienna from the Triumph Owners Club of Austria for services to the parent Club in the U.K. [A. Fenzlau]

order from my briefcase, the Customs man extracted a handful of cigars from the box, breaking the lid as he did so, and walked away. He weighed them, counted the remainder and asked for a duty payment which made me wonder whether he was on a commission bonus. I asked him to hold the cigars in bond, get the box repaired and give me a receipt. I would collect them in a week or two when I flew back to the Amsterdam Motorcycle Exhibition, taking with me the first machine of the 1100 order.

From the terminal building I made my way to the office of my friend Harry Stratton, Chief Engineer of the Heathrow vehicle fleet. Harry always permitted me to leave my car or motorcycle in the main repair garage and provided I returned from overseas between 5.30 and 7 pm my arrival was celebrated with a glass or two from my duty-free bottle. Invariably we were joined by the airport Public Relations Officer, Spike Mays, who became a best selling author with such books as *Fall Out The Officers* and *No More Soldiering*. Frequently we went on to the Peggy Bedford Inn on the Bath Road, where Spike always insisted that I played the piano.

By the third glass I had told Harry the story of the cigars and he advised me

Never a dull moment

Checking my 1907 Triumph at the 1954 Banbury Run. It completed the course, though somewhat late as I lost considerable time at the Bell Inn, Halford, on the Fosse Way.

to write to his friend, the High Waterguard Officer, to make sure they would be waiting when I returned to go to Amsterdam. The letter duly went and I sent Harry a copy. Some days later the High Waterguard Officer was having a drink with him and admired the Triumph Thunderbird tie he was wearing. The Thunderbird motif looked exactly like the BOAC Speedbird except that it was flying the opposite way. The tie once got me an invitation to a Trident flight deck when an air hostess thought I was someone important in BOAC. How could he obtain, one asked the HWO, and Harry thought it might be possible if some attention could be given to the Triumph man who had written asking for his box of cigars to be waiting when he returned with a motorcycle to go to Amsterdam. The HWO, not knowing that Harry had a copy of my letter, was unaware of our friendship and he much regretted that I had not been given the dispensation which was justified by such a large export order. Harry enjoyed telling me the story when I 'phoned to give him my Amsterdam flight date and which he no doubt passed on to the HWO.

After handing over the Triumph for loading on the Amsterdam plane, I went through passport control and was given a message to contact a senior Customs

Chapter Nine

Spike Mays, ex PRO, London Airport, and now the author of such successful books as 'Reubens Corner', 'Fall Out The Officers' and 'No More Soldiering'.

Official. My cigar box had been repaired, was handed over, and I was escorted to the VIP lounge. In return I gave an envelope containing a Thunderbird tie for the HWO. It was a fair exchange for the hospitality I was given in the lounge.

The Military Triumph was given pride of place on the stand at the Amsterdam Show and the news of the order was prominently featured in the UK Press. At the Show was the UK Minister of Defence, Roy Mason MP, and the photographs of him sitting on the machine proved very useful when they were sent to other potential customers overseas. On my return to Heathrow the following day, I entered a crowded customs hall carrying my crash helmet bearing the Triumph name motif. This time the Customs Officer, having seen the story in the morning paper asked if I had any connection with it. He was an enthusiastic motorcyclist and for some minutes we talked of the machines he had owned, Nortons, a Black Shadow, Triumphs and Velocettes. My bag was not even checked and it was a pity it contained no cigars. They had been enjoyed by friends in Amsterdam, which is exactly what had been prophesied by the secretary when the Stokvis Chairman gave them to me.

Never a dull moment

In 1960 I was given a trip to America to join Edward Turner at the convention of Western States Triumph dealers, and to visit the Triumph Corporation premises at Baltimore in the east. At the convention I met the enduro star and Catalina Grand Prix winner Bud Ekins who, in the following years, was to stay at my home several times. Bud did a lot of the riding in the Steve McQueen film 'The Great Escape' and I spent some time with him and Steve when they rode Triumphs in the ISDT. The last day of my visit to California was most enjoyable. Bud provided two Trophy Triumphs and we went rough riding in the desert country beyond the St. Gabriel Mountains. The next day I left behind the warmth of California and flew to snowbound Baltimore. A pleasant trip but my flight out of what is now Kennedy Airport was very different. During the war and since, I have had some worrying experiences in the air but nothing like that one. We took off in a blizzard after being towed to the runway which seemed curious to me. The 707 left the ground but did not climb and the usual thump of retracting wheels was absent. No cabin lights, no heat and when I looked out of a window and saw that the flaps were still down I knew we had a complete hydraulic power failure. Not so far below the lights of Long Island were dimmed by the driving snow. There was no announcement by the Captain and no doubt he and his crew were too busy keeping the flying machine in the air. The passengers were all huddled in blankets and the situation was somewhat tense. I had sometimes wondered how I would react if I was in a crippled aircraft and that night I found the answer — get the bar opened. An air hostess was hurrying past checking that all safety belts were fastened and I asked her to have the Chief Steward open the bar. He was reluctant but I convinced him it was the only thing he could do to help in the emergency. Two hours later, after dropping most of the fuel into the Atlantic, we made our return approach to the airport and I had what might well have been my last brandy for I realised that the 707 had no brakes. The apron lights appeared out of the snow and, as the plane touched down, the line of fire tenders and ambulances raced after it with sirens screaming. The jets went into maximum reverse thrust and the juddering 707 finally came to a halt past the red beacon danger marker. Back at the terminal I 'phoned Turner in Baltimore, who had heard on the radio of the emergency, and told him he still had an Export Manager.

Back at Meriden I had a letter asking if I would take the Military 500 to Sweden for demonstration. It was February and not the best time of the year to go to that part of the world, but I rode the machine to Hull and sailed to Gothenburg. I spent an enjoyable evening at Lerum with my friend Bengt Bjorklund, Editor of Swedish motoring and motorcycling journals. The next day a party of press men and military people in snow-tyred vehicles piloted me into forest country, pointed my way into a forest track and wished me a good ride. They were using the road route to a hotel beyond the forest and would be waiting

Chapter Nine

for me there. The track was narrow, deep in snow and as dark as night in the overhanging trees. My feet were rarely on the footrests, which had no rubbers, and my shins carry the scars to this day. It seemed hours before I saw light at the end of the track and finally I emerged to be greeted by a smiling group of Swedes. I badly needed a hot bath and a whisky, but Sweden was then an even drier country than it is now and the only bottle was in my haversack. I told Bengt that I was away to the bath and I thought he was joking when he said it could only be a cold one. He was quite serious, and explained that this was not exactly a hotel but a hostel for Swedish youth. There were not even baths but only cold showers. I have never been so cold and I was glad I had brought the whisky, though once the Swedes learned about it, the bottle emptied very quickly. The ride through the forest and those the next day proved to have been well worth while, for the Swedes bought many Triumphs and made a very nice job of fitting them out with skis on either side. My next ride to Sweden was to be my last on a Triumph, but there were many more to come before then.

To me, every Continental journey on two wheels promised new adventures along the roads I travelled to bring more orders to Meriden and, in later years, to Norton. One such journey produced an unusual experience in the French town of Fontainebleu, where the magnificent palace recalls the times of the Emperors before the revolution. I was on my way to Geneva with a Saint for demonstration to the Swiss Police, with a call at Fort Rosny, near Paris, to see the Garde Republicaine, who had a Saint fleet. In the early hours of a cold wet morning I had pushed the machine quietly away from my home near Stratford upon Avon, so as not to disturb my sleeping children and the neighbours, who had been disturbed enough when I moved into the lane and lowered the environment tone with motorcycles, four children and a noisy go-kart. I had to explain to the elected representative of the community that my doctor had prescribed motorcycling to help an old lung defect and my comings and goings on various machines were then tolerated. That is until the entire display team of the Royal Signals on unsilenced Triumphs rode in formation into my drive from the nearby Warwickshire County Show. Even that unprecedented disturbance of village tranquility might have been tolerated had the team not proceeded later to the village inn. On the way to the inn they passed by the church hostel for wayward girls, as it was known, and the residents took little time to locate the parked machines and fraternise with the riders. The event was a major incident in the quiet existence of a village as placid as the Avon which flowed gently past its lawns. The closure of the hostel soon afterwards may have been purely coincidental.

From my home to Paris the rain was incessant and did not relent until I left Fort Rosny in the evening to ride south towards Switzerland. I took the newly opened but far from completed Autoroute Sud, intent on covering as many miles as possible before stopping for the night. Darkness overtook me and I decided to

Never a dull moment

A Hertfordshire Police Tiger 110 on the M1 motorway.

leave the motorway and find a hotel. As I should have known, the smallest French villages have the longest names compared with the cities like Paris, Nancy, Nice and Pau. I took the exit to Saint Cricq D'Eglise Notre Dame Des Enfants Petites which surely had a hotel of some kind. In fact it had a cluster of cottages and an oil lamp lit Bistro from which emerged peasants to stare at the first British motorcycle they had seen since the Matchlesses and Triumphs of 1945. I pointed to the distant glow in the sky and asked which town it was. It was Fontainebleu. Several cognacs later, for it was a cold night, I rode away into the darkness and my hope for a room and food. The town was deserted as I entered the main street trying to remember the name of the hotel mentioned to me once by a NATO officer friend who had lived there. I recalled the name was the Aigle Noir, the Black Eagle, and there it was, dark and apparently closed for the night. A church clock chimed eleven as I parked the Saint and pressed the night bell button. Madame, who opened the door, looked like she had been around since the Louis Emperors hunted in the surrounding forests. She appeared to be unfavourably impressed by the late visitor in motorcycling clothes but agreed to find me a room when I explained that I was on a special mission to the Swiss Police. She regretted, however, that the kitchen was closed and no food could be provided. The Concièrge would show me to the garage and take me to my room.

Chapter Nine

A photograph from 1962 of the Fiji Police with a new fleet of 3TA models.

Never a dull moment

Ceylon Police and Speed Twins in 1964. The traffic Chief Inspector Jayatileke formed a display team after visiting England and seeing the White Helmets in action. Top spot of the show was a jump over a fully-grown elephant, which explained the complaint that one machine had trouble with buckled wheels.

Chapter Nine

Very few Triumph Tigress scooters were supplied to the Police, but here are two on beat patrol duty with the now defunct York City Police.

What this man was doing with a Tigress of the old Sheffield Police force is now a mystery. He is Bernal Osborne, who was then Midlands Editor of the journal Motor Cycling.

Never a dull moment

In this photograph, taken at the Metropolitan Driving School, Hendon, are three motorcycle instructors who have distinguished themselves in International competition. Standing on the left is Bob Wheeler, next to him on the Triumph is Len Farmer, and on the other Triumph is 'Bomber Harris'. The Author had the privilege of being piloted across London by each of them on his way to Continental assignments. In the centre of the photograph, under the crest, is Commander Norman Radford, then Head of the Metro Police Traffic Division, and on his right is the Author.

I shall always remember that Concièrge. He was the biggest man I ever saw, the previous biggest being the French wing forward who flattened me and broke four of my ribs when the British army played the French universities fifteen. As he pushed the Saint to the garage like it was a moped, his 100 decibel voice asked me if I was English. When I confessed that I was and apologised for troubling him so late, his reaction gave me hope for some food. He was very fond of English people he told me, because they made good whisky but as he hastened to explain, a poor Concièrge could not afford it. On my overseas journeys I have always made it a rule to carry a bottle of Scotch, primarily for myself but also for other people if necessary. When I disclosed to my Concièrge friend that I had a bottle which he could share if he could find some food, his nose quivered like a hunting dog and he was away to the kitchen. By the time I had unpacked my haversack he was in my room with the largest tray of French cuisine I had ever

Chapter Nine

seen. I opened the bottle and, as the level descended, I listened to his remarkable life story. He was a member of a noble Russian family destroyed by the revolution and had been a famous singer before he escaped westwards and finally settled in France. Quietly he began to sing the songs of his youth and with the encouragement of the whisky his repertoire began to reveal the old qualities of his deep bass voice. The church clock had chimed the second hour of the new day when I gave him the last remaining dram of what he insisted on calling wonderful English whisky. As he finally left my room he paid tribute to the empty bottle with an improvised aria. Imagine if you can a quiet French hotel in the middle of the night suddenly disturbed by a deep basso profundo voice singing 'I love the English people for their whisky is so good'.

The next morning I continued my journey to Geneva via Mâcon and at the French border I was held up for a long time by an official who informed me that he had been instructed to detain a radio-equipped GB motorcycle which a Police car had been unable to stop. This must have been the one I had passed after Mâcon and left behind through the twisty climbs of the Alps foothills. I had to wait a long time whilst he telephoned somewhere for instructions and came back to tell me I could not cross into Switzerland until he had been authorised to give permission and that could take several hours. I demanded that the Commandant of the Garde Republicaine at Fort Rosny be informed that I was being detained and he would certainly authorise my release. Ten minutes later I was on my way with the good wishes of the Commandant. The ride to Geneva did not have a happy ending. After being serviced by the Triumph distributor, the machine was handed over to the Police and several days later there was a major engine failure. An oil pump ball valve had become jammed by a particle of grit and that was the end of the big end bearings. A rare occurrence, but it could happen if the tank was not flushed out after an oil change. It proved to be my only unproductive order-hunting ride of very many.

Chapter Ten

The Turning Point

IN 1960, Jack Sangster handed over the BSA Group Chairmanship to Eric Turner after four years as the supremo, and a record profit balance sheet to which Meriden had made a major contribution. As long as Edward Turner, supported by Financial Director Charles Parker, continued to lead the Triumph team, excellent Meriden profits would be a foregone conclusion and so would those of the Daimler business which Edward had revived. As time went by and other companies in the Group began losing money, a Monday morning ritual was observed at Meriden. The Triumph income for the previous week had to be reported by Parker to the Group Financial Director at Small Heath and a good proportion of it transferred. The progressive profitability of the highly efficient Meriden operation was not only envied by certain individuals of the BSA Motor Cycles Limited staff but it led to their growing dislike of Edward Turner. They regarded him as a Director of both companies who devoted his attention to only one. This was utterly unfair for he did not ignore the BSA problems, but it was far beyond the ability of any one man to put them right, a fact which he had emphasised to me when he was first appointed as Automotive Division Managing Director. I fear that in his interesting book *The Giants of Small Heath* my friend Barry

Chapter Ten

Ryerson may have allowed himself to be misled by the views of certain BSA people in making his unjustified criticisms of Edward Turner. He would have been well advised to have ignored the comments and stories of the two men he quotes, Harrison and Hardwicke. We at Meriden knew well, and had the greatest admiration for, the man we called E.T., and I would be failing many people if I did not correct the impressions which Ryerson gives. Certainly E.T. was a hard taskmaster who demanded energetic effort from all his staff as a good Managing Director should, but to say that he was 'tyrannical and hampered by a sense of personal inadequacy which made him bluster and bully' is utter nonsense. It is equally absurd to attribute to E.T. what Ryerson dramatically describes as a massive breakdown of communication in the Automotive Division, by which he no doubt means between E.T. and Small Heath. He admits however that 'the Company did remarkably well despite it'. He overlooks the fact that there had never been an Automotive Division supremo until Jack Sangster gave the task to E.T. and perhaps as an apologetic appointment after bringing in the other Turner as Vice-Chairman. E.T. gave all the help he could to Small Heath, but his prior task was to revive Daimler, which he did so successfully. Anyone who wanted to see him had only to knock on his door and enter, whereupon even if he was dictating to his secretary Nan Plant, he would end a letter and give his attention to the visitor. Very few Managing Directors then or now could be so accessible as E.T. Ryerson is, however, right when he believes that Nan Plant understood E.T. and had an immense regard for him. She knew him better than anyone and consequently must resent as much as I do the unjustified criticisms of her old boss for whom, incidentally, she continued to work long after his retirement. After his untimely death she travelled the world meeting many of his friends.

In his book Ryerson went to considerable lengths suggesting possible reasons for what he called Turner's tendency to tyranny but, had he talked to many Triumph people instead of only several at Small Heath, he would have obtained the true picture of the man. E.T. was tough certainly, impatient with anyone who was inefficient, intolerant of anything less than complete commitment to responsibility, but never a tyrant. He welded together a Meriden team which was the finest in the industry and, from its humble start in 1936, led the Triumph company to the supreme position which it held until it was infected by the diseases carried from Small Heath by new management. These I will analyse later but a few more words are necessary to put the Ryerson record straight. It was unfortunate that E.T. ever became involved with Small Heath problems which had probably become insoluble by the time he was appointed Head of the Automotive Division. He did not seek the appointment but, not for the first time, he did as Jack Sangster asked him. He performed a remarkably successful operation on the ailing Daimler company but, as far as Small Heath was concerned, I well remember the words he spoke to me. 'If Sangster thinks that I can put the place right, he expects the impossible, but I must ensure that Triumph does not get any further ahead of BSA.'

E.T. was a perfectionist in all he did and he expected his staff to follow his example. Like all perfectionists he did not like to be told he was wrong but, quite contrary to what Ryerson has said, he would listen to anyone who had cause to believe that something was not correct. In fact he instructed me always to go straight to him and report any deficiency, whether in design or for any other reason, which I did on more than one occasion. Ryerson, again in the context of criticism of E.T., raises the old story of bad Triumph steering. Most of my million miles were on Triumphs and I can say with hand on heart and the other on the Good Book that never did I have a moment's worry. Ryerson writes of Meriden back room boys doing what they could to improve steering by 'judicious tinkering' to which one must ask how do you tinker with a frame? He goes on to claim that the problem was never solved until Hopwood and Hele took over. In fact they never altered the E.T. frame design for the 650 cc twins.

It is most regrettable that Ryerson, in divulging the confidential comments made by E.T. about his then young wife, should have added his own suggestion that instead of displaying the affection he felt for her, would have 'bawled her out at the top of his voice' on returning home in the evening. Here surely is an indication of unsound judgement which explains the inaccuracies of other criticisms which Ryerson makes of E.T., in a book which should have given him more credit for his achievements and exonerated him for any blame in the BSA decline to disaster.

Not long after he had begun the formidable task of building up the newly-formed Triumph Engineering Company, he suffered a dreadful personal tragedy which caused him to devote the next 22 years entirely to his work. Two friends, with their wives, were spending the weekend with the Turners and on the Saturday morning the three men were at the factory whilst the ladies went shopping in Mrs. Turner's car. The men returned to the Turner home near Coventry and, when their wives had not arrived after a considerable time, E.T. assumed that the car had given trouble and drove back to look for them. He did not have to drive far. All three had been killed in a head-on collision. E.T. was middle-aged when he married again and in all the many intervening years, when he must have been a lonely man, he gave his life to his company. It is time for me to return to the main theme of this chapter, but I must correct one more wrong impression which Ryerson gives of E.T. when he describes him as 'physically an unusually small man'. Everyone who met E.T. will know that this is untrue and, for those who did not know him, there are proof pictures in the Ivor Davies book *It's a Triumph*.

Moving on now to 1961, this was the year when Bert Hopwood returned to Meriden after an absence of 14 years. When he left Triumph in 1947 and joined Norton, he had been in charge of the Drawing Office and stories were told that he

Chapter Ten

At the Amsterdam Show, the first of the 1100 350cc military models supplied to the Netherlands Army. On the machine is the then Minister of Defence, Roy Mason M.P. Standing with me is Brian Jones from the Triumph Design Department.

left after a personal dispute with E.T. That would not be surprising for the blunt Hopwood personality did not provide for the shrewd diplomacy which was essential when dealing with the much more powerful personality of E.T. However, he had been Turner-trained and took his experience to the Bracebridge Street factory where he became a member of the technical staff under the famous Development Engineer Joe Craig. After only a couple of years or so he moved to BSA, where he stayed for seven years, before returning to Norton and becoming responsible for design following the retirement of Joe Craig. By this time, Norton had become part of the AMC Group and in 1958, after 42 years of distinguished service, Managing Director Gilbert Smith handed over to Hopwood. To be head of Norton was, or should have been, the pinnacle of achievement for a man who, eleven

The Turning Point

years before, had been standing at a drawing board working on Turner designs. However, it was too late to enjoy the position for very long, for the AMC Group was in trouble and the decision was taken to close the famous Bracebridge Street factory. Hopwood had seen the signs and was back at Meriden well before Norton moved to AMC at Woolwich. Whether or not he was invited to continue with Norton is not so important as the fact that he was wise not to do so, for otherwise he would have been faced with the Dennis Poore take-over and inevitably the two men would have clashed as they did many years later.

So Hopwood came back to Meriden and from him and E.T. I heard both sides of the story whereby the conditions of his Triumph appointment were finally agreed. On the one hand, the BSA Board required that E.T. should appoint a deputy to be responsible to them whenever he went away on his overseas journeys. His annual visits to USA and Australasia in particular took several months and they were expected of him. The Board request was not unreasonable, although the Meriden team was quite capable of attending to everything under the efficient direction of Financial Director Charles Parker. Hopwood had approached E.T. about returning to Meriden and the ensuing negotiations were typical of the past relationship between the two men. There was inevitably a gap between the position Hopwood wanted and that which E.T. was prepared to give him. As E.T. confided to me 'I have to bring in someone who will not interfere with things whilst I am away and Hopwood suits the situation'. As Hopwood then confided to me after he arrived 'If Turner thinks I have come back to start work with my pencil again, he is mistaken'. It was to be three years before E.T. moved out of Hopwood's way and it was bad news for Meriden when this happened and a new Managing Director appeared. Of him much will be written later.

Meanwhile, I had been appointed General Sales Manager, which involved responsibility not only for all markets but for production programming, the preparation of material purchasing schedules, creative publicity, supervision of product quality and other things. In all of these matters I was deputy to E.T. and the arrival of Hopwood did not change that status. This led to the first of my three major clashes with H.H. as I will now call him. Nobody at Triumph ever got around to addressing him as Bert. Occasionally E.T. would ask me to report on machine quality, knowing perfectly well that in addition to my long distance rides in the UK and on the Continent, I always used a new machine to and from home. I never told him that four times my lights had failed when the multi connection plug had pulled away from its headlamp socket on dark roads and on dark nights. Neither did I tell him that six twistgrips had come loose on the handlebars when they were needed to close the throttle hurriedly. Such things were normal test hazards and corrected accordingly, but I did become anxious about the twistgrip problem. When it happened for the sixth time, I rode into the factory that morning and, with the Bonneville engine revs halfway up the clock, I pulled the twist-

Chapter Ten

Geoff Duke and Percy Tait were two of the more illustrious members of the White Helmets Display Team of the Royal Signals, so I thought I would try to pass the beginners' test when the Team collected their TRW models from Meriden in March 1962.

The Turning Point

grip from the handlebar and offered it to the Works Manager, Bert Coles, who was talking to Syd Tubb, the Head of Test Department. The twistgrips of several machines were all found to be capable of moving round the handlebars and Coles asked whose job it was to tighten them. That person was a teenage girl, and even with a king-sized screwdriver she could not have tightened the mild steel twistgrip screw into a hardened steel handlebar. The problem which led to my first upset with H.H. was different, and it was to create a sensitive relationship between us, which never got back to normal.

One evening in September, I rode away from the factory on one of the first new season Bonnevilles to be produced for America. In Meriden village I slowed down to turn left up the lane which led to Berkswell and I almost overshot because of a poor rear brake. I stopped to check the reason and found that the rear brake operating rod had been altered. Instead of the straight rod which had been standard for years, it had been taken behind the frame down tube and had been given a U bend to clear the tube. Consequently, when the rear brake was applied, the rod tried to straighten out the U bend and there was no positive feel of brake application. I have always relied more upon the front brake than the rear one but it was my job to put myself in the position of a Triumph customer and I knew that he would expect a positive rear brake response. When I returned to the factory the next morning and rode into the test area, several testers came to me and asked, as they often did, if I had any comments to make on the machine. I told them what I felt about the new brake rod and not only did they agree but they urged me to have it altered as they had reported their concern without result. I went to Hopwood and told him courteously what the testers and I felt about the bent rod and how worried I was that its effect upon brake efficiency could cause accidents. I was told in no uncertain terms that it was my job to sell machines and not to criticise design matters. That evening I took another machine home with the intention of assuring myself that I had been unduly concerned, but instead, after using the rear brake many times, I had no doubt that the rod had to be changed back to its straight operation. For the first and only time I carried out the instruction given to me by Edward Turner that I was to go to him with any problem I could not overcome. He went with me to the Test Department, took one look at the bent rod and was angry at what he saw. 'Does Hopwood know about this?' he demanded and I replied that I had told him. The rod was put back to the original design, replacements were sent out for machines already despatched and my relations with Hopwood suffered. There were to be other occasions with similar results when I put company and customer before my own personal interests.

It was after this time that the Bonneville lost its separate gearbox and the new unit-construction model was introduced at the 1962 Earls Court Show. I had one of the first production machines and within five miles after leaving the factory I was regretting the change. Vibration had arrived and smooth power transmission

Chapter Ten

The famous Display Team of the Royal Signals has ridden Triumphs ever since the team was formed more than fifty years ago. New riders are trained each winter on the moors of North Yorkshire, to be ready for the first show in May. The 1981 Team which gave displays in Canada is shown performing the spectacular Six Bike Pyramid.

The bicycle was made for two but the Signals add seven more for this Nine Man Bomb Burst item in the programme. [Crown Copyright]

The Turning Point

The Fire Jump used to be the prerogative of the team sergeant, but scorched stripes have changed that tradition.

Chapter Ten

The Backwards Ladder foursome with the machine apparently on autopilot control.

Opposite: There is no margin for error when the four Triumphs and an Austin Princess have to be cleared in this salute to the Royal Air Force.

The Turning Point

Chapter Ten

had gone. It was generally believed that the American market had demanded the one-piece engine and gearbox because it would look better. Certainly it had been a time-wasting nuisance to adjust the primary chain and then have to tighten the rear chain, but it would have been far more sensible and much less expensive to have introduced a bolted-up gearbox with a chain tensioner. This would have obviated the problems which arose with the new arrangement, and which became worse when the engine became a 750.

The Tina scooter also made its debut in 1962 and it deserved to be successful. In his book, *Whatever Happened to the British Motorcycle Industry,* which seems to apportion blame to everyone but himself, Bert Hopwood uses the Tina as only one example of incompetence by Edward Turner. As the General Sales Manager totally involved with the machine even before its introduction, I am able to put the record straight. I rode a prototype for many miles and the only problem I encountered was whiskered plugs due to driving it much harder than the customers would ever do. The Tina was designed and built to sell at a very low price and indeed it sold very well. Better quality electrical equipment would have been desirable and would have improved it further but, of the two companies which quoted, Lucas lost out on price.

The Hopwood book reveals some remarkable lapses of the Author's memory and in particular the accusation that the Tina was to be launched without adequate testing. Advance production models were, in fact, sent out to important dealers to supplement the results of factory test programmes. The biggest mileage was undoubtedly done by Percy Tait and I remember well the occasions on which I rushed past him on a Saint or a Bonneville. I remember them all the more because I could never pass Percy unless he was on a Tina. One morning I was in a hurry on my way to the factory on a Bonneville and, climbing Meriden hill at around 80 mph, a hand slapped my back and a voice shouted 'Good Morning'. It could only be Tait. The Tina was officially introduced at a function held at the South Bank Festival Hall and attended by many important people. One noble Lord and his Lady rode around with the joy of teenagers and promptly ordered one each.

The Tina had one basic problem which did not take fully into account the fact that the type of customer for whom it was intended had no mechanical aptitude. It had been cleverly designed as the simplest form of personal transport next to the bicycle. All the rider had to do was to put the little switch to the position marked 'Safe', depress the easy starter pedal, move the switch to the 'Drive' position, rotate the handlebar accelerator control and move away to the shopping centre, the hairdresser, the railway station, or wherever the Tina was required to go. Nothing could be more simple.

I loaned one to my friend Chris Draper, best known as the Mad Major, who flew a plane under the Thames bridges. Chris, a pilot of very many years experi-

The Turning Point

ence, gave the Tina full marks by aircraft reliability standards. There had to be a snag somewhere for the customer who must always be the final tester. Said some customers 'I switched to drive and moved away like the handbook says, but when the engine stopped because I had not waited a minute for it to warm up, I started it again without remembering to put the switch back to the safe position. The machine went away without me and it was my fault, but you should prevent this from happening'. The customer was right and we tackled the problem. The most effective solution was complicated and expensive and so we settled for what we were assured was a clever idea from Small Heath. It was fool-proof we were told and it was to be demonstrated at the Blackpool Spring Show of the industry. A glamorous dolly bird was used to show how simple it was to ride the Tina without previous experience. With a Press audience she started the engine and the commentator announced that the Tina was now waiting for her to sit on the comfortable seat. She did so. 'Now,' said the commentator, 'Dolly is ready to go to the hairdresser and she will tell the Tina to go by turning the twistgrip throttle'. Dolly did so and the Tina did not move.

The reason was simple. Underneath the seat was the drive switch which was activated when the rider sat down, but Dolly was only eight stones and the seat pan required at least ten stones to depress it and activate the switch. The testers at Small Heath had been considerably heavier than Dolly. It must be said in favour of the Tina scooter that it was ingenious and the nearest the industry ever got to a successful and inexpensive personal transport machine. It failed to survive simply because there was no substantial market in Britain for scooters, and is never likely to be. It is traditionally British to wait in a bus queue for twenty minutes rather than ride home in half the time, and this would probably change very little if 50 cc machines were exempted from driving licence restrictions as in most Continental countries. One of the many mistakes made by Lionel Jofeh, the second successor to Edward Turner, was to believe that the absurd Ariel three-wheeled moped would revolutionise personal transport at the expense of tube trains and buses. It did not take long for Lambretta and Vespa to accept British resistance to scooter travel, the BSA Beeza scooter never did get to market and the Triumph Tigress models were short lived. The small BSA Dandy and Beagle shared utter failure with their companion, the Ariel Pixie. Whilst the Tina scooter must be recorded as a commercial failure, it is best remembered as a machine cleverly conceived and designed for a market which proved to be a mirage. It was the last project on the Turner drawing board before he left the factory which he had led to so many years of success.

Chapter Eleven

At Rotterdam airport on my way to the International Police Exhibition at Hanover. I am probably explaining the reason for the masking tape on the headlamp. [Fotodienst]

146

Chapter Eleven

The Beginning of the End

IN 1964, Edward Turner resigned his position as Managing Director of the BSA Automotive Division. Why he did so has never been defined, but it may well have been connected with his views on the Board move to engage the services of the McKinsey Consultancy organisation, a decision which proved to be an expensive and unsuccessful experiment. To lose E.T. from the Meriden which he had created, came as a shock to all of us and it was little consolation to know that he would remain on the Group Board where he and Jack Sangster would be the only people who knew or cared anything about motorcycles. We gave E.T. an affectionate farewell dinner at the George Hotel in Solihull and, as was expected of me, I wrote a suitable ode to recall the highlights of his Triumph years and especially his famous pronouncements. The June day when he called us to his office to say 'I have brought you here to discuss colour finishes for next year's models and these are the ones I have decided'. The occasion when he had his desk moved to the other end of his office and said to me, 'I am now sitting seven yards nearer to Small Heath and I do not intend to get any closer'. The occasion at the Cologne exhibition when the Editor of *Das Motorrad* was proudly showing E.T. the collection of historic German machines. Herr Editor was eloquent about the Africa

Chapter Eleven

Korps Zundapp sidecar outfit specification and capabilities. Shaft drive, desert tyres, Spandau machine gun mounting, panniers for ammunition, auxilliary drive to the sidecar wheel. 'It also has a reverse gear', he added. 'Ah yes', commented E.T., 'that must have been very useful in 1945'. Then, to my mind his best pronouncement of all, and one which he made to me one evening, 'It is my ambition to die when I am ninety, shot by a jealous husband'. He died much earlier and very quietly after a pleasant lunch with friends.

As General Sales Manager at Meriden, I was an early target for the McKinsey inquisition and I was instructed to drop all my work and devote my time to telling my questioner what was wrong in the Group organisation and what to do about it. The consensus of my advice was to divorce Meriden business from Small Heath interference, but I knew that this was impossible. In fact the final McKinsey recommendations went exactly the opposite way and that was the end of any lingering hopes for Meriden to regain the efficient independence it had enjoyed under the direction of Edward Turner. We awaited with apprehension the appointment of his successor and at one time it was thought that Hopwood might be given the job. However, as happened when Sangster brought in Eric Turner, who knew nothing about the motorcycle business, as Vice-Chairman, Eric did the same and appointed Harry Sturgeon. He had been with the Sperry Aircraft Accessory Company and then with Churchills, a subsidiary of BSA. A disappointed Hopwood was given the title of Deputy Managing Director, which proved later on to be a title of convenience and nothing more. Meanwhile, the McKinsey report proposals caused concern and discontent amongst senior men whose experience and ability were worth far more than the recommendations of any efficiency experts. Small Heath could not afford to lose the services of men like Bob Fearon, the General Manager, and Alan Jones, the Works Director. Both had done wonderful work for many years, but they could not reconcile their loyalty to BSA with a changing pattern in which they had no confidence. They resigned, and the manner in which the resignations were announced was, to say the least, distasteful. I well remember the day when senior executives from Triumph and BSA were summoned to meet in the Small Heath showroom to hear the McKinsey formula for restoring the fortunes of the Group, and I wondered what we from Meriden were doing there when Triumph business was continuing to make excellent profits. We listened to the formula of reorganisation which could have applied just as well to any kind of company, and the audience was as quiet as a church congregation listening to a funeral oration. A tolling bell would have been quite appropriate. It was in this unreal and ominous atmosphere that the departures of Fearon and Jones were announced by Chairman Eric Turner, and in a way which could have been construed to infer that there were no places for them in the new organisation. I walked away from the meeting with Ariel chief Ken Whistance, whose Selly Oak factory was due to be closed, and Ken confided to

The Beginning of the End

me that he too had decided to leave. So three first-class men were the immediate casualties of a very expensive experiment in the field of efficiency consultation. They were all good friends of mine, I admired their abilities and I was sad to see them go. BSA Sales Director Bill Rawson was another friend whose long term loyalty and excellent work were ill-rewarded by the consequences of the McKinsey exercise. Bill once said to Edward Turner 'I am BSA, Shilton is Triumph and that is the way it should be'. Bill died after a short retirement and I was amongst the many friends who packed the village church at Loxley near Warwick. It was a grey day, the BSA Group was approaching its collapse and as I walked away I said to Bob Fearon 'I think the next funeral will be of BSA/Triumph'.

One by-product of the McKinsey plan was the employment of market research specialists and soon we were again assembled in the Small Heath showroom to be lectured on the world market for motorcycles and how to secure the major share of it. According to the large multi-coloured graphs, which were revealed one by one by an assistant as the lecturer delivered a high speed commentary, the world was starved of motorcycles. All we had to do was to increase production at such a level as to keep pace with the rising birthrate. It seemed to me that he had brought charts and a lecture which had been prepared for a company in the food distribution business. However, like the McKinsey exercise, the market research report had been expensive and therefore it had to be implemented, as I found at my first meeting with the new Managing Director, Harry Sturgeon. He studied my Triumph production programme which had been running consistently at a weekly output rate of 375 Twins and 200 Cubs, laid down by Edward Turner as the optimum ratio of production to profitability. He was supported by Financial Director Charles Parker, whose knowledge of Meriden production costs was kept up-to-date on a meticulous basis. Sturgeon instructed me to issue a new production programme, increasing the weekly output by ten per cent in one month, and by twenty per cent in three months. I warned him of the principal danger. Our major suppliers of electrical equipment, tyres and wheel rims, petrol and oil tanks, bearings, carburettors, castings etc., could not step up deliveries without more notice and would be hesitant to commit themselves to more capital expenditure and labour costs in any case. Therefore, we would face the risk of producing incomplete machines which would certainly result in cumulative problems. Sturgeon was insistent that his instructions were obeyed and presumably he had already informed Hopwood of his policy decision, so I did as I was told.

There was to be a second serious occasion when he quoted to me his modus operandi, 'I am a professional Managing Director and must make decisions without wasting time listening to the arguments of other people'. This dictum well portrayed the character of the new man, determined to carry out his directives in the confidence that they were correct and necessary, but not prepared to take advice or even to identify the people who could give it reliably. It was to his, and

Chapter Eleven

our, disadvantage that his office was located at Small Heath, which did not help him realise the essential differences between the BSA and Triumph factories. He saw it as his task to bring them closer together and in so doing to destroy the traditional element of competition which had been deep rooted for many years. With no previous experience in the industry he could not be expected to understand that a motorcycle was a much more individual product than a machine tool or a Sperry compass, and was made by people to whom the name on the fuel tank was much more than a trade mark. To most people at Small Heath, the Sturgeon appointment was regarded as a most welcome replacement for Edward Turner, who had been responsible for the leading position which Triumph had achieved over BSA. We at Meriden however, were apprehensive and, no longer having a Meriden Managing Director since the company was formed, we feared changes which would undermine the close-knit structure of which we were so proud. Hopwood, as Deputy to Sturgeon, was based at Meriden but as his relations with Turner had always been brittle he was not expected to adopt the ideals of his old boss and resist policies likely to harm Triumph.

It was not long before I experienced an example of what was to become increasing control of Meriden affairs by Small Heath. The contract for 1100 machines to be supplied to the Royal Netherland Army promised excellent sales publicity and I prepared a suitable press release to be issued on the day I was to take the first machine to the Amsterdam International Show. I then had a visit from the BSA Publicity Manager who informed me that he had been instructed to handle all Group publicity in the future, commencing with the Dutch order. Although I knew that his first allegiance was to Small Heath, I trusted him to give Meriden the benefit of his expertise and I handed over the story of the contract. The £265,000 order was the big news of the Show and on the opening day I and my colleagues watched in the breakfast room of our Amsterdam hotel as my PRO friend searched through the newly-arrived British morning papers for his story. There was no mention. I discovered later that he had issued a Press Release for publication one week later, which inevitably killed it as an important news item. I believe that it was not an intentional mistake but he was a professional in his trade and should have done a better job. On my return to Meriden I put the matter right with my own story to the Press and was not popular at Small Heath in consequence. What mattered was the importance of good Triumph publicity for the Meriden factory and I continued to ignore the instruction to use the Group PRO.

Meanwhile, the early effects of the new Sturgeon policies were causing disquiet and were soon to lead to an inter-union dispute which stopped Triumph production for several days. The direct cause was the appointment of a Personnel Manager for the first time, and I became aware of this in a curious way. One morning, when I had ridden in from home on a new machine, I was walking past

The Beginning of the End

the office of Works Manager Bert Coles when he called me in. With him were the foremen from various sections, all of whom I had known for years. Over tea and cigarettes they were having one of the friendly chats which Coles convened from time to time to discuss any matters concerning production. He had been with Triumph since pre-war days and having worked his way up from the shop floor he was highly respected as a man who had a complete knowledge of every section in the factory, from machine shop to final test. The smooth running efficiency of Meriden production was a tribute to Coles, but he became an early casualty of the new regime when he was replaced by an inexperienced newcomer and, like Fearon and Jones, joined the list of early retirements. Unlike them, however, he died soon afterwards and many of his friends believed that his life ended when he left Meriden.

The morning he had invited me to join his tea party, he asked me to tell his guests how I saw the sales prospects over the next few months. I was able to tell them that I was about to issue a new production programme which would continue the current rate of output through the autumn and winter period right through to the spring. The forward order book was healthy, our markets buoyant and the prospects were excellent. As far as I was concerned, everyone in the factory was entitled to have this information. The following day I was sent for by Hopwood and told that I must not in future talk to factory personnel, and shop stewards in particular. For a moment I did not connect his instruction with my friendly chat of the previous day and I then said that if, in fact, any of the men I had talked to were union representatives, I had known them since I joined the Company and saw no harm in giving them confidence in their future prospects. I think Hopwood may have agreed, although he did not say so. But instead he informed me that a Personnel Manager was about to be appointed and all communications to the workers must go through the new man's office. Another outsider, and one who quickly disrupted the long established rhythm of the factory. Within a few days he made a bad mistake which cost the Company a lot of money. He filled a vacancy in the tool room with a man who was a member of the Transport and General Workers Union but, had he checked beforehand, he would have found that the tool room personnel were not only members of a different union, but operated their own closed shop against any intrusion from another. When the newcomer walked in on a Monday morning they all walked out, whereupon the intruder complained to the TGWU shop steward, who promptly ordered all of his members to cease work and they comprised the majority of the work force. An inter-union dispute was inevitable and neither side would give way.

Finally, the impasse was resolved quietly by paying the new man full wages to stay away and this went on for some weeks until he was given a generous sum in settlement and happily started a new job the next day. Meanwhile, the resentment against the new personnel relations dictum caused an immediate

Chapter Eleven

change in what had for so long been a happy factory. We had all been Triumph people, proud of the machines we produced, and with a mutual confidence between management and the entire work force. Now Edward Turner had gone, Bert Coles had gone and confidence had been replaced by apprehension and uncertainty. I had enjoyed my personal friendships with many factory workers and was especially happy to chat with the testers when I rode in each morning on a new machine. The new dictum changed all that and the morning after it was issued there was nobody to ask if the machine was satisfactory. I felt very sad that morning. Never before had I ridden into the test area without a cheerful welcome and a few words of enquiry about the machine.

It was not long before the warning I had given to Sturgeon about accelerated production proved fully justified. Machines began to come off the assembly line incomplete, as certain major suppliers had not been given enough time to meet increased orders. The head of the Material Ordering Department, Eddie Gough, and his excellent staff, used every means possible to overcome the shortages and every telephone was a hot line. His deputy, my good friend Alf Barker, died in the middle of a high pressure telephone conversation with the Lucas factory — and yet another fine Triumph man had gone. The alternative to a growing stock of incomplete machines was to slow down production, but Sturgeon was committed to his policy of increased output whatever the consequences. The results were expensively serious and, after the Spares Department had been raided for critical components, the stock of incomplete machines became too large for the space available in a factory which had never been designed to accommodate any interruption between final test and packing case. The green lawns in front of the factory were desecrated one morning by large marquees, which were soon packed with machines. Many of them were those built for my Netherlands Army order. The time was September, the days were warm and the nights were cold, the ideal combination for condensation under canvas. Maybe because of my personal involvement in the Netherlands machines, I found that they were the first to be affected. The brazing of the frames and the welding of the tanks began to show the first signs of rust so that, when the missing components finally arrived, a lot of work was necessary before the machines were good enough to be despatched to Holland.

Meanwhile, Sturgeon had turned his attention to marketing, a word introduced by the new regime, and he proposed a major step which threatened such damage to Meriden that I firmly refused to go along with it. He was eager to amalgamate the Triumph and BSA agency arrangements in both the UK and Overseas markets so that every BSA dealer or distributor would have Triumph and vice-versa. The idea was dangerous for the UK and quite unacceptable for the export markets but at least it was not so stupid as the one put to me by my McKinsey cross-examiner. That gentleman had said to me, 'Why not make the

The Beginning of the End

Kings of Oxford Group your UK Distributors? They would deliver them to the dealer network, do all the advertising and selling, you could dismiss your sales staff and simply take orders from Kings'. I destroyed the McKinsey idea with a few words but my debate with Sturgeon started one afternoon in my office and continued in the Meriden Manor Hotel until well into the evening. It was too intense to pause for dinner and in fact we did not even have a drink. I pointed out firstly that there were 435 Triumph dealers in the UK and, of these, more than half had the BSA dealership also. On the other hand there were more than 1000 BSA dealers and, as Meriden had no problem in selling its home market output, it was absurd to appoint an additional 800 or so dealerships. I gave some examples of how this would undermine the loyalties of dealers who had established their businesses on Triumph and what damage it would do to them.

One example was that of Bert Shorey of Banbury, the father of successful racer Dan who partnered Mike Hailwood when they won the Thruxton 500 miler on a Triumph. The Shorey business was entirely Triumph with a first class service, and close by were the BSA dealerships of Trinders and Eddie Dow. The three of them secured for the Group practically all the motorcycle sales in North Oxfordshire and South Warwickshire, so what was to be gained by interfering? Bert Shorey later wrote a letter of appeal to Sturgeon but to no avail and his was only one of a number of good Triumph agencies to go into decline as a direct result of the Sturgeon policy. As regards the overseas distributors, I said emphatically that there was no way in which the Triumph organisations would accept BSA and in some countries the BSA importers would not want to have Triumph. I confidently quoted the example of New South Wales, where the friendly relations between the separate importers in Sydney were such that they would throw out both makes rather than share. As for America, I assured Sturgeon that he would be very unwise to contemplate trying to make any change in the well-established arrangements. No doubt I upset him when I commented that not even Edward Turner could have made the major amalgamation we were debating. Sturgeon reminded me that he had to make decisions based upon his own judgement and I wondered why, then, the discussion had gone on for several hours. Clearly an impasse had been reached, he was determined to go ahead and he said so. I was equally determined not to accept his decision and he asked what I proposed to do. Before answering that question I enquired what would he do if the results of his decision threatened serious consequences. 'In that case', said Sturgeon, 'I promise you that I would revert to the original dealership structure'. 'Very well', I said, 'I will stay around and hold you to your promise but not as General Sales Manager. I would regard it as disloyal to the many Triumph specialist dealers to stay in that position when it is quite incompatible with my conviction that they will be damaged. Therefore I will resign and concentrate wholly upon UK and international Police and Military business until you have to change your policy,

Chapter Eleven

which I am certain will not be long'.

My forecast was to prove accurate and Sturgeon was to admit that he had been wrong. There should have been a more pleasant outcome of the agreement we reached that evening in the Meriden Manor Hotel and there would have been had Sturgeon stayed alive to keep his promise, which he certainly would have done. Meanwhile, many things were to happen and must be recalled before the final story of Sturgeon is told.

The amalgamation of BSA and Triumph dealerships was announced by Sturgeon at Meriden in a marquee erected on the lawn in front of the factory and crowded with dealers. Most of them were BSA ones and when the announcement was made they were the people with happy faces. To the others, the news came as a shock, and there was bitter disappointment with such a reward for their years of loyal support to Triumph. On that day Meriden lost the independence of which we had all been so proud and the Triumph flag flying over the factory should have been at half mast. I looked across at Hopwood and wondered whether, as General Manager, he felt the same way, or whether after his years at BSA he approved the Sturgeon policy. He had never discussed it with me but as he was deputy to the Managing Director I hardly expected him to give me any support, nor did I consider that he would be prepared to defend the basic interests of the Meriden operation. However, having made my own gesture by relinquishing control of Triumph commercial business to BSA which, incidentally, brought no comment from Hopwood, I was prepared to await developments. Except for Police and Military business, which was an important part of Triumph output, sales administration was transferred to Small Heath and two new appointments were introduced to fill mine. Sturgeon took the opportunity on this infamous day to invite all the newly-created Triumph dealers to ride Tina scooters and, for some of those who did, it was probably their first experience on two wheels except for a long ago bicycle.

In his book, Hopwood's memory is at fault when he refers to the launching of the Tina to dealers at a buffet luncheon in a marquee on the lawn at the Triumph factory. Only twice were marquees erected on the lawn, the first being for the Sturgeon announcement of agency amalgamation and the second for storing incomplete machines as was mentioned earlier. As for Hopwood's claim to have 'played hell' with Edward Turner about design faults of the Tina, only one man was ever capable of rebuking E.T. and that was his boss, Jack Sangster, who did so once when, in 1945, he questioned the cost of the sound-proof office in which his Managing Director had installed himself.

In 1965, some months after the Sturgeon appointment, I organised what had become a traditional Metropolitan Police day at MIRA, the Motor Industries Research Centre and test track near Nuneaton, in Warwickshire, and I invited him along. The programme was for three Metro riders to take three Saints through the

The Beginning of the End

timed quarter-mile strip and to achieve a minimum of 100 mph. They were accompanied by senior members of the Metro engineering branch and after the required performances had been completed, the visitors were entertained to lunch. On that occasion the lunch was arranged a few miles away in a Northamptonshire village, and I invited my friend John Gott, the Chief Constable of the County, who so tragically died at the wheel of his racing Austin Healey at the Lydden circuit. Sturgeon had one of his impetuous ideas and instructed me to have the prototype Trident brought along to show the Met. visitors. Note that this was 1965 and that the Trident did not commence production until three years later. I appealed to Sturgeon to forget his idea, pointing out that Metro were quite happy with their Saint fleet and I did not want them to postpone their new order and wait for Tridents. At that time it was by no means certain that the three cylinder model would ever go into production. The prototype was having problems and its development was costing so much money that financial director Charles Parker seriously questioned whether the project should continue, and I agreed with him.

It is difficult to reconcile the existence of the prototype Trident early in 1965 with the story in Hopwood's book that he and Doug Hele discussed a basic design late in 1963 and filed away their drawings in view of Edward Turner's reputed resistance to a three cylinder unit. In fact, Percy Tait had ridden thousands of miles on the prototype by 1965 and I well remember Bernal Osborne, the Midlands Editor of *Motor Cycling,* seeing it through my office window and having to be persuaded not to report it. Inevitably, Sturgeon insisted that the machine should be brought to the MIRA exercise and I told Tait to do so, but to stay on the outer circuit away from the timed strip. I almost got away with it but suddenly Sturgeon remembered and Tait was signalled to join the group. The clutch was noisier than the engine and this diminished any interest the Metro visitors might have had. It was a very long time before the Trident and its BSA counterpart, the Rocket 3, went into production and despite the brilliant work of the Doug Hele team which brought outstanding racing successes, there was negligible contribution to commercial profits, if any at all.

Following the amalgamation of BSA/Triumph agency arrangements in the UK market, Sturgeon flew to America to do the same thing there, and I awaited what I confidently expected to be the rejection of his policy and the justification of my own warnings. He addressed the Triumph Dealer Convention and before he got very far in outlining his plans he was interrupted by the elected spokesman for the dealers, who made it very clear that in no circumstances would they handle BSA. Sturgeon acknowledged defeat and realised that he would face the same situation in other export markets. He returned to England and soon afterwards became ill. He entered a hospital in Cambridge after consultations with specialists, and underwent a major operation to remove a tumour on the brain.

Chapter Eleven

He must have known that the chances of success were slight but it was typical of the man that he accepted the risk. The operation was apparently successful and in due course he was discharged from hospital. Having planned a holiday to recuperate, he made a visit to the Midlands and called at Meriden. I was leaving my office to go into the factory when I met him and Hopwood walking down the corridor. Significantly, I thought, Hopwood stopped a few paces away whilst Sturgeon spoke to me, and I remember his words quite clearly. He said 'You were right when we talked at the Meriden Manor Hotel, and I will keep my promise. As soon as I am back at work, I want you to restore the original UK dealership arrangements with my support, and to assure all overseas distributors that there will be no change in their franchise. Also I want you to know that you will be appointed General Sales Manager for both BSA and Triumph operations.' I thanked him and wished him a quick return, little realising as I said goodbye that I would not see him again. He had only a few days convalescent holiday before he was rushed back to hospital, where he died. I remember Harry Sturgeon not for his mistakes but for my conviction that he would have corrected them and been capable of averting the disastrous BSA slide over the next five years, which inevitably took Meriden with it.

With his death went my expectation that Triumph Sales Administration would revert to Meriden control, but with my Police and Military business running at an excellent level I was determined that this would continue, despite the clumsy efforts of envious people at Small Heath to sell BSA machines to satisfied Triumph users. The Saint reigned supreme in the UK and in many overseas countries. The Military versions of the 350 and 500 cc twins secured substantial business throughout the world and it was necessary to create a special section in the factory through which all official duty machines passed. After they had been subjected to the normal final test routine in the main factory, they were given expert attention by four highly skilled men who were as proud as I was of their work. No motorcycles before or since have ever left a factory with such excellent quality but I was to lose this valuable section, with serious consequences, as will be explained later.

At around the time of Sturgeon's death I had already planned my next and most ambitious ride, to underline the prestige which the Saint had achieved. The International Police Exhibition was to take place in Hanover and, as it had been some years since the last one had been held in Paris, it was to be a major event, supported by many Police Forces and their Governments. This was an opportunity not to be missed and not only must the Saint be there but it had to make the journey in a way which would ensure maximum publicity. If any further incentive were needed, it was to take the Triumph flag into BMW home territory. I had always regarded BMW as the only rival to the Saint and it had been very satisfying to compete successfully against the German machines in Continental

The Beginning of the End

Police markets like Holland, France, Belgium, Greece, Denmark and Sweden. Having calculated the road distance to Hanover, and checked on the Air Ferry service from Southend to Rotterdam, I estimated that by leaving Meriden at around 5 am I would reach Hanover by mid-afternoon.

The ride was to be made on 26th August 1966, the day before the official opening of the Exhibition. I contacted the Police Department of the Home Office and the Export Department of the Board of Trade to inform them of my plans. Both were very keen on the idea and the Exhibition organisers were notified officially of the ride. That was to prove useful. I also 'phoned my friends at Pye, Cambridge, who had loaned me the Westminster radio set already on the Saint, and they at once offered to have the company aircraft keep in radio contact with me over Germany and Holland and report my progress to Hanover through a set to be installed on the British Police Stand. When I was within 50 miles or so from destination I would be able to talk direct. Next I had words with the Metropolitan and Essex Police to notify them the time I would be in their areas, and with the Warwickshire Police to arrange for an Officer to witness my departure from Meriden village. As I did not want to lose any time finding my way out of Rotterdam, I 'phoned our Dutch distributors there and asked for a guide in a fast car. He proved to be a Monte Carlo Rally driver. As my ride would, in fact, start from my home at Stratford upon Avon, I arranged to carry a letter of greetings from the Mayor to the Burgomaster of Hanover. As I had found on past occasions, that was sure to get good publicity at both ends.

Several days before departure time I remembered that my friends the Royal Marines Motorcycle Display Team were appearing at the Essex County Show at Chelmsford during that week on their Triumphs. I telephoned the Team Officer with whom I had enjoyed several good sessions in the bar at the Eastney Barracks, and jocularly suggested that coffee and rum would be very welcome at Southend Airport at around 7.30 am on the morning of the 26th. I checked the Saint and thought it would look good on photographs to fly the British, Dutch and West German flags on the machine. It would have been wiser to have used flag transfers on the windscreen, for the Union Jack tore away before Southend, the Dutch one did the same by Arnhem, but the German flag survived the journey, though somewhat tattered at the end.

On 26th August 1966 at 4.30 am the Saint headlamp startled the herd of deer in Charlecote Park as I headed for Warwick and Meriden. By the village green was the waiting Police car and PC35 McCarthy who signed my log sheet at 05.05 departure time. Past the factory to what used to be called the Coventry bypass before the City extended way beyond it, and after a few dark miles I joined the night traffic on the motorway. Somewhere near the Toddington Service Area an ominous rattle developed in the fairing and I pulled on to the hard shoulder to investigate. It was the old trouble with the Avonaire, the headlamp retaining ring

Chapter Eleven

screws had worked loose and the lamp was coming adrift. Even in daylight the screws were difficult to locate and, with no time to spare, I used masking tape on the lamp and hoped it would hold. I exited the motorway on to what is now the M10 and at London Colney a Metro Police Triumph pulled out from the side of the road and the rider waved me alongside. I was delighted to see that he was my old friend Len Farmer, one of the elite members of the famous Hendon Driving School. Riders from the Police of many countries have been trained by Len and his colleagues, and when the Emperor of Japan made his State visit to England he was so impressed by the Metro Special Escort Group that, on his orders, Japanese Police come to Hendon each year for an advanced riding course. Len called out that he was to pilot me to the A12, and not for the first time, as I followed him, I admired the effortless way in which an expert Police motorcyclist filters through traffic congestion as though the road was empty. At the Metro Police boundary on the A12 a Triumph-mounted Essex patrol rider was waiting to escort me to Southend. I was being given very special treatment that morning, and I was to have more later on. I slowed down to wave thanks and farewell to Len and to continue with PC1296 Clare of Essex, but Len raced ahead and took the lead. As he explained later, he was enjoying the ride and it made a welcome change from training routine. The three Triumphs were soon at Southend Airport and, as the Essex Officer signed my log sheet at 07.40, I found myself in the middle of the entire Royal Marines Display Team. My telephone conversation had been taken seriously and Thermos flasks of coffee generously laced with rum were disposed of as the Saint was put aboard the Bristol Freighter. My happy association with the Display Teams of the Royal Marines and Royal Signals had always been one of the special pleasures of my years at Meriden and, when the Admiralty decided to axe the Marines team, I was privileged to play an active part in the appeal which resulted in the withdrawal of the decision.

The Freighter landed at Rotterdam soon after 09.00 and my Stokvis friends were waiting. With nearly 300 miles ahead of me I was anxious to leave quickly, but they insisted on having breakfast whilst the Saint was taken to their workshops to have the headlamp fixed. Also there were matters to be discussed in connection with the Netherlands Army machine. It was more than an hour before I got away, piloted by a very quick Porsche, and the Saint was at her maximum all the way to the German barrier. As the Porsche turned to go back to Rotterdam, I cleared Customs and began the last 200 miles. A German Police Porsche accelerated past me and I followed it for some miles at around 85 mph. I needed to travel faster to make up some of the time lost in Rotterdam and, with a courteous wave to the two officers in the car, I went past and the speedo needle steadied at 95 at which speed the Saint was quite happy and still had a little left. Immediately the Police car overtook and stayed at the 95 cruising speed, the observer signalled to me and I realised that I had another escort. An hour or so later the car turned off

The Beginning of the End

to a Police Post and the occupants waved me goodbye. The traffic was getting heavier on the two lane autobahn, the rain clouds were gathering ahead and I heard again the rattle of the headlamp. As the miles went by it grew worse and as the rain slashed down from a dark sky I pulled in to a parking area to do another taping exercise, only to find that I had left the tape somewhere on the M1 motorway. Two retaining screws had disappeared so I removed the other two, disconnected the wiring and put the lamp unit in my haversack. A GB car was parked nearby and the driver came over to ask if he could help. I saw that he had stopped for early afternoon tea and I said I would be most grateful for a cup. He was terribly sorry but the pot was empty. With some 50 miles to Hanover I pressed on through the rain and through the hazards of Germanic drivers who refused to move over from the outside lane, and certainly not for a motorcyclist. The time was approaching 3 pm as I slowed down at the Hanover exit sign and saw the waiting Police motorcycle escort, together with a couple of Triumph TRW-mounted British Military Police. A few minutes later we entered the Exhibition area where I was welcomed by Police Chief Karl Saupe. I remember well the conversation. 'I am surprised that you got here', he began. 'The machine is perfectly reliable, so why be surprised?' I replied. He went on 'The German car drivers do not like motorcyclists, especially Police motorcyclists, and my riders stay away from the autobahns'. I was to remember his words a year later when I did a ride from the Cologne Show to Denmark and was cut up a number of times for no reason except perhaps the GB plate. There is no speed limit on German autobahns and, as I have learned many times, a motorcyclist must not expect any courtesy warning from the driver who is determined to overtake.

My arrival at the Exhibition made the 435 miles ride well worthwhile. The Police Chief's welcome was followed by greetings from the Oberburgermeister of Hanover, who was delighted to receive the letter from the Mayor of Stratford upon Avon. The proceedings were filmed by ITV, to be shown on British television the same evening. I was taken to the German Police VIP centre and the hospitality was such that it was some considerable time before I rode the Saint to its prepared position on the British stand. There I met Alice Bacon MP, representing the Government, and she was grateful that somebody had done something to help the very poor British contribution to the Exhibition. I realised what she meant when I saw the magnificent exhibits arranged by the German, French, Japanese, Italian, Belgian and other Police forces. The British presence was evidenced by a couple of Dorset Police Officers and a portrait of the Queen. The German Press gave generous publicity to the ride and headlined the story 'Herr Shilton's Record Ride from Meriden to bring greetings from the British police to the Hanover Exhibition'. The Saint stood proudly on the British stand and was soon to be retired to its permanent place at the Metro Police Hendon Driving School. Man and machine had enjoyed many adventurous and successful rides, of which the

Chapter Eleven

Arrival at the exhibition, minus the headlamp. The Police Chief [fourth from the left] commented pleasantly that I was breaking the law.

The Beginning of the End

Hanover journey gave a great deal of pleasure. On the opening morning of the Exhibition I was on a tramcar crowded with Germans making their way there. One, who was reading the morning paper with the report of my ride and pictures of the arrival, recognised me from the crash helmet strapped to my haversack. He greeted me and, before the tramcar had reached the Exhibition, every occupant did the same and shook my hand. There is no doubt that had I done the journey by car, there would have been no publicity at all. As I write, I look at the log of the ride. Meriden to Southend 2 hrs 25 minutes, Rotterdam to Hanover 4 hrs 20, total road distance 435 miles, average speed 64.4 mph, which would have been even quicker but for the headlamp trouble. I returned to England to face the problems which were to lead to farewell to Meriden which followed my last long distance ride on a Triumph.

Chapter Twelve

Portrait of a Master. Freddie Frith on his way to victory in the 1937 Senior TT. [The Motor Cycle]

Chapter Twelve

Farewell to Meriden

THE TITLE of this chapter would be more accurate if the farewell was to the Triumph Engineering Company as, although I was to resign and leave in 1968, I was to return to Meriden several years later when the BSA Group had been taken over by Norton Villiers. After the death of Harry Sturgeon, we were anxious to learn who would succeed him and nobody expected that it would be his deputy Bert Hopwood, except Hopwood himself, who had been upset when he did not take over from Edward Turner. The Triumph executives were called to E.T.'s old office and informed by a disappointed Hopwood that the new boss was Lionel Jofeh. Having protested strongly against the Sturgeon appointment, which he regarded as a personal affront, Hopwood now offered his resignation but did not resign, having been assured by the Chairman that his support of Jofeh was essential. We were very soon to learn that to support the Jofeh policies was to hasten the collapse of the Motorcycle Division. He was yet another ex-aircraft industry man who not only knew nothing about motorcycle business but had a low opinion of those who had been involved in it for years. He was to say to me later on 'Shilton, if you possessed any real business acumen, you would not be in this industry'. Jack Sangster and Edward Turner were on the BSA Group Board, and

Chapter Twelve

they frequently criticised the way in which the Motorcycle Division was being run, but they were the only ones with any experience and they were outnumbered.

The Jofeh appointment was solely a Chairman decision, as had been the Sturgeon one, but I wonder whether Edward Turner ever recommended that Hopwood should take his place. Certainly he would have been preferable to Sturgeon and Jofeh, had he been prepared to accept the advice which was still available from Turner, but that might have been too much to expect. The man who would have collaborated with Turner, and so perpetuated the virility of Triumph, was Financial Director Charles Parker. He had all the qualifications and workforce respect to be the natural successor to his old boss. He had been with the company since its formation, prior to which he was with the motorcycling Press. He was a highly experienced accountant and a keen motorcyclist with a sound technical background. The Turner/Parker partnership had directed the Meriden progress along its outstandingly successful course and, when Turner departed but remained on the Group Board, he had given Meriden operations enough momentum to continue efficiently under Parker for a long time. Furthermore, the partnership would have continued, for Turner had been busy on his drawing board and Parker was the man to translate the results into profitable production. Everyone at Meriden, except Hopwood, would have been delighted had Parker taken over from Turner as Managing Director instead of Sturgeon, and this might well have changed the pattern of the next seven years which ended so disastrously. When Parker was ultimately asked to join the BSA Board he tackled the serious problems with little hope of success, and even his expert experience was not enough. He had been called up too late.

With the Jofeh appointment came more newcomers to add to those who had been brought in by Sturgeon, and it seemed that the most important qualification was to have had no previous experience in the motorcycle industry. I well remember the traditional Xmas luncheon in the senior staff dining room at Meriden in December 1967. We had enjoyed this function for many years, with Edward Turner and his co-Directors as the guests of the senior staff. Always we invited friends from the motorcycling Press, Bernal Osborne, Bob Currie and Cyril Quantrill, but a few days befor the 1967 luncheon we were told that the new Financial Director and two other BSA executives would accompany Jofeh, and that the Press would be excluded. The atmosphere was distinctly unhappy in the dining room that Xmas for we regarded the visitors as intruders, and I was expected by my colleagues to make some appropriate reflection in the Xmas address I always gave after lunch. My sense of humour was permitted some license by Turner and Parker, but it was to upset the new people. In referring to them as the Three Wise Men from the Heath I suggested that before they returned to the place from whence they came they should take a look at the book of the profits. I continued with a modified version of the old carol 'God Rest Ye Meriden Gentlemen

Farewell to Meriden

let nothing you dismay, business is good from Triumph but dreadful at BSA'. My colleagues were delighted but the Group Financial Director rebuked me for my discourtesy. The following Xmas there were no BSA visitors.

When I returned from Hanover I had my first collision with Jofeh. He had decided to move Tiger Cub production from Meriden to Small Heath and I protested strongly, as did the factory shop stewards. It was inconceivable that the Cub should be made anywhere other than in the Triumph factory, where it was born and where it had maintained a successful production programme which went as high as 275 per week. Hopwood should have been strong enough to have backed the resistance of the shop stewards, but there is no evidence that he was interested, perhaps because he had played no part in this Turner-designed machine. It may be for the same reason that he is so disparaging of the Cub in his book, and at the same time criticises Turner for developing the Cub from the 150 cc Terrier and increasing the capacity by 50 cc. The sales figures themselves proved the popularity of the Cub and Hopwood is quite wrong when he says that when he joined Triumph the machine was outdated and giving serious service troubles. Certainly the power output of its eager engine had recommended a more accommodating big end for hard driving and this had been done in good time. Many of the Military Cubs I supplied to the French Army before Hopwood joined the company are still giving good service, as I learned when I talked to an Army rider in France last year. He was proud of his Cub, so was I, and so were all the men at Meriden who made them. When I confronted Jofeh and told him he must not go ahead with his plans, as always he was incapable of listening to advice and he flatly refused to change his decision. He intended to move the Cub so as to make room for increased production of twins and, furthermore, he would move the twin assembly line to a new building to be erected behind the factory.

I found it incredible that a newcomer should be making major changes to a company which was operating so efficiently and so profitably. When I expressed my belief that the Cub would not be produced at Small Heath to the same standard as at Meriden, he asked if I thought the BSA factory workers were not so capable as those at Meriden. I replied that I would have the same doubts if the Bantam was produced at Meriden. There was more to a motorcycle than a blueprint drawing. Jofeh went ahead with his plans to move the Cub to Small Heath, but the shop stewards went ahead with their own. He had assured them that the move would result in higher wages from increased twin production and they insisted upon a signed undertaking to this effect. Jofeh gave it and it was waved in front of him whenever necessary. The shop stewards held him to his obligation and Triumph wages set an enviable standard in the Coventry area. There was supposed to be no break between the ending of Cub production at Meriden and its commencement at Small Heath, but this did not happen. It was a month or so be-

Chapter Twelve

fore the first Birmingham Cubs emerged and, when they did, they were all sent to Meriden where the engines were stripped, worked on, and rebuilt to acceptable standard. The little lightweight which had been so successful was subjected to new styling treatment at Small Heath and this effectively destroyed the compact appearance which was the hallmark of all Turner designs. There was no longer any sales effort behind it and it soon suffered the same fate as the Ariel Arrow, which never recovered from being moved from Selly Oak. When Cub production ceased, a black edged card appeared on a notice board at Triumph: 'In memory of T. Cub born at Meriden, died from neglect at Small Heath'. As to the new assembly building, it was another expensive mistake. Not only was it quite unnecessary, but engine units had to be transported a considerable distance in all weathers.

One morning I was informed that I was to lose the quality inspection section which was responsible for the final test of all Police and Military machines. It was to cease at once. I was particularly concerned about the Saint, which had earned such a high reputation, and which was doing fine business around the world. The instruction had come from the Financial Department at BSA on the grounds that the Police would have to accept standard machines and the extra cost of quality inspection was wasteful. I produced the records I had kept showing faults which had needed correction and which otherwise would have given trouble and resulted in expensive warranty claims. I urged that an analysis of warranty costs would show clearly that the work done by my quality check mechanics saved money as well as ensuring that we maintained our strong position in the field of Police and other official business. My appeals were in vain and my fears for the consequences were to prove justified. All the work which had established the Saint as the unrivalled Police and Defence Force machine in many countries was to be eroded and its reputation began to decline.

The first signs came from Australia which, apart from the UK, was the largest Saint market. An ominous telegram arrived from the New South Wales Police in Sydney, who bought 700 Saints each year. It reported an epidemic of burnt pistons with holes through the crowns, and demanded immediate action. I went straight to Hopwood, whose only comments were that either poor petrol was being used or the riders were responsible. Hardly the sort of answer I could send back to Sydney. I made one of my rare visits to Umberslade Hall, that extravagant folly which had been acquired to house the so-called Design Centre. There I consulted Hopwood's assistant, Brian Jones, and asked him if the material or construction of the pistons had been changed. The answer was negative, so back I went to Hopwood and suggested that Hepworth and Grandage, who supplied our piston castings, might know something. I was given the same answer as before, with the added comment that nowhere else was there any piston trouble. He was wrong, for a day or two later Rod Coates, the Service Manager of the Triumph

Farewell to Meriden

Corporation, Baltimore, arrived to see Hopwood about the same epidemic in America. I found the answer by talking to the man on the engine assembly section who fitted the cylinder block and pistons. He had noticed that the pistons were lighter in weight. More metal had been machined from the crown than the blueprint drawing specified and what remained was insufficient to prevent burning.

I cabled the facts to Australia, had replacement pistons sent by airfreight and decided to go there to give some help. With me went a very capable Senior Technician, Frank Baker, who had done fine work at Meriden for some years. We worked for two weeks in Sydney and enjoyed a day riding on the Police training circuit some miles away at St. Ives. This must be the most comprehensive training area in the world. Literally carved out of the bush country, it contained every condition to make experts out of novices on a programme lasting a month. The miles of circuit varied from rock strewn sections, mud and deep water, to a narrow road with such hazards as hump bridges and hairpin bends with adverse cambers. Finally there was a high speed circuit. Not until the student had done a non-stop course within the set time was he passed out and the Chief Instructor told me that some withdrew in their first week. I rode the course with him and wondered whether I could have got inside standard time after a month. On leaving Police HQ in Sydney I was given a farewell message by the Traffic Chief, 'We hope to see you here again sometime, but not if we have any more trouble'. Two years or so later, when another large fleet of machines had been supplied, there was a repeat epidemic of burnt pistons. That was the end of a long association between Triumph and the New South Wales Police. The Japanese eventually took over.

From Sydney, Baker and I went to Brisbane at the request of the Queensland Police, who used BSA twins and were having troubles with handling and suspension. We both took machines out in the hilly country and quickly found that the fork springs and rear units were much too soft. I had a cable sent to Small Heath for the required heavy duty units and a poor view was taken of what was considered interference. Subsequently there was some argument about payment and this may have been the reason why Queensland then changed to Triumphs. A visit to the Federal Capital of Canberra was next and I found myself in the awkward position of listening to rider demands for Bonnevilles, and the resistance of the Traffic Chief, who maintained that they were always riding too fast even when it was not necessary. I was given a Saint and went out with two officers intent on demonstrating that the machines were not quick enough. I found that there were only two roads in and out of Canberra and on my return I talked with the Chief and said that the answer was to equip the Saints with radio. No robbers or speeders could get very far before being stopped by a patrol car road block alerted by a motorcycle patrol radio. To my surprise the Chief told me that the riders refused to have radio. I left him with the problem and the next order was for

Chapter Twelve

The era of British racing supremacy. Frith [Velocette] leading Johnny Lockett and Artie Bell [Nortons] with Bob Foster [Velocette] completing the quartet in the 1949 Belgian Grand Prix on the Francorchamps circuit. [The Motor Cycle]

Farewell to Meriden

Bonnevilles. Melbourne was the next stop to see the Victoria Police and to renew a friendship with Frank Musset, who rode Velocettes in the 1939 TT races, finishing 10th in the Junior and retiring in the Senior. The 350 was still on display in his shop and looked immaculate. Our last journey was to Tasmania, the beautiful island off the south coast where I met several patrol riders who had come from UK forces and who were kind enough to lend me a Saint for a look round Launceston. The road journey to Hobart in the south was a rare experience, travelling for miles through uninhabited country unchanged, it seemed, since convicts were transported from UK to Tasmania last century. I was scheduled to fly from Australia to New Zealand, but the plan was changed when I was recalled urgently to the factory and found myself facing a difficult situation which had arisen during my absence.

For many months the Ministry of Defence had been running an evaluation programme of testing BSA and Triumph Military machines and a contract for some 2000 units was forecast. These were mainly for the Army, who had bought no machines for many years except for a very small number of the Triumph TRW 500 cc side valve models. BSA had submitted the 350 cc B40 single and Triumph the 350 cc twin, which was later replaced by the 500 to satisfy adequately the long distance two-up Ministry requirements. I had made several visits to the test areas at Chobham and Bagshot riding a Military model and satisfied myself that the programme was going very well for Triumph. I had also visited the Ministry of Defence (Wheeled Vehicles) HQ at St. Christopher House in London. The Assistant Director there was an old friend from the TRW days and, with the test programme nearing its end, he asked me to give him a reply to a confidential question. Having already had cost estimates of the two types of machine, he asked whether I thought that Triumph would be compelled to quote an appreciably higher price so that the contract would go to the BSA B40. He was wiser than I was, for the possibility had not occurred to me. However, I said that I was entirely confident that not even the BSA Group Chairman would dare to issue such an instruction, even if the B40 was near the Triumph price. Surely it would be much lower. I added several more comments. The Ministry could, if it so wished, issue a cost plus contract, which would entitle them to examine production costs and agree the profit margin. It would be simple for them to find out the price at which we at Meriden were already selling the Military model to various overseas Governments, and they probably knew this already. Therefore this was another reason why the price could not be loaded for our own Ministry. Finally, I gave an assurance that if, when I dealt with the official tender for the contract, I was told to inflate the price, I would refuse to do so. As I was leaving, my Assistant Director friend confided to me that the Danish Army would be placing a large order for whichever machine was chosen by our Ministry.

Whilst I was in Australia, BSA Sales Director Bill Rawson, having learned of

Chapter Twelve

the Danish potential from his importer in Copenhagen, pulled a few strings in certain quarters. I always had every respect for him and he was one of my very few friends at Small Heath, but on this occasion he went a little too far and created the problem which brought me back from Australia. Several BSA and Triumph Military models had been sent by the Ministry to a British Army unit in Germany as part of the user trials programme. Rawson had been able to arrange for a BSA to be taken to Denmark in an Army vehicle for demonstration. The Triumph importer got news of this and, when the demonstration began on an area of rough ground, a Trophy Triumph appeared ridden by Danish motocross champion Jacob Lynegaard, who gave a masterly display which made the British Army rider look like a novice, and the BSA performance like an old moped. Rawson was upset and, to the British Captain who had come from Germany to supervise, he made dangerously disparaging remarks about the Triumph importer. These referred to his involvement with the MZ motorcycle factory in East Germany, and cast doubts upon his personal character, his integrity and his loyalty to the BSA Group. Unfortunately for Rawson, the Captain relayed the remarks to the Military Attaché at the British Embassy and a report was made to the Foreign Office in London. Through some channel or other my Triumph importer friend became aware of what had been said and his reaction created a high risk situation for everyone involved. I was instructed to go to Copenhagen and try to defuse it, which I was finally able to do after discussions at the Embassy and with my Triumph friend. Also I talked with the Danish Army authorities, who confirmed that they would place a first order for 450 of whichever machine was chosen by the British Ministry. I had little doubt that the Triumph would be the choice, but having got BSA out of trouble with my diplomatic efforts in Copenhagen I was soon to regret it.

Tenders were issued by the Ministry and I prepared the Triumph one after getting approval from Financial Director Charles Parker of my costing, pricing and profit margin. Although I had estimted that the B40 price was bound to be at least £30 lower, there was no question of cutting our profit margin, for we were offering a 500 cc twin against a 350 cc single. Moreover, the Ministry knew that the twin had earned a first class reputation with Overseas Military authorities whereas the B40 had secured no business. The next day Parker sent for me and said that I had to increase the Triumph price by £30, on instructions from the Chairman. I protested strongly and flatly refused to sign the tender at an inflated price. Parker readily understood my feelings but he had to carry out instructions. I tried to help him by asking what explanations we would give to the Ministry if they questioned the price in comparison with the export figure for the same machine, which they either knew or could easily find out. His answer was that we would claim dislocation of standard production involving extra costs. He signed the Tender, a fact which I was later to emphasise to my friend at the Ministry.

Farewell to Meriden

Meanwhile, I 'phoned to ask whether price was an important competitive factor and the answer was affirmative. The Financial Department of the Ministry was more powerful than the technical side and, to them, a motorcycle specification meant nothing and was unrelated to the price. Which is why the contract went to Small Heath in accordance with the wish of the Chairman. BSA badly needed it whereas Triumph business was still healthy, but I debated this attitude with Parker and pointed out that if the Chairman was concerned about profits, he should have known that a Meriden contract would have produced much more than Small Heath. In fact he made another bad mistake when he gave instructions for maximum deliveries of the B40 before the end of June, so as to help the poor trading figures for the end of the financial year. The shortcomings of the B40 were emphasised by the hurry to obey his dictum, which left no time for adequate quality control and testing. Inevitably, the Danish Army ordered the B40 and a couple of years or so later, after the BSA collapse, I had a very difficult meeting with the Danish BSA importer. He could not obtain B40 spare parts, although the contract had contained a clause requiring parts availability for seven years. It is a sad reflection that the Danish Army now have Japanese machines, and the British services bought many Can Ams from Canada. I telephoned my Ministry friend a few days before his retirement and apologised for my mistake in believing that Small Heath would not compel Triumph to increase the Tender price. He had been as upset as I was and had come very close to having the Tender withdrawn on the basis that, as I had then pointed out, it was not a competitive quotation because the two companies were in the same Group. I should have 'phoned him when I was instructed to increase the Triumph price and I would have done so but for my respect for Charles Parker. It would have been difficult for Parker to have ignored the instructions from the Chairman although his integrity brought him close to doing so.

My diary reminds me to recall several interesting memoirs of this period. The first is a happy recollection of my long friendship with John Surtees. He was kind enough to agree to visit my son's Prep. School near Stratford upon Avon and talk to the boys. It was a very special treat for them to meet the World Champion and to see the film of his victory that year in the French Grand Prix. After the film, the Headmaster invited questions and they went on for so long that normal bedtime was deferred for the first time in the history of the school. Ultimately the Headmaster called a halt and began to thank John, who then asked permission to hear one last question from a small boy whose hand had been raised unsuccessfully many times. He was the fat boy of the school, the legendary Billy Bunter of Tuckshop fame. The assembly hall went silent for his question and, when it was asked in a nervous stammer, there was an eruption of delighted laughter from a hundred boys. 'Mr. Surtees, Sir', he said, 'do you have to be careful what you eat before you race?' John realised that upon his answer depended whether the boy

Chapter Twelve

would be ragged for asking the silly question of the evening. As the laughter died away John looked at the boy and replied, 'You have raised a very important subject. I have to be very careful what I eat even the day before a race. An athlete must, of course, do the same before a race which only takes seconds or minutes, and I must be equally fit for a Grand Prix which lasts for two hours or more. I thank you for your question, especially because it is the first time anyone has given the opportunity of explaining its importance'. The boy was happy and, as the assembly hall emptied, I saw him leaving between two friends who had their arms round his shoulders. He will be grown up by now but will always remember the happiness which John Surtees gave to him.

The next note in my diary recalls a very different memory. The Triumph distributor for New Zealand, an intensely loyal friend of Meriden, was Staffordshire-born Bill White, for many years the Mayor of Newmarket, near Christchurch. Regularly each year he came to the factory until the day he arrived after Jofeh had become the new Managing Director. At Meriden, where he had always been cordially welcomed by his old friend Edward Turner, Hopwood was too busy to see him. I 'phoned the Jofeh office at Small Heath and after a while was informed that Mr. White could be given five minutes. The offer was not accepted and it marked the end of a long association with Triumph. Bill went home and to keep his business going he was compelled to take the Yamaha distributorship. He later wrote to tell me of the visit he and his manager made to the Yamaha factory. There were two cars at the airport, one for the visitors and the other for their suitcases. As the cars approached the factory, the neon lights were switched on with the message: 'Yamaha welcomes our friends from New Zealand'. 'Somewhat different to England', commented Bill.

The next page in my diary deserves to have a black border of mourning, for it recalls the disastrous story of the device to become known as the Ariel 3, which was an insult to the once proud Selly Oak name which adorned the petrol tanks of the Red Hunters and Square Fours. The heavy losses written off against such failures as the Beeza scooter, Beagle and Pixie were negligible compared with this three-wheeled moped, which added the biggest nail to those which already awaited the BSA coffin. Designed by a man named Wallis on the principle of a tricycle which would go round corners with the two rear wheels staying firmly on the road, it was supposed to be the ultimate safety machine. He offered the manufacturing rights to BSA and, when I saw it, I recalled that the same principle had been tried out in Coventry very many years before the war and abandoned. However, Jofeh was impressed, and arranged a demonstration on the Small Heath test track attended by executives from Triumph and BSA. With its small wheels and the narrow track necessary to comply with moped licence regulations, the machine simply could not be regarded as adult transport and at best it could only be a fun bike for youngsters. After lunch there was a meeting with Jofeh pre-

Farewell to Meriden

siding and he quickly made it clear that he saw a vast market for the machine. It was the answer to commuter transport problems, it would reduce the bus queues and ease the pressure on the tube trains. On their side of the table, his BSA disciples supported him and when he turned to the Meriden contingent I was asked for my views. I said in a few frank words that it would not be acceptable as serious personal transport, an adult would look and feel absurd on such a small machine, and anyone brave enough to ride it on a dark wet night in city traffic would risk being killed by a driver who did not see him through a wet windscreen. Jofeh glared and said, 'Shilton, you are a motorcyclist and cannot be expected to understand this new dimension of mass transport'. He went ahead with his plans to manufacture and enjoy an expected demand for 100,000 per year. A first order was placed for 50,000 Anker engines made in Holland and in 1973, when Norton Villiers took over the BSA Group, one of my tasks was to find a market for most of them. The Jofeh 3, as I prefer to call it, was the biggest disaster of all those the Group had suffered and, even after its costly failure was clear to everyone, more money was spent on sending a team of salesmen and dolly bird demonstrators around the country. This Jofeh folly must have contributed generously to the £8 million loss announced by the Group in 1971. Sangster and Edward Turner would surely have stopped the Jofeh plan had they still been on the Board. As to the attitude taken by Hopwood, according to his book he left it to a consultant to criticise design geometry.

As the months of 1967 went by, Meriden morale continued to descend and the workforce had good reason to believe that they had nobody to defend them against the incompetent management. The once proud factory flag was at half mast and stayed there until it was finally furled. There was fertile ground for the rumour that the Chairman hoped to sell the Group motorcycle business to Tube Investments, who had more than enough cash to buy it after the Government took over their steel interests. That, it was said, explained the unnecessary new building extension at Meriden and the expensively useless Umberslade Hall, together intended to magnify investment prospects. Umberslade, which housed 300 so-called designers and reputedly cost £1000 per week rental, produced nothing of any use apart from a brood of cygnets hatched by a pair of swans on the lake. One of the bright young designers came to see me one day with a clay model of a petrol tank on which he had been told to get my views. It seemed to have been inspired by a Grecian sculpture of a generously-busted female, for the front of the tank was in the shape of two breasts which protruded like elongated headlamps. I told the young man that was certainly imaginative, but useless, as it left no room for fork movement and it was sometimes necessary for a motorcycle to go round a corner. He was very upset at having wasted weeks of work. He had simply been told to design a tank and nothing had been said about front forks.

In the early weeks of 1968, as I became more despondent about the future of

Chapter Twelve

Triumph, I decided to ask for a personal interview with Jofeh. Except for Charles Parker, I was the longest-serving Meriden executive and I felt that not only was I entitled to question him but it was time he was made to realise that the workforce had little confidence left in the management. The interview took place in Edward Turner's old office and at the desk which had been so admired by Stan Hailwood that, with Turner's assistance, he ordered a replica. I had written out my questions and I passed the list to Jofeh. The first asked him if he would convene a meeting of Triumph departmental heads and pointed out that he had so far not talked to any of them. The next asked him to divorce Umberslade from Meriden and to restore the autonomy of the Triumph Design and Development Department. The independence of Triumph sales operations was requested and the reinstatement of the quality test system for Police machines. There were other questions but above all would he issue an official statement to the factory workers about the position of the Company and its future prospects. Only to the first question was the answer affirmative, but in fact he failed to keep his promise. He prevaricated on the others, whereupon I handed him the notice of resignation I had prepared, to take effect at the end of May unless before that time he had taken positive action on the points I had submitted. I left the office with little hope that anything would be done but certain that, after the clashes with Jofeh about the Cub and the Ariel 3, he would not care if I left the Company. However, I had done what I believed I had to do in trying to help the factory which had been my life for so many years. I told nobody about the interview, nor about my notice of intention to resign.

In March I was honoured by an invitation to open the International Motorcycle Show at Stockholm on 3rd April. It would involve riding from Meriden to Immingham on Sunday 31st March to get the boat which arrived at Gothenburg the following afternoon. Then a ride to Lerum from where the long journey to Stockholm would commence the next morning at the offices of the Swedish motorcycling Press. I had a new Saint registered and asked that it should be given special attention, an extended run on the rolling road apparatus, followed by a few miles around Meriden and a final check. Normally I would have done the road testing myself but I had to be away on Police visits until a day or two before I was due to leave for Sweden. A year or so earlier I would have had no concern about riding a new Saint to Stockholm, but the days had gone when each one was checked to perfection. On the Friday evening before I was to depart for Hull on Sunday, I was in my office when a 'phone call came through from BBC Birmingham. A rider was urgently needed to rush to Belper in Derbyshire and bring back a film for showing on the 10 pm News programme. Meriden testers had often carried football match films from ground to studio at £5 per trip and I had earned a few pounds myself that way.

This time it was no football game. George Brown MP, later Lord George,

Farewell to Meriden

had that day announced his resignation and the ex-Foreign Secretary was on his way to Belper to speak to his constituency committee about his shock decision. A TV crew had gone ahead but only a motorcyclist could get their film back in time and that would be difficult enough. Belper was a long way from Birmingham and Meriden and the route was not easy. The time of the call was after 6 pm, all testers had gone away an hour before and so I said I would do the run. I was going to take the Stockholm Saint home anyway and Belper would put a few more miles on the clock. I was away at 6.30 pm and a couple of minutes later, at the bottom of Meriden hill, I hit a mild bump and had the first of the very many steering wobbles I was to experience before I reached Stockholm. Never since my Rudge days had I encountered what used to be called a tank slapper and all of my Triumphs had handled well, but this one only needed a slight bump to become dangerous.

A warm welcome on a cold day at Gothenburg en route to Stockholm, 1st April 1968.

Chapter Twelve

There were many bumps to Belper but I arrived there with a crowd still waiting for their MP. He made the grand entrance, parking his car as the TV crew dragged their camera and cables towards him, then dragging them away again as he decided to park somewhere else. I joined the crew as assistant cable dragger. The BBC interviewer did his best with a very rude George Brown and finally got an over the shoulder answer to his question 'Will you be making an official statement tonight, Sir?' 'I shall say thanks for my dinner', said Brown. For what it was worth I got the film back to Birmingham in time and had another bad ride. The next day, Saturday, I went back to the factory, hoping I could switch to one of the Saints which were being assembled for the Lancashire Police and put on my number plates, but none were complete.

Sunday was the day of the Triumph Owners Club AGM at the factory and I, as Vice-President, had a warm send-off as I left for Stockholm. In Allesley village, a mile away, I stopped to post a letter addressed to Lionel Jofeh at Small Heath. It regretted that nothing had been done following our discussion and I must therefore give irrevocable notice of my decision to leave the Company. I could no longer stay and watch the destruction of the once proud factory where I had spent so many happy years. This would be my last long distance ride on a Triumph and it seemed appropriate that the machine should be a bad one. I headed for Lincoln where Freddie Frith, four times TT winner, was to meet me and ride with me to Immingham. I always seemed to get the best escorts but I never dreamed when I watched the immaculate style of Freddie in the Island years before that I would one day be riding with him. At the rendezvous he was waiting with a Bonneville and after a brief chat we were on our way to Grimsby. Riding behind Freddie was a great experience and, as I told him at the end of the journey, his polished style was exactly the same as in his championship days. Arriving at Gothenburg the next afternoon I was given a VIP reception by Tor Line but, for the first and only time in my many overseas rides, I had to empty the panniers for a Customs search. As I rode away to Lerum I remembered that on the same day, 1st April, I had joined Triumph 23 years ago. I spent the evening in Lerum with my journalist friend, Bengt Bjorklund, who was to pilot me to Stockholm in his Volvo. The weather forecast promised snow, sleet and near zero temperatures, which was not surprising because winter continues beyond early April in Sweden. What most concerned me were the road surface conditions after the effects of heavy frosts and it was arranged that Bengt would use his brake lights every time he saw a rough section. There were to be many brake light warnings to help me stay aboard the Saint.

We left Lerum in mist and sleet and headed for Jonkoping, the first stop on the 470 miles journey. Press and TV were there at the Esso Motel but all too quickly we had to leave the warmth of the reception and be on our way to the next scheduled publicity stop at Norrkoping. The visibility worsened in the sleet and

Farewell to Meriden

half light of the winter afternoon and I was glad of the Volvo tail lights ahead of me. It was dark when we arrived at Norrkoping and pulled into the courtyard of the Rallye Hotel, well known to Monte drivers. After twenty minutes talking to the Press and trying to get warm it was time to start the last lap of 150 miles and I well remember how reluctant I was to face them. After nearly three hours of driving sleet and being blinded by the big heavies going south to the Continent, the lights of Stockholm began to appear and were more than welcome. The journey had taken nine hours, my hands and wrists were swollen from trying to prevent vicious wobbles and, as a hot bath restored my circulation, my old friend Mogens Beier stood by to make sure I did not fall asleep. 'Happy Birthday', said Mogens, who had arranged a birthday party for me in the hotel. I have always been very fortunate to have good friends at the end of my journeys. The next morning I rode the Saint into the Marble Hall where the Exhibition was being held, was greeted by the organising sponsor and Swedish racing driver Picko Troberg, and cut the ribbon to open the Show. One of the machines on display

Arrival at the Swedish Show held in the Marble Hall at Stockholm.

Cutting the tape to open the Show, with the assistance of Swedish racing driver Picko Troberg.

Chapter Twelve

was the very first Norton Commando, a much travelled prototype which had been shown in a number of countries. With it was new Norton recruit, Hugh Palin, whose few words to me reflected his annoyance at the publicity which my ride had achieved. Eight months later he was to try to prevent me from joining Norton and to make my life very difficult when he failed to do so. I would not ride the Saint back to England so I arranged for it to be returned to Immingham and asked Freddie Frith to collect it by truck, but not to ride it to his premises. When I went to Grimsby to pick it up I found that he had, in fact, ridden it and he was amazed that I had been able to complete the Stockholm journey. Meanwhile, at Meriden I had learned that it was one of a number of Saints, including those for the Lancashire Police, which had been built with wrongly machined front fork stanchions. Consequently, as I had discovered the hard way, there was no damping, and the result was very nearly a solid front fork.

I had brought back from Stockholm some 700 orders, but only as a postman, although when Jofeh got to hear of this he concluded that I did not intend to go ahead with my resignation. I was playing hard to get according to one report which reached me but, unlike Hopwood, I had no intention of changing my mind or being persuaded to stay around to watch the destruction of Meriden. On the last Wednesday of May I was given a farewell party in the staff dining room, best remembered because a television set had been installed and we watched Manchester United win the European Cup. The presentation of cut glasses was made by Brenda Price who, paradoxically, had been the receptionist when I first went to Triumph to be interviewed by Edward Turner. She graduated to the position of secretary to Financial Director Charles Parker and, in 1975, after a brief spell with Norton Villiers Triumph, went back to Meriden to become a well-known figure in the Workers' Co-Operative.

Friday was the last of my many Triumph days and it proved to be eventful. Charles Parker called me to his office before his daily departure to Small Heath and he asked me to withdraw my resignation. 'You cannot leave Triumph after all these years', he said. I replied that I would never have left if the Company had remained the one which he and I had served for so long, but it had become a BSA subsidiary, had lost its identity and any hope of survival. I added that I had no other job to go to despite the rumours that I was joining Honda, but I had decided to go now instead of waiting for the inevitable collapse of the BSA Group. Later that morning a telephone call from Small Heath gave a message from Parker to say that I must not leave the office before he had seen me. In the afternoon the same caller repeated the message and an hour later Brenda Price rang on the internal 'phone system at Meriden to say the same thing. I told her that, although I saw no reason for the calls, she could assure Parker that I would not leave the factory until he had seen me, no matter how late. In fact, I was not to see him again. At 4.45 pm my secretary distributed copies of the farewell statement I had

Farewell to Meriden

prepared for departmental managers, factory foremen and shop stewards. It said how much I had enjoyed working with them, how proud I had been to demonstrate their machines around the world and how I deplored the bad policies which had caused me to resign.

A photograph of a sad event. My 'Farewell to Meriden' party in May 1968. Centre front is Brenda Price, who was to become a well-known personality when the Workers Co-operative took over Triumph.

Within minutes the TGWU steward came to my office wearing on his shoulder the red cloth which he always displayed when on union business. He had heard earlier rumours that I was leaving and now he had the confirmation. He proposed to call for industrial action against the irresponsible policies. I advised against it and recommended instead that a statement should be issued to the press giving the reasons why there was no confidence in Board level management. However, as I pointed out, it was too late for this to make any improvement and it was only a matter of time before the entire BSA Group faced financial collapse. After personal farewells to my colleagues, I continued to clear up my work whilst waiting for Parker to return from Small Heath. At 8.30 I was still waiting when the Security Officer looked in and I was astonished when he told me that Parker had come and gone an hour before. He added that on his rounds he had found that the safe in Brenda Price's office was open and he 'phoned her home. Shortly

Chapter Twelve

afterward she arrived with Parker in his Daimler, they locked the safe and left. My office was next to hers and was the only one with lights burning. It was a curious end to my last evening at Triumph and it has remained curious, for when I 'phoned her the next day there was no explanation as to why Parker had to see me but quite obviously avoided doing so. I switched off my office lights for the last time and walked through the deserted factory which, until a year before, had been noisy with night shift work.

My goodnight to the security man was, I thought, my farewell to Meriden and the end of my very long association with the motorcycle industry. I had sacrificed my hard-earned position in the conviction that Harry Sturgeon would revert to the well-proven policies of Edward Turner but his malignant brain tumour had put an end to that. I had resisted the ill-fated schemes of Jofeh to the point of final confrontation and could do no more. On my 25 miles homeward journey I realised that I had been conducting a lone crusade, unsupported by anyone else. Sangster and Turner had been critical of Board decisions but were disregarded as was Turner's serious warning of the Japanese threat. I had been particularly disappointed with Hopwood who, as deputy to Jofeh, should have demanded radical changes and resigned if they were not made. He could have enlisted not only the support of the entire Triumph factory but that of worldwide distributors. I have kept the letters I received from many of them, from Police forces and the press. In his USA journal *Cycle World* Joseph Parkhurst was particularly generous when he described my resignation as that of 'The leader of the progressive element in the British motorcycle industry'. I only wished that the element had been stronger. As I left Meriden that night I could not imagine that I would return when Norton Villiers took over the wreckage of the BSA Group. When that happened I was once more to make every effort to protect the future of the Triumph factory.

Chapter Thirteen

The Interpol Story

AFTER LEAVING Triumph I had no plans for the future. I had been invited to join Honda UK by my friend and ex-Raleigh Director Jim Harrison, who was the one man capable of establishing the first Japanese Company in the UK market. His personal reputation throughout the retail business was such that, when the first Honda 50 was shown at Earls Court, he booked orders for the entire allocation of 50,000 machines and paved the way for the future predominance of Honda in Britain. That was the Show when the quip went around that anyone on the BSA Group staff visiting the Honda hospitality bar would get the Saki. Jim 'phoned my home one day in 1968 to ask if I was going to the funeral of our old friend Joe Shearsmith, the Triumph/Honda dealer in York. If I was, would I like to ride the new electric starter 250 Honda there and tell what I thought of it. I collected the machine from the Honda Nottingham HQ, where it was handed over by my friend Alf Briggs, whose wife Molly was a well-known International rider on Triumphs. The day was very wet and windy and top gear of the five-speed gearbox was useless in a head wind. On the return journey from York I stopped at a 'phone box in Nottingham to call Jim who had invited me to dinner. I switched off the ignition key but the engine continued to run til I stopped it by

Chapter Thirteen

engaging bottom gear and applying the brakes. The 'phone was out of order and, when I went to the next one, the same thing happened when I switched off. I told Jim of the problem and decided to ride home to Stratford, but by Rugby the battery was flat and I finished my journey by taxi. When I 'phoned Alf Briggs the next day I learned that he had experienced the same trouble with several of the first 250 models. The starter motor circuit was independent of the main loom and, when the drive pinion jammed, the starter continued to turn the engine until the battery was exhausted. Those were the days when even the Japanese made mistakes. I was tempted to join Harrison and might have done so had he been the real chief of Honda UK but, as he confided to me, there was a little man from Japan on his shoulder who was the big boss. At the Amsterdam Show some two years later I shared a bottle of whisky with Jim in his hotel room, after he had told the little man where to go. He had done a fine job for Honda but he would prefer my view that he did a finer job for his many dealer friends who made much money from the Honda 50.

Five months after I left Triumph, I attended the annual TT riders reunion luncheon at the Connaught Rooms in London. The guest speaker was Roger Dennistoun Poore, better known as Dennis Poore, and as he plays a significant part in these chapters I ought to introduce him properly. Born 1916, he was educated at Eton and Cambridge, where he took an MA degree. He served in the RAF and in 1950 was British Champion in car hill climbs. Chairman of Manganese Bronze Holdings Ltd., since 1963, he was also Chairman of two finance companies and Director of another. He had also been a Member of Lloyds since 1950. In 1965 MB Holdings had taken over the Villiers Engineering Company at Wolverhampton and in the following year acquired the bankrupt AMC Group at Woolwich, which comprised AJS, Matchless, Norton, James and Francis Barnett. The new company became Norton Villiers and Dennis Poore added another Chair to his collection. At the luncheon I met many old friends and was introduced to RDP, as I will now call him. He asked me to talk to him after lunch and the outcome was an appointment to see him at his offices in London. I was invited to join Norton Villiers and create a Police Norton. After my bitter experiences at Triumph I was not eager to return to the motorcycle business, but there were three deciding factors. Firstly, I was fond of my home near Stratford upon Avon and the Building Society wanted me to continue paying for it. Secondly, Triumph Police business was failing quickly through unreliable machines, deliveries and parts service. Thirdly, was the assurance I requested from RDP. Would I have full responsibility and authority not only to create the Police machine but also to ensure production and quality. The assurance was given like the blessing of a priest and it was agreed that I would join the company at the beginning of January 1969, reporting at Woolwich to W.B. Colquhoun the son of an MBH Director.

The Interpol Story

Things went wrong from the very beginning. Bill Colquhoun, soon to become a good friend of mine who rode with me in the International Circuit des Pyrenees, had been sent off to the States and I had to report to his substitute, Hugh Palin, who had been unfriendly when I opened the Stockholm Show the previous year. For reasons which did him no credit, he clearly resented my appointment and, when I arrived at Woolwich, he told me to return home and wait until he sent for me. I was standing in front of his desk and was about to turn it over when I realised that it was exactly what he hoped I would do and resign before I had even started work. I was to have many more problems with Palin before he was moved to a position of minor importance, after which he found himself a job with the Skoda people.

Before I could start work on a Police prototype I had to help clear the stocks of machines which lay in the Woolwich factory, and it was a long time before the last of them went. The old factory awaited the attention of the demolition contractors and only a few staff and testers were left. RDP had decided to drop everything except Norton and AJS. The end had come for the proud names of Matchless, Francis Barnett and James, and AJS might well have been included, for the name did not deserve to appear on the tank of a two-stroke engined scramble machine which was a waste of time and money. Norton production was to be shared between the old Villiers factory in Wolverhampton manufacturing the engines and gearboxes, and a new building at Andover, where machines would be assembled. An excellent arrangement for the transport company which operated two trucks each day on the long haul from Wolverhampton. In Edward Turner's era the distance from engine building to final machine assembly was 20 yards, Jofeh increased this to 120 yards, but RDP set an all-time record with 120 miles. It would be interesting to know why, but sufficient to recall that Andover was a Government-assisted development area. Norton Villiers was to become the first company to reverse the process.

From January to September, when assembly work began at Andover, I worked at Woolwich and lived in a guest house run on military lines by the permanent residents, who were officers and senior civil servants on the staff of Woolwich Arsenal. Anyone not present in the dining room at 7 pm went without dinner. Every evening I returned to the factory occupied only by a security guard and his alsatian, who we trained to come to my office if I had not left by midnight. To walk through the dark factory and up the creaking stairs was always a strange experience and I could almost imagine the ghosts of the famous Collier Brothers surveying the dissolution of the business they had founded so long ago. From this factory had come the first machine I rode, then the one I raced at Syston Park, and those which served me so well during the war. My long nights in the old factory were nostalgic. The one man, and in fact only man who gave me any help with the creation of the Police Norton, was Wally Wyatt. He was a

Chapter Thirteen

brilliant Development Engineer, with abilities like those of Freddie Clarke and Doug Hele. We worked late hours on a 750 cc Atlas, until it resembled a Police model and I used it to commute to Stratford upon Avon at weekends.

When September arrived the last people left Woolwich, some to Andover and the others to collect redundancy pay. Wyatt was offered an unimportant job, which was an insult to his ability and his loyal service. Several new men had made sure that he would be no threat to their own ambitions, and he joined the young and progressive Rickman Bros. at New Milton, where his skills were welcomed. Two years later I was asked to persuade him to return, but I did not try very hard and, wisely, he declined. He would have been out of place amongst the new regime which made a poor copy of the Atlas motor, installed it in a new frame, and called it the Commando. The method of installation was called the Isolastic System, intended to isolate the rider from engine vibration, but unfortunately, as time went by, the system was expected to take care of inherent defects in engine quality.

In September I began work at Andover and enjoyed the 200 miles return ride, over the Cotswolds to Stratford, on the Atlas. If Wolverhampton could have reproduced the quality of this Woolwich-built engine, there would have been no need for the Isolastic System, which was to prove a very questionable innovation. On my travels, the machine had attracted the interest of Police patrols and several times I had been stopped for polite questioning as to Norton plans to produce it. One weekend I invited Warwickshire Officers to my home for test rides, with very encouraging results, and I was anxious to get busy with a full Police version of the Commando and have it ready for production by the spring of 1970. It became necessary to live nearer to Andover, though I was most reluctant to move from my Stratford home where I had entertained many famous riders and well-known people in the motorcycle world. 'All removal and legal expenses paid', promised Palin, 'and a temporary house whilst you look for one you like.' This was the formula enjoyed by Palin and which he arranged for two of his friends who he brought to the company from Coventry whilst I was still busy at Woolwich. All of which I quoted unsuccessfully to the Andover Housing Manager with whom Palin was well connected. For the second time I came near to giving up and then became more determined to do the job I had set out to do. I lived in an hotel for three months, and at my own expense.

As the winter weather arrived I began work on the Police Commando, starting with the bare carcase of the machine from which to build a pilot model. I secured a corner of the wartime aircraft hangar at the Thruxton Airfield where the Norton Test Department was located, and was given the services of one mechanic who had not been Woolwich trained. He worked overtime until 10 pm, when I took him home, and I then returned until midnight. There was no heating and my hands were as cold as the tools they were using. One major problem was the need

The Interpol Story

Building the first Norton Interpol in a hangar at Thruxton in February 1970.
[Cecil Bailey]

for a steel petrol tank in place of the standard fibreglass type, which was unacceptable to the Police. It was also illegal in a number of overseas markets and was soon to be prohibited in Britain, but nobody at Norton had taken any steps to have a steel tank made. I 'phoned my old friends Homers of Shirley, near Birmingham, who for many years had made tanks for the motor and motorcycle industries. They had also made big losses from business with Norton, AMC and other factories, so they were not very keen on any more risk business. They still had the press tools for the Atlas tank and I asked whether they would produce a pilot quantity of thirty tanks, using the Atlas top and side panels, but hand-making the base section so as to clear the large diameter top tube of the Commando frame. I felt confident in supporting my request with the assurance of

Chapter Thirteen

substantial future business and asking them to go ahead with press tooling for the new base panel ready for production in the spring. Homers were more than helpful and, but for them, the Police Nortons might never have been built. I was able to reward them with good orders over the following six years, but when steel tanks were finally used on standard production Commandos, they were made in Italy, as were all frames. Unkind to Homers, but at least they did not lose so much money when Norton Villiers went into liquidation in August 1975.

My negotiations with Homers had been conducted on my own initiative and when RDP saw the first steel tank he was surprised, but complimentary. With him was designer Bob Trigg who, having done nothing about it, was somewhat annoyed that someone else should have gone ahead. Said RDP, 'This is just what we urgently need for the USA', and Trigg replied that he disliked the shape. The Atlas tank was, in fact, quite attractive and I could not resist commenting that Trigg could design whatever shape he wanted, but tooling would cost around £10,000 and there would be six months before production. I was to annoy the Wolverhampton Design Department more than once by using my own initiative, but that was only one of the obstacles which had to be overcome before the Police Norton finally started production.

Having built the prototype I rode it to a number of Police Forces and made a point of having it examined by their workshop staffs, whose observations were very useful in making improvement modifications to effect easier servicing. Warwickshire Police were kind enough to arrange for a rider to be photographed on the machine beneath the International signpost at Birmingham Airport, and this gave me the idea for the name I was seeking for the machine. It had to be as good as the name Saint which I had given to the Triumph and I decided upon Interpol, after checking with the appropriate authorities that there was no objection. Thus was the Interpol created and I had taken another step towards achieving the target I had undertaken a year or so earlier. Using the airport photograph, the Interpol was announced on the front page of the journal *Police Review* and I mailed copies to many Police connections overseas. My calculations of Interpol production costs showed that the selling price would be some £70 more than the Saint and, as the Triumph was not yet quite finished, I needed to do something about this difference. The answer was simple, but was bound to upset those dealers who had enjoyed generous profits from Police Triumphs sales though they had done nothing to secure the orders. I informed all UK Police Forces that, if they so wished, they would be able to obtain Interpol direct from the factory. Furthermore, the machines would be complete with Police equipment, instead of having to fit everything themselves, and the Company would provide all service support. I rode the prototype to ten Forces in little more than a week, and many riders tested it.

The first order came from the Sussex Police for 17 machines and they had to

The Interpol Story

The Tomos Interpol which I demonstrated in Yugoslavia. [*Cecil Bailey*]

be delivered by 31st March, the end of the Police financial year. Only four weeks remained but I was refused the use of the Andover assembly line. With the help of an ex-Woolwich mechanic, and without even a workbench, 15 machines were completed and delivered with two days to go before the end of March. The other two I delivered myself by trailer on the last day of the month. The Department of Industry had heard of the Interpol and they arranged for BBC TV to film the scene as the Sussex riders paraded in front of headquarters at Lewes and rode away in an impressive formation. I went along from Andover on the prototype to watch the proceedings, which were shown on National TV the same evening. The publicity gave a valuable boost to the Interpol and the order income was very encouraging. The Works Manager at Andover agreed that I could have a number of machines built on the assembly line and they began on the day when John Pedley, the Works Director at Wolverhampton, made his weekly visit. He was angry; Police business was a nuisance and should not interfere with normal production. America could take all the output for a very long time and we did not need any Police markets. I decided that this was the time for a showdown and, after all the problems I had faced in creating a machine which could recover much of the International business being lost by BSA/Triumph, it was either going to

Chapter Thirteen

take a proper place in the production programme or be abandoned. I asked Pedley to telephone RDP immediately and get a decision. He backed down and agreed that the Interpol would be given the same treatment as the standard Commando. The time was to come when Police machines were the only ones being built for which orders were in hand.

During my last year at Meriden I had begun an attempt to rid Police machines from Purchase Tax, as it was called before VAT took its place. It seemed wrong in my view that, as essential public service machines, they should be subject to that tax whilst Military and Fire service vehicles were not. The Motorcycle Industries Association declined to support my case and so did the Car Manufacturers Association, the SMMT. At Norton Villiers I decided to try again and this time I did so as a private individual and rate payer, whose rates contribution to Police services included VAT. I presented a case to the Treasury through my MP, emphasising that Norton Police motorcycles were specially manufactured and supplied direct, as distinct from cars which were supplied as civilian models through dealers. The Treasury resisted, but my MP pressed the case hard and one morning sent me a copy of a letter he had received from Terence Higgins, Financial Secretary to the Treasury. It announced that, as from 1st April 1971, VAT on Police motorcycles would be recoverable, which meant that after being paid it would be reclaimed by the County Council. I had aimed at total VAT exemption but had achieved what Kenneth Steele, Chief Constable of Somerset, had considered impossible. 'Should you be successful', he told me, 'try then to do the same with petrol tax which is one of the biggest demands on Police funds.' Quite recently I talked to C.J.Anderton, Chief Constable of Greater Manchester Police, and undoubtedly the most outspoken of all the 54 Chiefs in Britain. With Whitehall demanding severe reductions in local Government spending, they could have no case against the exemption of all Police vehicles from VAT, car tax and petrol tax. The total amount involved nationally for Police authorities, and consequently for rate payers, runs into millions. Mr.Anderton saw the whole subject as one which was long overdue for action and I hope that he will have been successful by the time this book is published.

During 1970, the Interpol order book grew steadily, and so did my mileage riding the demonstrator around more UK Forces. I was invited to take it to the Royal Ulster Constabulary in Belfast and, on arrival at Liverpool, I took the machine aboard the Ulster Prince, which brought back memories of June 1940 when I got away from St.Nazaire on the ship of the same name. I knew that she had been dive-bombed and sunk off Crete and, in the dining saloon of this, her successor, I found the brass plate inscribed with her wartime history. I entered the bar as we cleared the Mersey Lightship and spoke to the elder of the two attendants. He had been with the old Prince at St.Nazaire and we shared a bottle as we recalled the night when the bombs fell as we waited for the mines to be cleared

The Interpol Story

from the harbour channel so that we could go home. It was a nostalgic reunion, which lasted well into the Irish Sea.

At Belfast the next morning, I rode the Interpol away from the docks and found my way to the Police Traffic Workshops at Lislea Drive, where I was confronted by a security fence, armed guards and the disbelief that I had ridden the machine from the docks. It seemed that, especially along that route, a Police machine was an attractive target and certainly I would not be allowed to ride it back. It was taken to the docks at night in a van, whilst I went by a car which narrowly avoided destruction by a booby trapped lorry parked with steel girders blocking the road. The next entry in my journey log book recalls another unpleasant experience. Having regularly ridden a Triumph Saint to the Cologne Show, I decided to do the same with the Interpol, but even more quickly, and display it on the Norton stand. I planned a six hour hourney from Andover, using the air ferry service from Southend to Ostend, and would be met on arrival at Cologne by RDP and Bill Colquhoun. As I boarded the Bristol Freighter I waved farewell to my old friend and Southend Norton dealer Bert Saunders, and to this day only he believes the reason why I was three hours late at destination. The aircraft reached flying speed but, at the moment of take-off, the pilot's seat collapsed. The boundary fence was very close by the time we came to a halt. No reserve flying machine was available and repairs took several hours, during which time the airline had promised to telex the British Embassy in Bonn with a message for the member of their staff who had arranged to meet me at the autobahn exit to Cologne. The message was not sent and, when I finally met RDP and Colquhoun, they did not believe my story but were convinced that I was covering up for trouble with the Interpol. After the Show closed, I rode the machine to Odense and Copenhagen for demonstrations to the Danish Police. An unpleasant ride on dark and wet autobahns, which I was glad to leave when I reached Schleswig and crossed into Jutland.

The Interpol was by now attracting interest from overseas Police and Defence authorities. From Yugoslavia we received an enquiry and request from the Tomos Company in Koper, who manufactured lightweight motorcycles and imported Citroën cars. They were anxious to arrange for an Interpol to be demonstrated to the authorities in Belgrade and it had to have their name on the tank. I had a machine prepared and personally painted the name Tomos above the Norton tank transfer. The Tomos Norton was sea freighted to Koper on the Adriatic and I followed it. I was to be met at Trieste Airport, not the easiest place to get to in those days, and I was not able to telex Koper my arrival time until several hours before I left London to fly via Venice. The telex arrived a few minutes after 2 pm, which gave my Tomos friends six hours notice to make the one hour journey to Trieste, or so I thought. I did not know that the working day of the entire Tomos factory was from 6 am to 2 pm, a pleasant arrangement to

Chapter Thirteen

With ex-Yugoslav Champion Ivanisevio and his Norton in Belgrade.

enable everyone to enjoy the adjacent Adriatic beaches. My message stayed in the unattended telex machine and I stayed in the empty airport, having arrived on the last flight of the day. I made my way to the office of the airport Commandant, presented my card and produced a bottle of whisky, which I suggested we should sample whilst I explained my problem. The suggestion was warmly welcomed. I told him that I was going to Belgrade on Police business and should have been met with a car from Koper but something had gone wrong. Could he advise me how to get to Koper? It would be arranged, replied the Commandant, and did he have my permission to invite his deputy to share the rare pleasure of the scotch? I reciprocated his courtesy by asking if I had his permission to offer him the bottle with my compliments, and next time in his airport I would bring several. His deputy was instructed to telephone for a certain taxi driver, who arrived and

The Interpol Story

stood to attention whilst he was ordered to drive me to a hotel in Koper and to charge the fare to the Airport. I figured that the journey would have cost me the equivalent of at least twelve bottles of scotch.

After a couple of days at the Tomos factory, where I managed a few quick laps around the test track on the Interpol, I spectated at the Yugoslav Grand Prix and then made the long journey to Belgrade. The Interpol demonstration had been arranged in the equivalent of Hyde Park and, within only a few minutes, the Police had cleared everyone out and closed the park. To do that in London would have required an Act of Parliament. I was introduced to a charming character who made an impressive arrival on a 650 SS Norton and who was to be the official tester of the Interpol. He was the Surtees of Yugoslavia, many times National Champion Ivanisevio, a dedicated motorcyclist who had been to the old Norton factory in Birmingham and talked with affection about the Manx models which had given him many victories. He greatly enjoyed his rides on the Interpol and went round the narrow roads of the park much quicker than I dared to do. Lunch was a prolonged affair, with generous supplies of wine, and Ivanisevio addressed the officials with a report on the Tomos Norton Interpol which left them in no doubt that it was the machine they had to order. A nice ending to an interesting day, a pleasant time in Yugoslavia and a memorable meeting with a fine rider.

After a week working in Athens, instructing unskilled mechanics on the assembly of Interpols for delivery to the Greek Gendarmerie and Armed Forces, it was time to ride again to Copenhagen. The British Trade Week, organised by the UK Government, was to be opened by the Duke of Kent and this was, in fact, to be the last time any British motorcycle appeared at a Scandinavian Show. I rode the Interpol along the roads which I had first enjoyed with the Triumph Saint, and it had pride of place on the Norton stand. At 11 am the Duke began his tour of the stands, prior to opening the Show at noon, and each exhibitor was naturally eager to have him photographed with their products. Lord George Brown was representing the textile company Courtaulds and, after the Duke had been welcomed by the Lord at 11.30, it seemed evident from where I was standing that the ex-Foreign Secretary did not intend that the Duke should have much time left to visit other stands. I had a few words with his equerry to the effect that, having known the Duke at Catterick when he was an Army Subaltern, I felt sure he would like to renew our acquaintance and might be more interested in motorcycles than in textiles. The equerry quietly conveyed the message, the Duke exchanged the Courtaulds stand for Norton, and as I looked at the Lord's expression I remembered the night of his discourtesy at Belper to my BBC friend.

The Duke stayed on the Norton stand until it was time for him to open the Show and we chatted about Catterick, his courting days nearby, and about motorcycle engineering on which he was quite knowledgeable. He admired the Interpol and asked when would it have shaft drive, a good question to which there

Chapter Thirteen

The Interpol Story

Left: With the Lady Mayor of Andover the day before my September 1970 ride to the Cologne Show. The picture is her gift of an old map of Hampshire to the Mayor of Cologne. [C.E. Wardell]

Bottom Left: Talking to H.R.H. The Duke of Kent at the British Trade Fair in Copenhagen 1972. Looking on is Norton Importer Jorgen Aagesen.

Below: John Surtees and Mike Hailwood, two honoured guests at a Norton Press Day held at Silverstone in 1973. The machines are two of my Pyrenees mounts.

193

Chapter Thirteen

could be no favourable answer.

Soon after I had returned from Denmark with the Interpol, I negotiated a substantial contract for machines to be supplied to the security forces of Nigeria,

Now a Director of Norton Andover Ltd., ex-Greeves scrambler Mike Jackson is pictured testing his AJS at Saddleback Park, California, in 1971. Mike rode this machine in the Baja Desert Enduro and finished 4th out of more than 1,000 starters. [Dennis Greene]

The Interpol Story

which was a good opportunity to recover the serious losses which resulted in 1970 when a colleague let his 165 Nortons go to a Nigerian importer without making certain of payment, a precaution which is just as essential now as it was then. This time the order and payment were confirmed by an old established British company, despite their German name Brunnschweiler, based in Manchester and with an establishment in Lagos to teach assembly and maintenance to Nigerian mechanics whose main interest was in getting smart overalls and tools, not necessarily to be used for their intended purpose. I must resist the temptation to describe the methods of getting business in Nigeria because Cyril West is still there, but it is sufficient to say that the entrepreneurs I have met in the Middle East are amateurs in comparison.

I had a meeting with the Chief of Traffic Police, Colonel Adiseba, who invited me to look at the large number of Triumphs which were out of action waiting for spare parts, but fortunately he gave me his official card which was to prove most useful when I went through Lagos airport on my way home. My bags had been cleared through Customs by arrangements facilitated by Cyril West, but not even he could arrange for me to avoid the so-called security check control. A large Nigerian lady studied every document in my briefcase, whilst an even larger gentleman with kingsized revolvers searched me. He pointed to the pineapple with its spikes sprouting from my bag and demanded my export licence. Without one, he said, I would have to pay him an exemption fee. This is known in Nigeria as 'Dash' and is one of the main ingredients of the Nigerian economy. I took out my wallet, which pleased him, and extracted the card from Colonel Adiseba, which did not. 'OK, you can go,' said the deflated security officer. A few months ago I saw that Triumphs had obtained a large order from Nigeria and I hoped they had made sure of payment, but from what I learned later it seemed that they had repeated the Norton mistake.

It is now time to pay attention to an entry in my personal log book which reads 'The International Circuit des Pyrenees', and to recall the most enjoyable of all my million miles of motorcycling.

Chapter Fourteen

196

My first ride in the International Circuit des Pyrenees. Entering the first of the two tunnels between the Soulor and Aubisque mountains. My favourite caption to this photograph is 'Neale Shilton [Norton], third from the left'.

Chapter Fourteen

The Circuit Des Pyrenees

ONE HUNDRED and twenty miles south of Bordeaux is the charming town of Pau, renowned for its Château where King Henri 4th was born, its golf course claimed to be the first in Europe, its wonderful views of the Atlantic Pyrenees and for its warm welcome to motorcyclists who travel far to ride the mountain roads in the third week of June. In the Boulevard de la Paix there is a lovely house and on the white gate of the driveway is a brass plate which bears the name of Roland Roussel and his title, President of the Club Motorcyclistes Palois. To meet Roland is to meet a charming man, a highly skilled engineer, and utterly dedicated to preserving the unique event called the International Circuit des Pyrenees.

He is to be found in his workshop at the end of the tree-lined drive, bent over one of the belt driven lathes and machining, to micrometer accuracy, anything from a crankpin for a Norton to a connecting rod for a Renault. On the walls are fading posters of old AJS and Norton race victories, and others of the successes of Roussel sparking plugs, which he and his father once manufactured. Adjoining the workshop is an assembly room in which British and other visiting Circuit competitors are entertained each June, and fed by Roland's wife, the charming Ginette. The walls are covered with action photographs of riders, mainly British,

Chapter Fourteen

Seven check points and 150 miles later, at the British Police refuelling point in the Basque country village of Espelette, near to the Spanish frontier. Next to me is ex-TT rider Phil Heath, who was to have ridden a Gold Star BSA in this event but it had major engine trouble on the way from England.

and of pictures which recall Roland's own exploits on two wheels. There are plaques and presentations given to Roland by competitors from British Police Forces, and in pride of place is the citation and medallion from the French Government in recognition of his services to motorcycle sport.

I first met Roland in 1971, when he came to Norton Andover with Inspector Alec Smith of Metropolitan Police, who was one of the Metro Police Team which began what later became the annual pilgrimage to the Pau event by Police and Club riders from Britain. My Norton Interpol had begun production, Roland was a Norton enthusiast, and Alec was a fine ambassador for the Circuit Pyrenees they called the Pau Rally (which remains its official Auto Cycle Union designation) and my visitors recommended it as an excellent publicity media for the new Interpol. I had visions of a very pleasant gathering of motorcyclists which it was, and a gentle ride through the mountains, which I later discovered it certainly was not. Roland sent me the entry form, I paid the ACU for my National and one day

The Circuit Des Pyrenees

International licences, and prepared my Interpol for departure.

From Le Havre to Pau is over 500 miles and in those days the Tours to Bordeaux motorway had not even begun construction. Leaving the Saturday night boat and Le Havre at 8 am, I was still more than 100 miles from Pau when I 'phoned Roland at 8 pm. My inadequate French was not improved by a poor telephone connection and I did not understand that I was not to go straight to my hotel but was to call at his home no matter what time I arrived. Consequently I went to the hotel and bed. The next morning I discovered that, as from midnight, all Police patrols between Bordeaux and Pau had been instructed to search for a Norton with a GB plate.

On Monday morning Roland, on his Norton Atlas, piloted me over the first fifty miles of the circuit route, from Pau through the first check point at the village of Ferrières, where the road narrows and begins to climb steeply round countless hairpins to the top of the Col du Soulor. Roland was moving very quickly, disappearing round the hairpin corners which were familiar to him but blind to me, and I stayed just behind him only because of my complete confidence in a rider who was so clearly an expert. We reached the top of the Col du Soulor at 6000 feet, and pulled in to the tourists' café owned by a remarkable character named Poulo, who became a great friend of mine in the following years. Roland had a coffee, but I needed something stronger. I casually commented to Roland that on the Rally day I should welcome the opportunity of climbing more slowly from Ferrières and enjoying the wonderful scenery, which I could not look at during our racing speed approaches to the hairpins. Roland was very kind and gently explained to me that, compared with the speeds demanded by the Rally schedule, we had been riding at touring pace. He added even more gently that the climb up the Col du Soulor was an easy section of the circuit. As the practice week progressed I found he was right. The dangerous sheer drop and gravel strewn corners of Soulor were easy compared to the Houratate and Spandelle treachery.

Roland pointed away across the snow slopes to the Col d'Aubisque in the far distance, before which point on the course are two tunnels cut through the rock. He warned that many cattle sheltered in the longer one during the cold night and early morning. They would be there when the riders went through for two hours from 6 am. They would not move even if pushed by a big Triumph, as Police Sgt Ron Hawkins was to find out on the Sunday. *Moto Revue* of Paris described the event precisely when it reported 'The Circuit des Pyrenees confronts the riders with many hazards and to cross the finish line is itself a fine reward'.

By the end of the practice week I had decided that this year I would treat the event as a warm up for next year and would ride until I reached a control point where I was too late to check in. I could always blame a slipping clutch or some other impediment. Meanwhile, there were the receptions to be enjoyed. On the

Chapter Fourteen

At the weighing-in for the 1972 event.

Friday evening the Roussels always give a garden party for all competitors and the Press, with Armagnac and Champagne predominant. No waitress has ever succeeded in getting as far as the tables with anything but empty glasses on her tray, but it is exciting to see them try. The scene is a colourful mixture of French, German and British Police and Army uniforms, as riders meet again and discuss experiences of last year and the conditions around the circuit. Photographs are taken and hurried away for publication the next day with the list of riders and their countries. The three newspapers of Pau give more space to this event than the UK Press gives to motorcycling in a year. As dusk becomes darkness, the guests drift away and the Maison Roussel is quiet again.

Saturday morning is traditionally spent in a final check and polish of machines, ready for their afternoon presentation at the Place Royale in the centre of the town. By 2 pm riders are arriving at the enclosure under the trees and specta-

The Circuit Des Pyrenees

On a brief stretch of good road in 1971 after the second check point in the ski village of Gourette.

tors are gathering. Place Royale begins to look like the Isle of Man in TT week. As machines are ridden past the barriers guarded by Gendarmes, the commentator announces the names and countries of riders from overseas. In my case he used to add the title of Le Veteran until, after a year or two, he promoted me to Le Patron. On my first ride there were very few machines below 500 cc, but now there are not many above. Gone are the days when the Garde Republicaine team rode from Paris on their Nortons, and the Metropolitan Police rode from London on their Triumphs. Now the British Police Team bring their 175 cc Japanese machines along in a transporter truck. Always difficult, the course has been given new sections and many kilometres of track more suited to a tractor than a motorcycle. However, there are British Club stalwarts who still ride their big machines to Pau to enjoy the event. As Allan Jefferies used to say say about another form of sport, they have a lot of fun without laughing.

After all machines have been checked by official scrutineers, all is ready for the grand parade through the town, with streets lined with spectators and Gen-

Chapter Fourteen

darmes stopping all other traffic. Where else could this happen except in Pau. The once sedate parade is now marred by wheelies and, by the time the first machines are back at the Place Royale, local riders have enthusiastically joined in, hoping to get admission to the civic reception given to all competitors in the Town Hall, where the long tables are decorated with glasses of wine, le vin d'honneur as it is courteously called. Speeches are made, the traditional presentation is made by the British Police to the mayor, the wine bottles are emptied and the reception is over for another year. Outside, we look at the distant snow-covered peaks of the mountains, soon to be covered by clouds as the sun sets beyond the Bay of Biscay and the warmth of the day retreats. Before the sun rises again over Soulor and Aubisque, many riders will be climbing in the dark, hoping that headlamps will pick out the gravel patches and fallen rocks. The only disadvantage for the riders of the smaller capacity machines is that they are the first to start. Number one is away at 5 am, but even earlier are the officials who have to be at their control points around the morning half of the circuit. Like the Marshals in the Isle of Man, they are dedicated and indispensable.

At one minute intervals, riders are signalled away from the start in the Avenue des Touristes, until the last man leaves around 7 am. He is followed by two Gendarmes in a Peugeot and they will check at control points for any missing rider whose machine they have not seen. They are the first in a relay of expert drivers who will have accounted for every competitor by the end of the circuit. Ambulances are standing by and a Police helicopter is ready for any rescue emergency. The whole circuit is covered by Police radio.

Beyond the second control point, in the ski village of Gourette, the road descends into the river valley and is one of the few sections where the larger machines can use top gear, but not for long. Back to the narrow twists and turns to the Badgers Wood climb, which has maintained its challenge for many years and where many a rider has come to grief. A minimum time is set for the climb and each rider is electronically timed, with penalty marks for each second beyond the time limit. After the first left-hand bend, where Metro Police Officer Clive Thomas broke a thigh on his first visit to the event, the machines accelerate to 70 mph and brake to 20 mph on the short straights between corners. There is no room for mistakes between the high banks of Badgers Wood. With enough snow it would make an excellent bobsleigh run. To achieve the set time demands courage, rare ability and fine judgement. Each year I have been determined to do the four minutes twenty seconds allowed, and each year I have failed.

Many difficult kilometres beyond Badgers Wood is a timed climb called Houratate which leads to the forest of Assau, and becomes more difficult each year after the rock falls of the winter thaw. I once stopped in practice at the top and realised that the complete silence was because it was too high for birds to live there. Only the June motorcyclists, and the tree fellers, disturb the silence. On

The Circuit Des Pyrenees

A pause in practice, at 5,000 feet, overlooking the ski slopes of Gourette. Centre is Norton Director Bill Colquhoun and left is Mike Jackson, who joined Norton from Greeves.

this climb the fastest man sets the standard time and traditionally he is so brilliant that he is likely to win the event. Northumberland Police Officer Bill Emmerson demonstrated this formula on two occasions, and so did a Corsican.

At the half-way mark, back at Pau after 165 hard ridden miles in the Pyrenees Atlantiques, the surviving riders have a short break before heading for the second part of the circuit in the High Pyrenees terrain. The morning run is quite good enough for any test of man and machine, but not for the organisers of the Circuit des Pyrenees. Several years ago they included the formidable Col Spandelle, where machines are upright for only a few metres, and sheer drops are the penalties for careless mistakes. Somewhere below the mountain lie the remains of a BMW sidecar outfit, and circling above the summit are the constantly vigilant vultures. I told Bill Emmerson they were looking for dead sheep but Bill said they were attracted by motorcycle crash possibilities. A few miles beyond Spandelle the course looks down on Lourdes, then veers away to tracks unmarked on any map and which have to be firmly memorised in practice as time lost by a wrong turn is impossible to recover. It always seems that with another eighty or so miles

Chapter Fourteen

At 7am in the Avenue des Touristes, awaiting our one minute interval starting signals. A nine hour race against the clock lies ahead.

The Circuit Des Pyrenees

The Author on the Bois de Bager [Badgers Wood] timed hill climb. More than three miles of hairpins, abundant gravel and no escape roads. Five marks were lost for each second over standard time, which was little more than four minutes. The one year I managed standard time, I broke a footrest.

Chapter Fourteen

to go to the finish, the concentration and effort are beginning to weaken. Certainly the organisers have plotted a course and distance which demand optimum limits of effort and endurance. Few riders would wish to go any further than the 325 miles, although ex-scrambler Mike Jackson did confuse the timekeeper when he finished his one ride in the event. He handed in his route sheet and asked in his best French if there was another lap.

At the finish, with Roland Roussel waving the chequered flag, and crowds of spectators lining the avenue, the commentator announces the names of the tired riders. I have been very relieved to hear my name and been grateful for the much-needed drink. Another Circuit des Pyrenees completed to add to those which followed the first, when I said that there would not be a second. It has a remarkable attraction to which I succumbed on nine more occasions, and so have many others. At the end of the Sunday evening announcement of results and dinner in the crowded restaurant of the Elf Petrol Headquarters, the words of farewell are always the same. In French, German and English, they say 'until we meet again next year'. At Pau, the Club Paloise with its Circuit des Pyrenes, maintains the cameraderie of motorcyclists year after year. 1980 saw the twenty ninth anniversary of an event which has nothing of its kind anywhere in the world. I only wish I had discovered it many years earlier, when perhaps I might have made standard time on Badgers Wood and overcome my apprehension of the Soulor and Aubisque hairpins. However, I have six trophies to show that I tried.

My plan to retire after a reasonable distance in the 1971 event did not work out, although after the second control point, the Norton gave me real problems with a sticking throttle, which would have justified giving up. I had earlier decided to finish at the third control in the village of Montory, by which time the café would be open for coffee cognac. After all, I would have done the Soulor-Aubisque mountain sections, Badgers Wood and the unpleasant swervery through narrow lanes to Montory. This would be enough for my first experience of a course which combined the essentials of an Enduro with Motocross, and here and there a few kilometres where the Norton tachometer briefly approached the top gear red line. Next year I would come back, spend many practice hours on the most difficult sections, and ride to finish.

With these thoughts in mind I accelerated away from the start, past the Grandstand of the Formula Two Grand Prix Circuit, and away to the snow-capped mountains rose-tinted by the rising sun. Motorcycling at its best, and with the thrill of riding in an International event. Village children had left their Sunday morning beds to wave to the riders, as they always do. On through the town of Nay to the village of Asson, where the signboard shows whether the Aubisque Pass is open or closed by snow. On the 1972 practice Monday, I waited with other riders for the snow plough to break through.

I checked in on time at the first control and on to Arbeost, the last village

The Circuit Des Pyrenees

My boss Bill Colquhoun relaxes and permits me to work on his machine in Pau for the 1972 event.

before the mountains, and where the first of countless hairpin corners climb steeply away from the church. Beyond the tree line, the narrow road, damaged by the still-lingering winter, twisted its way along the side of the mountain to the top of the Soulor, then down through the tunnels and up again to the summit of Aubisque. Cook Nielsen, Editor of the American journal *Cycle,* and a Daytona racer, who came over and rode with me several years later, described the road as 'like chimney smoke ascending on a windy day'. The descent from Aubisque is even steeper than the climb and I was relieved to check in at the second control in the square at Gourette, with brake drums as hot as the engine. More miles of downhill bends bring the road down to the valley and at last the Norton could use its top gear performance, which was when my sticking throttle problem started and gave me anxious moments, growing worse as the course left the good road and began its twisting way to Badgers Wood. There was only one method of tackling the steep swervery of Badgers, and that was to leave the Norton in second gear and rely upon the brakes to fight the sticking throttle. After all, I would only need the brakes for another thirty miles to my retirement point at the next con-

Chapter Fourteen

trol. Before then I had some satisfaction in passing a French rider on a sharp corner, but only because the Norton throttle stayed open when he sensibly closed his.

I rode into the Montory control and switched off. This was also the refuelling point for the British Police Team and my Norton. Ready with petrol container and funnel was Norman Vanhouse of BSA, a top class International Six Days rider who came to Pau year after year, but for some reason never rode in the event. Norman had been a personal friend in my Triumph years, but a business rival in keeping with the strong competition between BSA and Triumph men. Humorously, perhaps, he expressed surprise that I had got as far as Montory but surely I would not need petrol to go much further. My resolve to retire was thus forgotten and I demanded a full tank. It is to Vanhouse that I owe my completion of the circuit on my first ride.

In those days the course crossed the frontier and climbed into Spain up the formidable Col Lizerietta, down through Irun to the halfway check at San Sebastian. Once down the mountain the big machines enjoyed fast roads but, several years later, the Spanish section had to be excluded. To have a crash in Spain and need hospital treatment created the same problems then as it has done ever since. Furthermore, the fast climb out of Spain led to the top of the mountain with its fine views of the Bay of Biscay, which attracted hundreds of San Sebastian motorists for a Sunday afternoon. The police closed the road until the last competitor had made his climb and by that time many Spanish families and Spanish motor horns were voicing their objections. I need nothing to bring back memories of my ride in the last event to include Spain, but sometimes I look at my very attractive Sportsmans Trophy presented then by the Spanish Club Guipuzcoa. Decorating the plinth are green stones from the Pyrenees, and the name of the club.

Four hours later I rode into the finish of my first Circuit des Pyrenees and the painful right hand did not matter as my route card received its final stamp. Later that evening, as I walked up to the top table to collect the Veteran Trophy, I knew that I would return next year to enjoy the cameraderie which Roland Roussel and his Club Paloise have created and preserved. Nowhere else in the world of motorcycle sport is there any event which gives such a welcome and so much pleasure to the competitor. When I returned to England I wrote the story of the event for a motorcycling journal and a number of readers contacted me for entry details. More British riders have since made the journey to Pau and, like myself, they have been back year after year. On my first ride, there were 65 entries and by 1980 this had nearly doubled. At various motorcycling functions, you may see someone wearing a tie with the letters C de P below the outline of mountain peaks. He will tell you he has been proud to take part in this remarkable event.

I went back to ride each year from 1971 until I decided at the end of the 1978

The Circuit Des Pyrenees

Checking the Interpol in 1973, observed by a French gentleman who seems curious.

event that it would be my last. As I rode away from the finish, I looked back for what I thought would be the last time at the spectators in the Avenue des Touristes, but in 1979 I rode my BMW to Pau to help as a travelling marshal. To be there on a machine without a racing number plate was very strange and so I was back in June 1980 with a BMW R100T wearing number 77. The newspapers announced the return of Le Patron. Joining me in Pau were two young friends from Denmark, Kim Reinhardt and Bo Foenss, whose mileage to and from Pau will long be a record. Kim on a Suzuki 850, and Bo on a 500 Yamaha, first went to the TT races via Esbjerg and Newcastle, then to Southampton via London and to Pau via Cherbourg. The day after the event they rode back to Copenhagen via Switzerland and Germany in a day and a half. Total mileage around 2300 plus, more than 800 in the event and practice. They both made brilliant performances and were awarded a special trophy. For several days I piloted them around the course and I was very apprehensive about their ability to finish a circuit which faced them with conditions they had never experienced before. I need not have

Chapter Fourteen

worried. Kim was riding 76, one minute ahead of me, and Bo one minute ahead of him. After the first checkpoint of the morning circuit I never saw them until the halfway stop and, after the first control of the afternoon course, I did not see them until the finish. Their performances deserve this special mention, for they showed the true spirit of motorcycling.

The exit from the second mountain tunnel between Soulor and Aubisque.

In the years which followed my first 1971 ride I had many experiences, mostly pleasant ones, but I do not look back with any pleasure at 1975, when I crashed on the Aubisque. It was 8.00 am when I was brought down the mountain to the small town of Eaux Bonnes. The pharmacy was, of course, closed and no doubt the proprietor was enjoying his late rise Sunday as it took him a long time to unbolt the door. He looked at the rash of gravel on knee and face and reached for a bottle which I was convinced a few seconds later contained sulphuric acid. Later at the hospital in Pau, the treatment included the longest injection needle I have ever seen. 1975 was not the most enjoyable of my rides.

Early in 1974 I had a telephone call from Margaret Benton of the Central Office of Information Films Division. A series of TV films was being made called 'Pattern of People', which featured personalities from various industries and was aimed at promoting overseas business through those personalities. The COI

The Circuit Des Pyrenees

A Garde Republicaine Norton rider nearing the top of the Lizieretta climb to the Spanish frontier in 1973. The team from this elite squadron was unbeatable in those days.

American Cook Nielson and Norton on Badgers Wood, in the 1973 event. Well-known racer and journalist, Cook came to Europe specially to ride in the Pyrenees International, and on his return he wrote a fine story about it for his journal Cycle.

211

Chapter Fourteen

Receiving the Veteran Trophy and a French embrace from Madame Ginette Roussel, wife of the Club Paloise President.

The traditional Friday evening reception at the Maison Roussel. In the photograph are competitors from the French, Belgian and British Police, the German and British Armies, club riders from France and Britain, civic dignitaries and the Press. Near the top of the stairs, wearing his uniform as Commandant of the Surrey Special Constabulary, is well-known commentator Allan Robinson, a regular competitor at Pau. [Photo Eclair-Pyrenees]

The Circuit Des Pyrenees

wanted to help Norton and would I agree to play the lead or words to that effect. I asked what would be involved and Margaret explained that I would have to be at COI disposal for two weeks. I declined, as I could not spare the time. Would she get someone else. She came to see me and she was at her persuasive best. I compromised, with the offer of one week in UK and the other week at the Circuit des Pyrenees. That would be too expensive I was told, and that was where the project should have ended. It would have saved the tax payer £23,000. However, Margaret went back to COI and put forward the Pyrenees idea. Once each week she 'phoned to say that she had an affirmative from one department and was working on the next. One morning came her call of success. The top man had approved the cost of a film unit flying to Pau, complete with Director, Producer, researchers and all the other people involved. Margaret herself would fly down in advance, to make preparations.

In June, at the beginning of practice week, Ginette Roussel in a Renault, and myself on a Norton, met Margaret at Lourdes Airport and two hours later I rode away to the mountains, with Margaret as passenger: she had to fix camera points in a hurry before everyone else arrived. Returning from the top of the Soulor she went to sleep twice and I must be the only motorcyclist to have ridden down that mountain with a sleeping pillion rider.

The COI party duly arrived on the Wednesday of practice week and suggestions were made by my rider friends about the high fee I was being paid. They never did believe my denials. In fact everyone was being paid, except me. On Thursday, the camera and sound crews set up their equipment at the 65 degree hairpin on the steep climb out of Ferrières, a section I have always disliked intensely. However, unlike the countless other corners on the circuit, there is a safety guard against the sheer drop down into the village. It is a thick stone wall and with one camera pointing down the road on the approach to the hairpin, and the second one at its apex, I was signalled to start my run from the bend by the church. Faster than I had ever approached this corner before, I braked hard for the full lock turn, and harder still to miss the dog which chose that moment to appear. As I went back to try again, Margaret coaxed the half starved animal away from the road with a sandwich. Within several minutes half a dozen more dogs arrived and the entire proceedings were held up whilst she went down to the village to fetch enough food to keep them away from the hairpin.

Then away we went to the Poulo café at the top of Soulor, and subsequent events there would have made a top laughter show on TV. The Film Director wanted a sequence of the Norton coming up the mountain and stopping at the café, where I was to walk through the entrance, remove my crash helmet and greet my old friend Poulo, who was standing behind the bar. It was sandwich and wine time for half a dozen shepherds, who watched with curiosity as cameras and sound equipment were set in place. I did the trial run, greeted Poulo in my best

Chapter Fourteen

Near the top of the Spandelle Mountain, I pause to check the route on the first practice day of 1976. This was my first BMW ride in the event and the machine had already done the Paris to Teheran Rally, ridden by John McDermott, then BMW Concessionaires' Publicity Manager and now the Editor of a motorcycling journal.

Climbing Spandelle in the 1977 event. Near the top the narrow road is always strewn with rocks.

214

The Circuit Des Pyrenees

French and said I had returned once more, as I had promised last year. The Director had the camera moved a few inches and, with the clapper board signalling 'Café Poulo, take one', I walked through the entrance and spoke my lines again. The shepherds looked on with increased curiosity, more light was needed, decided the Director, and for the third time I walked in and told the patron I had returned once more. This was altogether too much for the shepherds and they roared with laughter, helped by the bottles of wine we had substituted for their empty ones. The scene did, in fact, come out very well in the film.

For the Sunday event, the first camera was located by the sheer drop bend above Arbeost and a few hundred metres after I passed I entered thick fog, which persisted right across the mountains and down beyond the Gourette control, where even the timekeepers' table was difficult to find. Long before the Soulor summit I raised my goggles, and then removed my spectacles. Mountain fog has always been the worst hazard of the Circuit and has accounted for many retirements. As I emerged into clear weather, but still not seeing clearly without glasses, there was the second camera and the film has a good shot of the Norton being passed by a couple of BMW riders. Had its commentator Shaw Taylor been told that I was riding half blind, he might have mentioned it as my excuse for being passed, and I would have felt a little better each time I have seen the film. The rest of the shooting took place at the Thruxton track and at the Norton factory, but, even before the film was finally edited and issued, the end of Norton production was looming nearer. I had been certain, when Margaret Benton first contacted me, that the purpose of the film could not be successful. However, those countries in which it has appeared on TV will have enjoyed the scenes from the Circuit des Pyrenees. It is ironical that its first showing in Saudi Arabia should have helped me secure the million pounds' order for Nortons, too late to make the difference between closing the factory and giving some hope of survival. My presentation copy of the film, which was the one shown in Arabia, is labelled, 'Neale Shilton The Motorcycle Man'. It holds many memories, especially the laughter of the children and of the shepherds of the Pyrenees.

In the 1976 event I had the most enjoyable of all my experiences in the Pyrenees, and repeated it in the following year, when I rode BMW. A few kilometres beyond Nay, and in the shadows of the foothills, there was a school which I subsequently found out was for orphans and deprived children. As riders passed they would rush to wave from the playground wall and the Nuns would look up from their needlework. One practice morning I stopped, and childrens' faces shone as I talked in my limited French. On Saturday I made up a parcel of sweets and rode away from the start the following morning with it strapped to the tank. As I slowed down on the approach to the school at 6.45 am it was too early for the children to be at the wall and I threw the parcel into the playground. The afternoon circuit follows the first few miles of the morning course and passes the

Chapter Fourteen

school, before heading for the Spandelle mountain. There were the children leaning over the wall and looking down the road as the Norton approached. As they recognised the racing number there was the sudden waving of paper union jacks which, as I learned the following year, they had made in the time between their breakfast and the second lap. In the parcel I had enclosed a note addressed to les enfants heureux, the happy children. The Monday morning newspaper report of the circuit made me very happy too. Evidently the Nuns had telephoned the Eclair newspaper about the parcel and sent thanks from them and the children to the kind English rider. I resolved to do even more next year.

To the 1977 event came London Harley-Davidson agent Fred Warr, and shook everyone by bringing a 1200cc monster Harley. It was destined to frighten timekeepers as it rushed towards them, with Fred using his feet to help the fading brakes. He also had the distinction of pushing a small Citröen into a ditch when there was no room in the narrow track for both of them. The Harley was much heavier than the car and it was undamaged. Fred and I stopped in practice to talk to the Nuns and children, to whom we promised two parcels. On Friday, two days before the event, we called at the shop in the last village before the school and rode away with parcels which contained most of the stock of sweets, plus fruit, also balloons which madame threw in as her own gift when she knew where the parcels were going. The Nuns and children were delighted, and we were assured of many 'bon voyage' waves as we passed the school for the second lap on Sunday. Fred and I were on consecutive riding numbers and we made a point of being together when we passed the school.

The sight of those waving children will long remain a very happy memory, and even the Nuns joined in. After the finish back in Pau, I talked to my commentator friend who, as a reporter for L'Eclair newspaper, asked me whether I had been involved in any incidents. I told him of the waving children and said a television recording of the scene as Fred and I passed by would have been fine publicity for the event. Had I not seen the TV camera, he asked? The waving children and the Nuns had indeed been filmed and were shown that evening on the news programmes. I looked forward eagerly to calling at the school in 1978 but, as I stopped the BMW, I found it closed. Grass was growing in the playground, the windows were shuttered and the children had gone. For me, something special had gone from the Circuit des Pyrenees and in vain I looked for the happy faces and waving hands as I rode by in 1979 and 1980. I hope les enfants heureux are happy somewhere else.

The 1978 circuit produced an unusual surprise. I was asked by a friend who is a professor at Pau University if I would return to my hotel early after practice. The reason was important, but secret. He duly collected me and we drove out to the town of Jurançon, which is the centre of the wine industry of the area. At 7 pm we entered the headquarters of the industry and were greeted by a group of

The Circuit Des Pyrenees

gentlemen wearing clothes which were fashionable at least three centuries ago. Then I learned that I was to have the rare honour of being initiated as a Dignitaire of the Viguerie Royale of Jurancon, an order founded by Henry IV. The ceremony was recorded and broadcast on radio the following day. I was presented with a parchment scroll and a silver chalice bearing the royal cipher which, with its red silk ribbon, decorates my 1974 Sportsmans Trophy. It seemed that I was the only non-titled Englishman to be so honoured.

Before leaving Pau after the 1978 event, there was one more pleasant surprise. The University of Pau presented me with a large and quite beautiful relief map of the French Pyrenees. The contours of the mountains and valleys are geographically perfect and all are named, Soulor, Aubisque, Bouezou, The Forest of Issaux, Badgers Wood, the Valley d'Aspe. I shall not see them again as 1980 had to be my last ride. Twice before I have decided the same thing, but as June has approached, and the entry forms have arrived from Pau, the call back to the Pyrenees could not be resisted. After the 1980 event, I had to accept that I was having to try too hard to reach the control points on time. I realised as I finished, and without a clutch for the last 40 miles, that the time had come at last when I would not return. At the award presentation dinner I was surprised to receive a Trophy, which presumably was the Veteran Cup to add to the others, and I remarked to the President that I would much rather be having the novice award. I called it the Adieu Trophy for it had to mark the last of my ten years visits to Pau. I was sad to say farewell to the companions with whom I had shared many experiences in this wonderful event and, as I left Pau on the road to Bordeaux, I looked back to see the snow covered Pic du Midi towering above the narrow ribbon of road with the hundreds of hairpin hazards which challenged us on the Soulor and Aubisque mountains. I took home a plate given to me by my friend Poulo when I said goodbye to him at his Soulor café. The hand-painted inscription reads, in translation, 'To my friend Neale Shilton whom I shall remember each year'.

In April 1981 I received the regulations and entry forms as always, but the temptation to go back just one more time had to be resisted. The accompanying letter from Roland Roussel explained with regret that this, the thirtieth anniversary of the event, would almost certainly be the last. For many years the costs of organisation, amounting to some £10,000, had been met by SNPA, the Elf Petrol Company, and they were unable to continue sponsorship. Roland and his wife Ginette would have been fully justified in cancelling the 1981 event but, despite many problems, they went ahead. It was won by French rider Vanhelube from Bayonne, inevitably on a below 200 cc machine, but Roger Jackman from the Metropolitan Police was a creditable third. A London friend, Jonathan Vickers, who made his annual pilgrimage to Pau on a BMW, wrote to tell me that the traditions of the event were no longer there. No Friday evening reception at Maison Roussel, no grand parade through the city, no Vin d'Honneur in the town hall

Chapter Fourteen

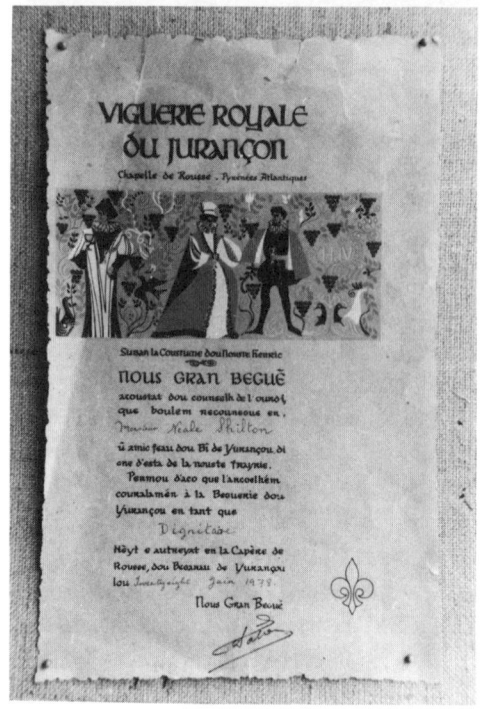

The ceremony at Jurancon, when I was made a Dignitaire Viguerie Royale.

The parchment scroll of the Viguerie Royale. Written in old French of the Henry IVth period, it measures two feet by one, and is beautifully coloured in red, blue, purple and gold.

The Circuit Des Pyrenees

and no award presentation dinner at Elf headquarters. So it seems that the mountains of the Pyrenees may no longer echo to the sound of motorcycles in the third week of June and, although I said goodbye in 1980, I should greatly regret the end of the event I enjoyed so much. My feelings were best expressed by the words I spoke at the end of the COI film, 'In my office I am over 60 years old but in the Circuit des Pyrenees I am 21'.

A Circuit des Pyrenees montage display at the Police Guest Day which I arranged for Norton in November, at Earls Court. [*Fox Photos Ltd.*]

Chapter Fifteen

A shot from the COI film 'The Man of the Motorcycle'. Peter Williams on a John Player Norton shows the Author the line into Thruxton chicane.

Chapter Fifteen

The End of the Commando and Trident

MY ENJOYMENT in the Pyrenees had been lessened in 1974 by the realisation that things were not going so well with Norton Villiers. As had happened at BSA/Triumph, quality was seconded to production quantity and there developed a constant feud between the experienced ex-Woolwich testers at Andover and the factory at Wolverhampton. Rejected machines continued to increase at the Thruxton test establishment and they were not due to problems which could be cured by the rectification staff. There were serious faults like porous crankcases and cylinder heads, main bearings turning in their housings, and poorly finished cylinder bores. The trucks which brought engines and gearboxes from Wolverhampton no longer went back empty, and the hangars at Thruxton were crowded with machines waiting for major attention.

Despite this deteriorating situation, RDP went ahead with what was known as the Combat engine, intended to increase the standard power output by 5 bhp to 65 at 6500 rpm. The already high compression ratio of 8.9 : 1 went up to no less than 10 : 1 and camshaft contours reached maximum, but the only concession made to the overstressed bottom half was to substitute a roller bearing for the ball race on the timing side. I had heard, and disbelieved, rumours of this engine until

Chapter Fifteen

one day at Andover I was called into a meeting by RDP. Present from Wolverhampton were the newly-appointed Works Director, the Production Director, and several senior technical men. 'Your Police customers will want the new Combat engine', began RDP, and my answer did not please him. I made full use of the opportunity to emphasise that the Police wanted more reliability, not power, and far too many major engine and gearbox failures were being reported. It seemed that this kind of news had not been made known to him, or perhaps he thought I was exaggerating, but I left him in no doubt that the Combat engine must not be used on the Interpol.

When the meeting had ended, the new Works Director had a quiet word with me and, after confessing that he knew nothing about motorcycles, he asked if I could explain in simple language what the debate was all about. I summed it up very simply 'No more new wine can be put into the old bottle'. However, nobody ever stopped RDP from doing what he had decided, except the Meriden factory pickets several years later. He went ahead with the Combat engine and it was a major disaster, not only financially because of the avalanche of warranty claims, but it did great harm to the name of Norton. By the time the inevitable decision was taken to discontinue the Combat, several thousands had been produced.

Then followed a second error, which compounded the effects of the first one. To achieve the higher compression ratio and still use the standard pistons, the joint face of the cylinder head had been machined down. It was then decided at Wolverhampton to revert to the original ratio by using an alloy head gasket. Around 1000 Combat-engined machines, which had not been despatched, went down the Andover assembly track for the second time, so that the engines could be removed and trucked back to Wolverhampton for the head gasket to be fitted. They were then returned to Andover to be put back into the machines. This programme kept Andover in work for some six months, but the closure of the assembly track and the redundancies of the workers were not far away. The Combat disaster, like the Ariel 3 debacle at BSA, was another classic example of individuals choosing not to risk their own positions by challenging a higher level mistake. I had been the only dissident when Jofeh decided to make the Ariel, and once again my objections had been proved justified, though ineffective. I had prevented the Combat being used in Interpols but I did not know of the alloy gasket in time to preclude the serious damage it did to machines supplied to the Jamaica Police and the Defence Forces of Kuwait and elsewhere. I was to learn later that the alloy material deteriorated through burning, causing the cylinder head joint to leak, which resulted in weak mixture and the consequent overheating and burning of the valves and valve seats. The so-called engineers at Wolverhampton must have known this would happen.

The closing down of the Andover assembly operations and Thruxton Test Department was a badly-handled and expensive affair. Most of the workers were

The End of the Commando and Trident

I cannot remember the reason for this Andover photograph of my boss Bill Colquhoun, but it may have been in connection with my appointment as a Director in 1973.

those who had moved their homes from the Woolwich area into sub-standard houses on the Andover industrial estate, and with the promise of employment continuity. The announcement of closure came as a shock and the workers occupied the building, refusing to allow any material to be taken away and barring anyone from entering. The Press and TV media gave full treatment to the sit-in, which dragged on to an impasse situation. Union demands for very substantial redundancy payments were finally successful and a few workers were left to clear up the debris of an ill-fated factory. It was later to be used as a spare parts depot and as a warehouse for large stocks of unsold machines. A new subsidiary company was formed with the name Norton Villiers Europe Ltd., of which I found myself a Director, and from one of the few offices which still existed I continued to operate until my ultimate resignation.

Meanwhile, I had kept in touch with Triumph friends, who gave dismal reports on the outlook at Meriden and Small Heath. In two years the BSA Group had made losses of more than £11 million and I was somewhat surprised to have a 'phone call from old friend the Triumph importer for Scandinavia, asking me to meet him at the Royal Lancaster Hotel in London, where he would be attending a banquet and ball given by BSA for international distributors and Press. Friends of mine attended from many distant countries at BSA expense, and the whole affair was extravagant, even for a profitable company. Nobody understood the purpose of the extravaganza but my Danish friend agreed my own view when I said

Chapter Fifteen

that, when a company owed millions, what difference does another £50,000 make.

Shortly afterwards my boss, Bill Colquhoun, informed me that RDP was negotiating for Norton Villiers to take over the BSA Group with Government support. I could hardly believe his news, for the problems of NV were serious enough without taking on more. A few months later Colquhoun dropped another bombshell, when he asked me if I thought RDP would be doing the right thing in closing Meriden. I urged him to dissuade RDP from even considering such an idea. I knew the Meriden workers; they had been dragged down by the BSA wreckage, and if any plant had to be closed it was Small Heath. It was an outdated, sprawling collection of old buildings which should be sold to the Birmingham Corporation and demolished to make room for new housing. This was, in fact, done much later. On the other hand, Triumph Meriden was ready for revival and if RDP was to attempt to close it he would meet fierce resistance and would be defeated. I hoped that Colquhoun would convince him, and I am sure he tried but, as I was to learn by September, he was not successful.

I went back to Meriden that month to take over export Police and Security Force business negotiations. On my arrival I was sent for by Colquhoun and shown a Press statement which was to be released that evening. It announced that the Meriden factory was to be closed and production moved to Small Heath. I was stunned and asked what had been the reaction of the union representatives. Unbelievably, they had not been told, let alone consulted, and they would not know until they saw the morning papers. I was tempted to breach the confidence which Colquhoun had enjoined and show the statement to the shop stewards. This would at least have enabled them to give a statement to the *Coventry Telegraph,* who would have put it out immediately to the National newspapers and the Norton announcement would have appeared in a different context. However, it could not have altered the subsequent events which are too well known to need repeating. The so-called rescue of BSA/Triumph entrusted to RDP by the Government had started in the worst possible way and this first mistake foreshadowed failures which were to close not only the Small Heath factory but the Norton plant at Wolverhampton. Good business was assured for the Official Receiver and I was to be very much involved with his subsequent operations at both places.

Meanwhile, Interpol orders from UK and overseas continued to increase. New markets were achieved in Mali, Trinidad, France and Venezuela, most UK Police Forces operated substantial fleets, the RAF ordered a quantity and so did Scotland Yard, although theirs were never put into operational service. One order which gave me special pleasure came from Oman. One morning I received a cable from a British official working with the Oman Government, who had been given my name by a Major with the Oman Scouts Regiment. This Officer and I had

The End of the Commando and Trident

been good friends when he was in charge of the Royal Signals White Helmets team several years before. The cable asked if 20 Interpols could be delivered in time to lead the Sultan's birthday parade. The date was little more than two months away and I cabled back affirmative, provided there was a ship leaving UK within three weeks. From various shipping agents and from Lloyds List I got negative results but, from telephone enquiries to continental agents, I found a ship loading at Antwerp which would be calling at London docks and would have space for twenty cases which must be there in two weeks. I booked the space, gave instructions to Wolverhampton and cabled the news to Oman. Back came a message of warm thanks and nice comments on being able to rely upon a British factory.

The machines were given priority on the assembly line and I rode there to check that all was well. Shipping documents were prepared and the road transport arranged. On the morning of collection the transport people 'phoned me to report that their driver had been refused permission to load by a picket, on instructions from his shop steward. I rang the Works Director and appealed for his help, but he could do nothing. There was a dispute in the tool room, pickets had sealed off the factory, and nothing could move in or out. I made one last attempt and talked to the one remaining shop steward at Andover, asking him to call his brother steward at Wolverhampton. To permit the loading of the machines for Oman could not possibly do any harm to whatever case was the cause of the dispute, so would he make a personal appeal on my behalf? I handed him my telephone and left him in my office. When he emerged some minutes later he passed me without speaking and I demanded some explanation. All I got was a routine speech on the need for workers to stand firm and show their strength. I lost my temper and made disparaging remarks about his intelligence and that of his misguided colleagues, who could be proud of their ability to wreck a valuable export order. By the time the dispute was over, the ship was on its way to Oman, and I spent some time trying to prepare a suitable cable until I decided to send one which gave the true facts. I sent a copy to the appropriate shop steward at Wolverhampton, who maybe recalled his day of power when the factory was closed for ever a year or two later.

My next overseas journey was to Iran, where I appointed an importer who was an old friend of the Royal Enfield company when it existed at Redditch. At the Asia Festival Exhibition, which was in progress, Enfield machines were being shown by Enfield India, who manufactured them in Madras. They were the Villiers-engined two-strokes and the 350 cc Bullet, which was almost the same in detail as those which had been made in Redditch. One of RDP's Director colleagues had a financial interest in the Enfield India Company and I was commissioned to go to Madras and examine the prospects for importing the Bullet into UK, also the 200 cc two-stroke as a Police beat patrol machine. I spent an inter-

Chapter Fifteen

Discussing business in Dubai during my tour of North Africa and the Middle East, with a Government-sponsored trade mission.

esting week or so at the Madras factory and was impressed by the enthusiasm of the workers and their pride in their products. After examining the two-stroke I had to say that, with its flywheel magneto and direct lighting, it was not suitable for the British Police.

Next morning I was asked to look at a machine which had been modified and I found that, during the night, a new crankshaft had been machined and a rotor fitted, the crankcase had been welded to accept the stator, the wiring harness had been reworked and a battery installed. The men who had done the work anxiously awaited my approval, and I much regretted having to tell them that, being a 6 volt system, it was unacceptable as the UK Police used 12 volt radio sets. I regarded

The End of the Commando and Trident

the Bullet as a good prospect though with an out-of-date electrical system. The machine was well-made, looked attractive, and the price was low enough to provide a worthwhile profit margin for importer and retail dealer, especially as no duty would be payable into UK. I carefully calculated all cost figures from factory to Wolverhampton, including port charges at both ends, freight, road transport in UK, insurance and even a margin for warranty cover. Related to a reasonable retail price the Norton profit figure would be around £170. When I returned and confidently submitted my figures, I had been wasting my time, for the profit margin was not enough. It was, in fact, much more than was being made on Nortons.

At the Madras factory I rode the Bullet and borrowed a crash helmet from one of the testers. He was a Sikh, and no doubt a devout one, but his religion did not interfere with his work as a tester for which a helmet was compulsory. An interesting recollection in view of the still active helmet controversy in UK. On my way back from Madras I flew to Kuwait, where I had an appointment with the Police. I was met by an important Kuwaiti businessman named Ali Karam, who drove me straight to Police HQ. The sentries presented arms smartly, which is why I knew he was important. After meeting the Chief, I was introduced to the man who trained the motorcycle patrols and supervised the maintenance of their machines. They were BSA twins and he had problems which had put most out of action because spares could not be obtained. He was an interesting character from Syria and had toured Britain as a Wall of Death rider in a circus. As I had watched a number of performers on the Wall it seemed reasonable for me to assure him that I must certainly have seen his act and he was delighted. He was invited by the Chief to join a very pleasant lunch party and when Ali Karam drove me away I took with me an order for 25 Interpols. Afterwards, I was to regret the results of my visit to Kuwait and my meeting with such charming people who had shown me generous hospitality. The machines proved to have the infamous reworked Combat engines and they all had the inevitable overheating trouble. Ali Karam later visited London, and I met him at the Churchill Hotel. I enquired about the Interpols and learned of the troubles. When I offered to go to Kuwait and take corrected cylinder heads plus all the other necessary components, he was embarrassed to tell me that the machines had been disposed of. They lie somewhere on the bottom of the Arabian Gulf.

Before I became involved in what was to be my largest and last export contract for Norton Villiers, now with Triumph added to the title, I was sent back to Meriden with Bill Colquhoun and a legal man, carrying writs to be served on the pickets unless they permitted vehicles to enter and collect equipment belonging to NVT. I found it strange to ask permission to go through the gates of the factory where I had worked for so many years, but none of the pickets had been there five years before, when I left. It was my second visit to the closed gates, the previous

Chapter Fifteen

Judging an immaculate entry in the Concours d'Elegance at the Woburn BMF Rally of 1973. The British Motorcyclists Federation does fine work for the interests of all riders and, as far as I am aware, there is no comparable organisation in any other country.

one being a few months before, on Xmas Eve. I had made a diversion on my journey south, purely to wish any of my old friends a good Xmas and a brighter New Year. Behind the gates were the figures around the glowing brazier, one of whom detached himself to ask what I wanted. When I told him he said, in the correct union manner, that he would report my message to his committee and I felt that my visit had been wasted.

After the Workers' Co-Operative was formed early in 1975, and paradoxically only a few months before the Wolverhampton and Small Heath factories closed, I visited Meriden several times. The Government loan of more than £4 million should have enabled the new organisation to make steady progress, but it

The End of the Commando and Trident

lacked a competent leader with authority to set a sound course. It was of paramount importance to restore goodwill and confidence amongst dealers and overseas distributors, and the first essential was to produce spare parts for the machines supplied before the factory was closed. Large numbers were unserviceable and their owners needed parts to restore their faith in the dealers and the factory.

Spare parts would, in any case, have been very profitable, and it was a serious mistake not to give them priority. A small company across the road from the Meriden factory, and directed by Jack Shortland, ex-Spares Manager of the old Triumph company, has done volume international parts business with Triumph distributors. On one of my visits to Meriden, I enquired about the prospects for producing the 350 and 500 cc mediumweight twins which sold so well in those markets for which the 650 models were too large. I was told that all the jigs and tooling had disappeared. There had been talk of an East European deal when NVT took over, and I recall having to send a couple of machines to Poland for some obscure reason when I was at Andover. Several gentlemen from Wolverhampton went behind the Iron Curtain for undisclosed reasons, and Russia was the popular guess, but whatever the purpose might have been, nothing came of it.

In March 1975 I was invited by an old established City company, Anthony Gibbs Ltd., to discuss a very large potential contract for machines required by the Saudi Arabian Defence Force. This company specialised in Middle East business and the spade work they had already done on this prospect offered business which was badly needed at Wolverhampton. I was asked to take an Interpol to Riyadh, the Saudi capital, and demonstrate it to General Aloufi and his staff. The Interpol was prepared and taken to Heathrow to be loaded on the Saudi airline's Tri Star, which was to take us to Riyadh the next morning. Heathrow was closed that night by the fog which killed Graham Hill and his companions a few miles away. The plane landed at Riyadh at dusk and I finally found the Anthony Gibbs representative, Sabeh Bijani. There was no way of getting the machine through the complex Customs procedures that night and, as the next day was Friday, the Arab holy day when Customs closed, it had to wait until Saturday morning. This meant that it had to be presented to the General by noon, when he left his HQ for the day. We began negotiations early on Saturday for the release of the machine away and they were frustrating and costly, as one official after another had to be satisfied. With much less than an hour to go before the noon deadline, I finally wheeled the machine away and began to fit the windscreen. A Customs official ran up waving the import documents and said the machine could not be released because the radio set was not mentioned. More duty would have to be paid after the radio had been examined. In vain I tried to explain that it was not an operational set, it was of no value and was only on the machine to show how it was mounted. He was adamant and I had no more patience, so I detached the set and made him a present of it. I asked Bijani for the tin of petrol, and he

Chapter Fifteen

Testing on the Thruxton circuit in 1975 the Interpol which I took to Saudi Arabia. I made a bad mistake in fitting a fairing, for the engine ran too hot in the Saudi temperatures and I had to cut away a lot of fibreglass in Riyadh.

had forgotten to bring it. We rushed, in his car, to the filling station a kilometre away and the only can they could find had a hole in the bottom. Not much was left when we got back to the machine. There were fifteen minutes left when I started the engine and then found that I could not engage the gears because the clutch was solid. I switched off, put the machine into gear, and hoped that it would get moving on the starter plus leg power and an Arab push. It did, and I rode to Defence HQ in bottom gear. As I arrived, the Staff Officers were lined up ready to salute the General when he departed. I just had time to put the machine on the centre stand and take off my helmet as he appeared and, in Sandhurst English, apologised for keeping me waiting. He studied the white Interpol and discussed it in French with an Officer whose uniform and badges of rank were familiar to me and I had a feeling that I had seen him somewhere before.

The General left, after inviting me to bring the machine to the Military Tat-

The End of the Commando and Trident

too the next day, and I turned my attention to the French-speaking Officer. He was attached to the Defence HQ as a motorcycling instructor and had trained a display team which was to make its first appearance at the Tattoo. Mutual introductions revealed that he was Major Jean Gujon of the Garde Republicaine Paris, to which distinguished service I had supplied Nortons several years before. I asked if we had met at the Fort Rosny HQ and got a negative. Then I remembered the Garde Republicaine team of 1971 in the Circuit des Pyrenees, the first year I competed. He was the Captain of the team which had been so successful that year. Our reunion, so far away from our last meeting, was very cordial and was to prove most useful to me. That evening was very pleasant, as we sat in the courtyard of the villa owned by Bijani, sharing a bottle of whisky, which was forbidden in Arabia but which he had acquired by some means. The afternoon I had spent dismantling the clutch in a temperature over 100 degrees, which made it painful to handle tools. How different, I thought, from the frozen fingers which assembled the first Interpol in the Thruxton winter.

The next morning the road from Riyadh to the new and magnificent stadium was crowded with people going to the Tattoo, which was to be attended by HRH Prince Aziz, the Defence Minister. With blue lamps flashing and two tone horns sounding, the Norton made an impressive entrance to join Jean Gujon and his display team. I asked him if it would be possible for me to ride round the perimeter track as a compliment to the Prince and he thought it an excellent idea. I would never have expected to open the Tattoo, but that is what happened. When the Prince arrived and took his seat with the General, Jean had an announcement made over the public address system that Captain Shilton brought greetings from England to the Prince and the Saudi Arabian Forces, and had been invited to ride round the arena to signify the opening of the Tattoo. The packed stadium applauded as the ride began and cheered as, when I approached the Royal enclosure, I stood to attention on the footrests and gave a Sandhurst eyes right salute. I felt that I was getting closer to the contract order. The Tattoo was a colourful spectacle and the Gujon display team gave a performance which was a credit to him. In the cinema at Defence HQ the following day the COI film 'Neale Shilton the Man of the Motorcycle' had its première when it was shown to the General and his staff. It was the first copy to be released by the COI and had been collected for me by a Metro Police rider just in time to be brought to Heathrow before my plane left for Riyadh. Predominantly featuring Nortons and my Interpol ride in the Circuit des Pyrenees the previous year, it set the seal on the contract I was seeking. Several days later I flew back to England with my biggest order ever, worth around a million pounds. The news was very welcome at Wolverhampton and by my friends at the Anthony Gibbs Company.

In my office at Andover I had a busy two weeks tying up all the arrangements for the Arabian contract before departing for France and another

Chapter Fifteen

ride in the Pyrenees event with the British Police team. It was to be less enjoyable than usual for I had a problem engine, which lost me several minutes by the time I reached the highest point on the mountain section, and tempted me to make up time on the steep descent to the second check point. I braked without seeing the ridge of gravel, and that was the end of the ride. Back in England a week later I was called to a meeting at Wolverhampton in early July, and was asked to produce all details of the Interpol orders which I was holding. With the Arabian order, the total was impressive and I presented the details with some satisfaction, which was promptly shattered by Director John Pedley who chaired the meeting. He announced that when the factory closed for annual holiday at the end of the month it would not reopen. The Company was going into liquidation with immense debts, reputed to be around £5 million, no more material could be bought and none of my Interpols would be built.

I departed in a mood of deep depression and three weeks later the factory workers, unaware of the news, went away to enjoy their holidays. They returned in August to find the factory gates closed and I wondered whether it would have been less cruel to have announced the news before they went on holiday. However, the timing had been convenient for the management, which had been responsible for letting the situation deteriorate until it was interpreted into the prescribed formula of voluntary liquidation, though the word voluntary was hardly accurate. Meanwhile, a Parliamentary question had been tabled by R.E. Eyre MP, asking the Government for more help for what was left of the motor-cycle industry. The new Labour Government, having seen how wasted had been the millions invested by the Conservatives in the Manganese Bronze takeover of BSA, was unlikely to have any confidence in Norton Villiers. However, I felt that Mr. Eyre deserved to have support for his efforts and I sent him a telegram to Westminster on the morning of 7th August 1975, the day on which his question was put to the Minister for Industry Eric Varley. I did this without reference to anyone, and the NV management never became aware of it. The day was the Thursday before the Wolverhampton workers were to return from holiday on Monday and find the factory gates closed. The telegram was lengthy and I quote some extracts.

FROM NEALE SHILTON FLEET SALES DIRECTOR NORTON TRIUMPH DESIGNATED IN DAILY EXPRESS LAST WEEK AS WORLD NUMBER ONE POLICE MOTORCYCLE SALESMAN STOP SINCE I CREATED THE NORTON INTERPOL MACHINE FIVE YEARS AGO IT HAS PROUDLY SECURED MORE AND MORE MARKETS FROM THE JAPANESE AND GERMANS STOP NOW IN FLEET SERVICE WITH 48 UK POLICE FORCES AND OVERSEAS IN GREECE, FRANCE, MALI, GAMBIA, JAMAICA, NIGERIA, KUWAIT, DOHA, ABU DHABI, ARABIA ETC STOP URGENT ORDERS NOW HELD WORTH MUCH MORE THAN MIL-

The End of the Commando and Trident

LION POUNDS AND CONTRACTS BEING NEGOTIATED WITH MORE COUNTRIES ENSURE PROGRESSIVE FUTURE BUSINESS PROVIDED ASSURANCE CAN BE GIVEN OF CONFIDENCE IN COMPANY PROSPECTS STOP UPON THE OUTCOME OF YOUR QUESTION TODAY DEPENDS NOT ONLY THE FUTURE OF MANY WORKERS AND FAMILIES BUT WHETHER WE ABANDON FOREVER REPEAT FOREVER ALL MOTORCYCLE BUSINESS TO JAPAN AND GERMANY STOP MANY IMPORTANT CUSTOMERS WAITING FOR NORTONS ARE ANXIOUS TO BE INFORMED THAT PRODUCTION RESUMES ON MONDAY MORNING STOP MONDAY IS THE MOST IMPORTANT DAY THE INDUSTRY HAS EVER FACED AND THIS IS THE MOST IMPORTANT TELEGRAM I HAVE EVER SENT STOP MOST GRATEFUL FOR YOUR HELP.

Mr. Eyre was not successful and the House was warned that the day might come when its Ministers would be escorted by foreign machines. That day was not long in coming but it is doubtful whether any Minister ever noticed, or was concerned to see, that their Police escorts were riding machines with BMW on the petrol tank. I do know that HRH Princess Margaret not only noticed them but made very favourable comments on their quietness when she spoke to the Metro Police Special Escort Group.

After learning the expected news from Westminster I decided to make one more personal attempt to get production resumed at Wolverhampton. Having carefully analysed my order figures and contract negotiations, I came to the conclusion that they could keep the factory going for at least 30 weeks on an output of 70 machines per week. Whilst this would involve a much reduced labour force it would give time for recovery action and would enable me to satisfy important orders. I learned the name of the Wolverhampton Solicitors who had been appointed to act for the Liquidator and I 'phoned them, asking for a meeting as quickly as possible, at which I would present what I believed were helpful proposals. The meeting was agreed and would be held on Monday morning in the board room at the factory. Once again I was acting solely on my own initiative and risking the anger of my superiors for whom the Wolverhampton factory was a corpse in the hands of the official undertaker.

On Monday morning I rode from Andover through heavy rain on an Interpol and arrived to see a depressed crowd of workers at the factory gates. In the board room were the liquidator, his lawyers, an official from the Department of Industry and Union Representatives. The Liquidator was a Cardiff man and we had a mutal friend in the Lord Mayor of that City, which was a useful start to my petition. I put all my order facts and figures on the table for examination and appealed for the factory to be opened for at least the time required to complete the order commitments. By then there would be more orders and I felt confident that I could promise a continuity of production on a limited but profitable scale.

Chapter Fifteen

The petition was well received but the Liquidator pointed out, as I knew already, that it was his responsibility to convert the assets into money for the creditors and not spend more money in the process. I suggested that by completing all unfinished Interpols and making as many more as possible from material stocks, more money would be available for creditors. Furthermore, would they not be prepared to supply more components on secured credit terms guaranteed by the Liquidator? Finally, I offered to ask for a substantial advance payment from the city company which was underwriting the Arabian contract and to obtain deposits from other major customers who were waiting for machines. The Liquidator promised the fullest consideration and the official from the Government Department went away to 'phone London and seek support. I had done all I could and it was the last hope for the Wolverhampton workers, whose Union representatives were very grateful.

I rode away on the 120 wet miles journey to Andover and approaching the Bristol exit from the M5 motorway at rather more than the legal limit, the engine locked up without the slightest warning. I had experienced engine seizures before but always with a few seconds to declutch as the pistons tightened up. This time it was different, the rear tyre squealed before I could grab the clutch lever and get to the hard shoulder. After two cigarettes I was able to turn the engine over and continue the journey very slowly with the generator warning light glowing red and headlamp beam becoming dimmer. For 50 miles I rode on the parking light and for the remaining 20 miles with no lights at all and only enough current left in the battery to feed the ignition. The next day I found, as expected, that the rotor had seized on the stator due to main bearing wear and the two components had been locked together by a two second electrical welding process. I can confidently claim the quickest ever stop from 80 mph.

I was working on the engine as the telephone call came through to give the results of the Wolverhampton meeting. The proposals were admirable but one obstacle defeated them. The Liquidator could not be given authority to go ahead with production because he could not become involved in what is called Manufacturer Liability. I had met this before and remembered one case of an American who had been severely injured when the front brake cable failed on his Triumph. His lawyers sued everyone involved, the supplying dealer, the Triumph Corporation of Baltimore and the Triumph factory. There had been other cases and the premium a manufacturer has to pay to insure against claims is very high. My efforts had failed and I could do no more for Wolverhampton, but was there anything I could do about the Arabian contract in particular? Those machines were expected by General Aloufi to be in Jeddah by December, in time to escort important people on the Mecca pilgrimage, and I had given my promise. I was concerned also about all other orders, but this one was paramount. The only possible solution was to offer the 3 cylinder Triumph Trident which was being made for

The End of the Commando and Trident

NVT in the Small Heath factory.

I went to London and talked to my Anthony Gibbs friends who agreed that the Trident should be offered. We could hardly tell the Saudi authorities the true reason and so I wrote to explain that, since my visit, comparative tests had been made of the Norton and Triumph under simulated Arabian conditions at the MIRA establishment. These had proved that the oil-cooled Trident was much more suitable. I was not proud of this move, although technically it was justified, and the Saudis agreed to accept the Triumph at an increased price. The first quantity of 175 machines was programmed to be built at Small Heath for delivery to Jeddah in November and they would be flown out in a Jumbo freighter at Saudi expense to meet the Mecca deadline. Assembly began in October and stopped suddenly when a creditor, tired of waiting for some £23,000 payment, issued an application for the winding-up of the new company which had been created to replace Wolverhampton. The promise of an immediate cheque was in vain as, once the application had been made, it was too late. The Official Receiver was appointed and all activity at Small Heath stopped. When nothing had happened in the next few days, I demanded a meeting at the factory with the Receiver's lawyers and the Directors. I appealed for the urgent completion of the machines and there was no apparent interest from the lawyers, Cork Gully of London. Neither was there any support from my Directors and I was seriously inclined to abandon my efforts and 'phone Anthony Gibbs asking them to cancel the whole deal.

Later events caused me to regret that I did not do so. I went back to Andover and after 'phoning Small Heath for three days I spoke to Production Director Alistair Cave, emphasising that only a few days remained before the machines had to be at Heathrow. To cancel the Jumbo would mean paying some £20,000 penalty and would he ask the Receiver how he felt about paying it. Assembly work commenced the next day and I learned that by some complex arrangement known only to experts in such matters, the machines would be bought back by the Company from the Receiver at a price which satisfied him and which gave an excellent profit to the buyer. I spent several days progressing deliveries of all the accessories required and finally the 175 machines were transported to Heathrow. My problems seemed to be over, but they were to get much worse.

I flew to Jeddah several days later with one mechanic, to start assembling the machines, but they had not arrived. It had been found when the Jumbo had been loaded that no equipment existed at Jeddah airport to handle it. Consequently it went into Beirut, where the cargo was transferred to a couple of 707 freighters. The financial documents on which the payment of more than £200,000 depended had clearly specified direct flight to Jeddah and no transhipment was allowed. This was a problem I had to deal with later. Eventually, the cases arrived and were taken in trucks to a deserted Army camp some miles out in the desert and I soon discovered that, when a Saudi Army camp has been vacated, it is no place to

Chapter Fifteen

Testers at Enfield India, Madras. I was greatly impressed with the enthusiastic activity I saw at this factory and the workers were intensely proud of their machines.

assemble motorcycles or anything else. No electrical power, no water, no workshop facilities, only empty barrack rooms invaded by sand and by Arab families breaking open the cases which littered the desert. My colleague and I worked from dawn to dusk, but made slow progress. Many parts were missing, others did not fit, and the quality of the machines reminded us that they had been built by workers who were about to become unemployed. D-day for the Mecca pilgrimage grew nearer and it became essential for me to fly back to England to obtain replacement and missing parts. I had already used my one visa and when I arrived at Birmingham I found that it would take at least a week to get another, so I decided to fly back and bluff my way through Jeddah airport. After all, I was on Saudi Defence Force business.

At the end of three long days at Small Heath I went back with many cartons and at Jeddah I joined the hundreds of pilgrims being checked by the military passport control. Maybe because I was obviously not an Arab, my passport received special attention. An Officer was called and despite my explanations, which were ignored, I was marched away under arrest and spent the night in very unpleasant conditions. It was many hours before my demands to see a senior Officer were successful and, when he came, he would not believe that I was known to his General. I assured him that he would be court martialled if I was not released to deliver my cartons and eventually I was given 24 hours parole. In that time we

The End of the Commando and Trident

managed to get only a few machines completed and at 2 am I was escorted to a Tri Star to return to England. Three hours later, over the Mediterranean, it dived from 30,000 feet almost into the sea, which promised a suitable end to my Arabian experiences. There was no explanation except from a scared stewardess who announced that we were about to land in France. The Captain corrected her after he had regained control of the aircraft and we later went into De Gaulle airport for inspection of the flying machine.

Back in London I first went to the Anthony Gibbs offices and was asked to 'phone Dennis Poore, who had been demanding news of payment. I called him and was in no mood to be pleasant when I said that the money would be paid when the Saudi Bank in London reopened after the Ramadan Arab holiday. I added that we did not deserve it. I had by this time decided to resign my Directorship and leave the Company but before doing so I wanted to find some means of satisfying the outstanding Interpol orders. The time was late December and the Andover premises were over-flowing with unsold Commandos. I recommended that as many as necessary should be converted to Interpols, but this was rejected because of cost. After expressing my conviction that it would be more profitable than selling the stock at an inevitable cut price, my proposal was accepted and conversion work could start immediately after Christmas. Several of the original assembly workers were available, having been employed in the parts warehouse, and they looked forward to the change.

At the beginning of January I saw the General Manager, the son of a main Board Director, and told him that all was ready to begin conversion work. It would have to wait several weeks, he said, until spares stocktaking had been completed. This was the end of the Interpol and I went to my office to make a number of telephone calls. They were to the Police Forces still waiting for deliveries and I had to tell them there would be no more. The last call I made was to my boss, Bill Colquhoun, telling him that my resignation was being mailed. He asked me to stay on and promised his personal support to make a fresh start with Police business.

Not even my good friend Colquhoun could persuade me to continue risking the personal integrity I had built up over the years and, reluctantly but inevitably, I said my farewell to Norton and closed my office door at the end of January. In my desk were orders for many hundreds of machines which would never be supplied. It was the end of my Interpol dream and the end of another personal battle against incompetent management. If the Japanese Emperor were to give awards for services to the motorcycle industry, then several of the people I have mentioned should be at the top of his list. As for those misguided individuals who believe that the British industry was destroyed by the Japanese, I destroy their error with one answer. The industry was doomed in 1964 when the only man capable of preserving it left Triumph Meriden. His name was Edward Turner.

Chapter Fifteen

Police Constable 629 Edwin Baker of the Staffordshire County Police photographed at Leek Police Station in 1928. His mount is a 490cc Model 18 Norton. PC Baker later retired in the rank of Sergeant and has since died.

Opposite: Police Sergeant 'T' 5526 John Baker of the West Midlands Police, photographed at Brierley Hill Police Station in 1976. Like his father he too rides a Norton, in this instance an 850cc Commando Interpol model. Both rider and machine are still serving on the Western Traffic Department.

The End of the Commando and Trident

Chapter Sixteen

My Chiswick team. On the left, Leslie Walker, and on the right, Kay Fallon, with Gordon Maggs [ex-Commander Metro Police Traffic Division].

Chapter Sixteen

Per Ardua ad BMW

IN 1977 I attended another annual reunion party of the original Triumph staff at the Coventry headquarters of what used to be called the British Motorcycle Manufacturers Association. The walls are adorned with the photographs of illustrious past Presidents, whose names someone once described as inscriptions on the tombstones of British motorcycle factories. The building is itself a monument to the dead industry and now, as the UK Marketing Directors of Japanese, Italian and German machines climb the stairs to the well-appointed board room, they ought to look gratefully at the pictures of the men whose factories created the Association and provided these comfortable headquarters by Coventry Station.

At the Triumph reunion that year I met, or rather was confronted by, Geoffrey Robinson MP, the Meriden Co-operative Chief Executive who, in fact, had no right to be at the party. I was talking to a group of old friends about the increasing use of BMW by the Police when Robinson, whom I did not know, walked in and interrupted to say that he would ensure that BMW Police sales would soon stop. He commented on my 22 years with Triumph, my 7 years with Norton and questioned my loyalty in joining BMW; I answered that my loyalty was to my mortgage and I would willingly return to Triumph if I could be sure of

Chapter Sixteen

paying it. That was quite true.

Leaving Meriden had been an intensely sad experience but I had few regrets when I moved from Norton and joined BMW at Brentford. My Saint business with international Police forces had been destroyed by the BSA Group Management well before Meriden itself was destroyed. Having created the Norton Interpol, I spent six years recovering much of the business lost by the Saint, but when Norton ceased production I had to decide whether and how I should preserve the integrity I had built up in UK Police circles at least.

My very good friend of many years, Neasden dealer Bill Slocombe, provided the answer. Bill, one of the most loyal supporters of the British motorcycle industry, had finally accepted a BMW dealership and had been consulted about Police sales potential by Richard Styer, the General Manager of the BMW Concessionaires Motorcycle Division. Bill 'phoned me in January 1976 and, when he learned that I could do no more for Norton, a meeting was arranged with Styer at Brentford. An appointment was offered, though not on very generous terms, as Styer and his directors did not expect that I could sell more than a hundred machines. Beyond that figure, commission would give a reasonable income, but it was obvious to me that even if I could exceed the target, it would be a considerable time before I could earn as much as my Norton salary.

I considered the pros and cons of the situation. On the debit side was the realisation that there would be a great deal of political resistance to the purchase of non-British machines for the first time by UK Police forces. This later proved to be quite true. However, the resistance would also apply to Honda and Guzzi, both of whom I knew were keen to develop Police sales. Honda, in fact, scored the first major success in February 1976, with the Greater Manchester force. The situation at Meriden was still to be settled but the possibility of Triumphs recovering Police business could not be ruled out. At Wolverhampton, due to political pressure from the West Midlands Council, headed by a determined Chairman, Sir Stanley Yapp, the Norton Liquidator had agreed to a fleet of Interpols being produced for the West Midlands Police. These were some of the factors I had to face when making the decision, in late January 1976, as to whether the time had come to say goodbye to a life with motorcycles.

I decided to join BMW and I reported to Brentford at the beginning of February. The premises on the Great West Road were occupied almost entirely by the car side of the business, which was selling around 12,000 units per annum very profitably. The Motorcycle Division was the poor relation, not yet selling 2,000 in a year and operating from one office area only. When someone was away I borrowed his desk, and to get letters typed was a problem for a long time. No Police demonstrator machine existed and I was indeed starting once again at the beginning, as I had done at Norton and to a large degree at Meriden also. My first move was to contact all of my UK Police connections, tell them where I was, and

Per Ardua ad BMW

why. Joining BMW was, I explained, the only way in which I could offer reliable machines, backed by efficient service and delivery undertakings which would be honoured. I was reasonably confident about the reliability of machines but took a chance on the other two commitments and a considerable time was, in fact, to go by before I could honour them. At stake was the personal integrity I had built up over many years and there were to be occasions when it was at risk.

The early responses from Police authorities to my approaches were encouraging and I was anxious to make a Police machine available so that I could start a programme of visits. As supplied by the factory, the 600 cc or 750 cc model fully-equipped with all components required for UK Police service would be far too expensive. Furthermore, certain parts were not suitable and they could not offer the essential calibrated speedometer, certified as it had to be, to an accuracy margin of plus or minus two per cent. Securing Police orders was one problem, and supplying complete machines at an acceptable price was another. For some years I had enjoyed the personal friendships I had made amongst the suppliers of Police equipment, panniers, blue flashing lamps, stop warning signs, radio carriers, auxiliary wiring harnesses, fairings and speedometers. Everyone was keen to help and needed the business anyway. A standard R75 was obtained and, with ready co-operation from my supplier friends, it was prepared to Police specification and became my demonstrator. Once again I was able to add to my riding mileage and start an order book. The price to the Police was several hundred pounds more than they had paid for Triumphs and Nortons and this made it more difficult for Chief Constables to obtain buying authority from their council finance committees. I therefore eased the problem with a letter which emphasised the value of the UK components and labour, pointing out also that accessory factory workers would continue to be employed after suffering the effects of the Triumph and Norton problems.

Orders for the R60 and R75 began to arrive and I then had to face the question of where, and by what means, the machines would be assembled. Two BMW specialist dealers in Berkshire and Monmouthshire were very helpful and assembled the first few, but this could be only a temporary arrangement. It was decided to set up an assembly scheme at Brentford, using part of the car service area, and this was later to create serious difficulties. I was given the services of one mechanic who I found was a car electrician and somewhat reluctant to become involved with motorcycles. However, the two of us unpacked the first machines when they arrived from Germany, and began to prepare them.

The Brentford Workshop Manager was not merely unhelpful, he came close to stopping BMW Police business before it began. No tools, no workbench and insufficient space were only some of the handicaps which evidenced his objection to the trespass of motorcycles on his car territory. There was one other, and more severe, handicap. Labour time was charged at skilled car service rates and meant

Chapter Sixteen

that even with my own assistance work, each machine was costing more than £70 to prepare. My protests were ignored and I would have left BMW there and then but for the delivery promises I had made to the forces who had supported me and had placed orders after overcoming political objections. There was also another reason which made me determined to carry on with the project I had undertaken. The Midlands newspapers, which had so often given generous coverage of my Triumph and Norton sales achievements, had headlined my BMW appointment. I quote from the Coventry Telegraph. 'After 29 years in the British motorcycle industry during which he became an international figure, Neale Shilton has joined BMW. A BMW spokesman said that this appointment signifies a new phase in our Police busines policy.' I never discovered who that spokesman was but certainly he was not the Brentford Workshop Manager.

As the weeks went by, there was no improvement in the situation and, with the income of orders increasing, there was no way in which Police business progress could continue as long as it depended upon Brentford output. I was already in arrears with deliveries to such Forces as Hertfordshire, South Yorkshire, Essex, Leicestershire, Kent and the City of London. I paid a visit to an engineering company in Andover which employed some of the men who had been made redundant by Norton, and of whom several had worked on my Interpol assembly line. My talk with the Managing Director had the precise results I had hoped for. He was seeking more work and the prospect of assembling BMW Police machines was very attractive. We agreed a labour rate which was considerably less than I was paying and the next day I had a confrontation with Brentford. The Workshop Manager declined to attend and his deputy had no answer to my criticisms of the problems of labour inefficiency and high cost. I was, however, threatened with the personal consequences of taking the work away from Brentford, but a week later I moved the operation to Andover and advised all Police forces that BMW Police machines would now be built by the same mechanics who had assembled Nortons. The Hampshire press publicised the story and BBC television showed film of BMW machines being tested only a few yards away from the premises where Norton Interpols had been produced.

It was now nearing the end of 1976, and less than ten months after I had joined BMW to sell a hundred machines, orders had been received for three times that figure. The Kent Police alone had ordered more than seventy and I invited trouble from the management by signing a fixed price contract shortly before the rate of exchange between the pound and the D-mark worsened abruptly and considerably reduced the BMW profit margin. Instead of being complimented on the Kent order, I was rebuked for risking a lowered profit, but I had the last word in the interview with my director. Had I not agreed the fixed price which came only marginally within the Kent Police financial budger, the order would have gone to the much cheaper Honda. He was not impressed and I was left wondering

Per Ardua ad BMW

With John Thaw [The TV Sweeney]. I had the pleasure of driving him in a BMW Police car, when he opened the new premises seen in the background.

whether Police business was of any real importance to BMW Concessionaires. Meanwhile, I was back in the saddle of a demonstration machine for long hours and long journeys, selling as I had always done by personal example, which was often illustrated by a ride of 500 miles a day and return journeys which started from Northumberland or Durham after 6 pm and ended in London at midnight. I did for BMW what I had done for Triumph and Norton and I knew of no better way of showing my confidence in the machine which I was selling.

BMW orders reached the 500 mark and it seemed to me that the delivery of machine number 500 should be celebrated. It was one of a fleet supplied to the City of London Police and they were kind enough to agree to a ceremony by the Tower of London. The machine was handed over to the Chief Superintendent by

Chapter Sixteen

A familiar sight to all regular users of the A30 and A303 roads in Hampshire. PC Pat McCarthy, who has probably ridden as many miles as I have. After finishing his hours of patrol duty, he often goes for a pleasure ride on his own BMW. He spent his 1981 leave touring Canada by motorcycle.

the Chairman of Tozer Kemsley and Milbourn Ltd., who owned BMW Concessionaires, and through whom years before I had supplied all the Triumphs I had sent to the Australian Police in New South Wales and Queensland. At the lunch which followed, I met the Australian who had handled that business and whom I had last met in Sydney. From him I learned that the 1000 Triumphs I used to sell each year had been replaced by the Japanese and what could BMW do about it? Later on I tried, but the German factory was not interested in my offer of assistance.

Neither were they interested in a £2,000,000 order I was offered early in 1977. I had a 'phone call from my good friends Anthony Gibbs Ltd. in the City, with whom I had negotiated the Saudi Arabian Norton Triumph contract two

Per Ardua ad BMW

years earlier. After the problems they encountered with that business, I was happy to be given the opportunity of collaborating again, and more successfully. They had been invited by the Saudi Defence Authorities to arrange the supply of 500 cars with full service support logistics and, with UK manufacturers excluded for unfortunate but firm reasons, the order was open to BMW. My boss and I went immediately to the Managing Director and within minutes he was talking to Munich at top level. The answer was an emphatic negative and it was repeated when another call was made the next morning appealing for reconsideration. The factory had committed its entire production for the year and was not prepared to break delivery promises. An admirable policy but a great disappointment to my friends in the City and to me. Shortly afterwards, they tried again, and this time 400 motorcycles were required for the same Defence Force. I felt that a direct approach to Germany by the Anthony Gibbs company might be more successful than involving BMW Concessionaires, whose business was restricted to the UK market. My director friend from the City agreed and flew to Munich. He was back in London the same evening with another negative, but for different reasons, which I found difficult to accept. As time went by I received other enquiries from UK and overseas connections anxious to satisfy Police and Defence authority orders, but finally I ceased to take any action. I later made an exception when the Eire Police, the Garda, was interested in a BMW motorcycle fleet. This followed a course at the Metropolitan Police Hendon Driving School by a Garda Inspector. I was asked to quote for machines exactly as supplied to the Metro and other UK Forces. Having supplied them with many Triumphs in the past, I was anxious to help with BMW and, as the Eire market was directly controlled from Munich, I telexed for permission to negotiate. The reply was unfavourable. I have always found it difficult to understand why BMW Germany did not take the same advantage of my overseas connections as they have done with my UK Police associations. I offered my services soon after taking up my Brentford appointment but maybe my offer did not reach a high enough level. I would have enjoyed keeping the Japanese out of some of the Police markets I created for Triumph and Norton.

In 1977 the Motorcycle Division moved from Brentford to premises in the Chiswick High Road, a move which was made to give more room to the car operation but which suited the Police Department very well. My office quickly became a convenient morning coffee stop for Metropolitan Police riders on Triumph Saints, which I had supplied years before. I felt sure that one day soon they would be BMW, a thought which gave me commercial satisfaction but some personal regret. My office became a reception point for deliveries of pannier boxes, speedometers and radio carriers which I then took to Andover. Often there was barely enough room to move and many a Police Officer sat on a stack of panniers whilst drinking his coffee. Orders came in at an increasing rate and I issued a pro-

Chapter Sixteen

duction programme to Andover which covered deliveries towards the end of 1977.

In my mail one morning came the order from Scotland Yard which I had been hoping for and which sent me straight to my boss, who was kind enough to offer me a free lunch when he realised what was in my hand. I knew that the Metropolitan Police had been quietly testing Japanese, Italian and BMW machines for many months on a test programme equivalent in efficiency to any formula in the aircraft industry. Many thousands of miles had been covered in all conditions, by very experienced riders, who had changed over machines until each had been evaluated for performance, handling and reliability by the whole team. As I learned later, BMW had been given top marks, with the 750 Honda second and the 850 Guzzi third. On the pure basis of price and performance comparison, Honda might well have obtained the order if the machine had been shaft driven. Rear chain adjustment was all too frequent during the test period and chain life was very limited in London traffic conditions. Strange that this was never a serious problem with the Metro Triumphs, although they had no efficient chain lubrication system. The rear chains on my own Triumphs were still good at more than 40,000 miles and I have always believed that this was largely due to the efficient engine crankshaft shock absorber which was used in those days. Certainly chain life was reduced when the alternator rotor displaced the shock absorber which had worked efficiently for years. Compressed rubber segments in the clutch were a poor substitute. I have often wondered if we should now be seeing all Metro Police riders on Honda, had the evaluation test machine been shaft driven.

The Yard order was for a first fleet of twenty machines and upon their behaviour on everyday duties in various Metro divisions would finally depend whether the total fleet of some 500 machines would be BMW. That was unless the Triumph factory overcame its serious problems and was then able to produce satisfactory machines. The hundreds of Triumphs still being used by Metro had given good service but were now getting old and expensive to maintain. Meriden could not supply spare parts and to keep the fleet operational was a major problem.

The man who carried this burden was a friend I had known and admired since my Meriden days, Jack Clarke, who arrived at the Metro Police garage Walworth before 7 am each day from his home near Guildford. He and his team of three riders combed the country for Triumph parts and it was entirely due to their determination that the Metro Police divisions were able to continue essential motorcycle patrol duties. Not until late 1980 were their last Triumphs disposed of and these were the machines of the Special Escort Group which were in such excellent condition that they were sold at a higher figure than they had originally cost. Jack Clarke richly deserved his award of the OBE in 1979. He was due to

Per Ardua ad BMW

The first BMW machines supplied to the Metropolitan Police were 600cc and 750cc models, the larger capacity type being later standardised. Here is a 600 fitted with the Avon Fairing which was common to both and widely used on Continental Police BMW's until superceded by the Munich-designed fairing in 1979. [Commissioner of Police of the Metropolis]

retire at the end of 1980 and when I was leaving BMW, on 30th November, that year, I 'phoned him to say farewell and to thank him for all the help he had given to me over the years. Especially the expert support he gave when I took him to Munich for a meeting to demand action on various problems of design and quality. This quietly spoken engineer, whose appearance belied his ability, achieved improvements which I had been unable to obtain. Soon after I had said farewell, Jack died, having had a painful two weeks of his retirement.

During 1977 I encountered an unpleasant aspect of departmental politics which brought me very close to leaving BMW Concessionaires and giving the rea-

Chapter Sixteen

son to all Police Force customers. I had an apparently friendly visit from the Dover-based Parts Manager, who was keen to learn the future prospects of Police business. The outlook was bright and I was well on the way to achieving 1,000 sales. I regarded his visit as a demonstration of his wish to ensure adequate cover for Police parts requirements and I gave a forecast of deliveries for some months ahead. I was soon to discover the real reason for his interest. A week or so later, following a Brentford meeting from which I was excluded, I received a memorandum of instruction from the Parts Director to which I took strong objection. I was to hand over immediately all stocks of Police components to Dover and I was to give details of their prices, the addresses of the suppliers and the names of my contacts. All future orders would be issued by Dover and I would draw my production requirements from there. Dover Parts Department would increase the component prices by 15%. Quite clearly the sole object of the plan was to increase the parts turnover.

I objected strongly in a note which emphasised the complications and what to the Police would be an inexplicable price increase of £25 per machine, not long after I had announced prices for the rest of the year. There was no response to my objections and I ignored the instruction for a month or so until I was told by my boss that I had to comply with a director's ruling. In a two-hour meeting with him I repeated all of my reasons for refusing. I had built up the Police business, had negotiated lowest prices with the component manufacturers, had organised supply schedules on a reliable system which required no stocking finance, and to have everything sent to Dover with additional transport costs was a quite absurd proposition. He agreed entirely with all I said and so, finally, I asked him why he would not support my case. His answer was simple and sincere. He had a wife, two children, a large mortgage and could not afford to upset a Director. Now an executive with a Japanese car company, he was the nice character who arranged my BMW appointment and for him I gave way, for the first and only time, to a policy which I knew was wrong. There was soon to be plenty of evidence to prove this. However, I did not increase prices to the Police and I would have welcomed an enquiry into the reasons why the profit margin had reduced.

Over the following few months, the new supply arrangements caused chaos and several times the incompetence of the Parts Department stopped production of Police machines. I reached the point at which I urged that components should be sent direct to the Andover assembly point by the manufacturers and Dover could enjoy their profit margin for doing nothing except sending me their invoices. My appeal was rejected because the Dover computer programme required the components to be taken into stock before they could be supplied. The computer and its servants were more important than the proper conduct of Police business. The consequences were absurd. For example, urgently needed panniers made in London were sent by rail to Dover with considerable delay, taken into

Per Ardua ad BMW

This is one of the early Metro Police 750cc fleet. [Commissioner of Police of the Metropolis]

stock then taken out again to be sent to Andover by road transport. The same system applied to Police signs made in Blackpool, blue lamps from Bridlington, fairings from Durrington, only ten miles from Andover, wiring harnesses from Warwick and speedometers from Nottingham. There was nobody at Dover capable of checking component quality and so when any were found to be unacceptable at Andover, they had to be returned to Dover, and from there back to the supplier who replaced them to Dover, and so on. To the sheer inefficiency of the system had to be added all the extra carriage costs but, most importantly, assembly work at Andover was held up and deliveries to Police delayed. The most extraordinary of many absurdities concerned the mounting brackets used for the Police speedometer. These were manufactured by the Andover engineering company where the machines were assembled. They were then sent to Dover and, having gone through the system, they were returned to Andover.

After a few months of complications, of frequent frustrations and of protests which were ignored, I decided to take my own course of action. Having contacted my supplier friends I reduced the quantities on my orders to Dover and

Chapter Sixteen

ordered the required balances directly on the suppliers. Deliveries were again made to my office at Chiswick and I took them to Andover. This put an end to production delays. As the months went by, I further reduced the Dover orders and finally stopped them completely. The Parts Manager must have realised this from his computer print outs of Police component turnover and I expected to be asked for an explanation. My answers were always ready and I would have had great satisfaction in giving them, but they were never asked for. Another struggle to overcome the obstacles in developing BMW Police business had succeeded, but it should never have been necessary.

Chapter Seventeen

The Chiswick Chapter

1978 WAS a good year for BMW Police sales and from my very small office space on the ground floor of the Chiswick premises came results which fully justified the determined resistance against people who were more concerned with their own personal interests than with the Company and its customers. Over my years in the industry I had been faced on a number of occasions with the choice between personal popularity or becoming disliked by opposing someone with whom I disagreed. If I felt that something was not in the best interests of the Company and the customer, then I would not accept it. That was always my code and, as at Triumph and Norton, there were those at BMW Concessionaires who had different ideas.

February and March of 1978 brought many orders, some from existing Police customers and others from new Forces. The financial year of local authorities commences in April and it was soon evident that, by the middle of the year, deliveries would reach the 1,000 mark. Following the initial order, Metro Police had placed a contract for a substantial number of 800 cc models and I arranged to visit Germany with two of their top engineers to ensure that the highest quality standards would be satisfied. There were to be similar visits later on when Metro

Chapter Seventeen

and other Forces substantiated my 1976 warning to the factory that British Police riders would discover faults which were not previously recognised.

The number of UK Police BMW fleets was now 35 and the delivery total was near to four figures. I decided that there should be some celebration to mark the delivery of machine number 1,000, and my Sales Director not only gave me full scope to make arrangements but offered generous help. A fleet order for 28 machines was on the books for Hampshire Police and one idea led to another. The Thruxton circuit in Hampshire was booked for a test day and many Forces were invited to attend. Delivery number 1,000 would be ridden from Andover to the circuit and handed over during the day. Something more impressive was considered and the suggestion was made of delivery by helicopter. My Director had good connections with a helicopter hire company and negotiations went ahead. They were passenger charter operators but could lift a motorcycle provided an acceptable sling could be obtained. We located a specialist company which made equipment capable of carrying a tank and we had what we wanted in a few days.

Next, we thought how appropriate it would be to have at Thruxton the first BMW machine supplied to a UK Police Force. It was supplied to the Thames Valley Force and was still in daily use at 100,000 miles. The Chief Constable agreed that it would be ridden to the circuit. The final idea was to invite actress Susan Hampshire to be present and hand over the keys of number 1,000. This charming lady had visited us at Chiswick on the R100 BMW which she owned and she was kind enough to accept our invitation.

On the morning of the function, a test lift was carried out by the helicopter near Andover and the results were ominous. The machine swung like a pendulum and the pilot had his hand close to the red buton which would jettison the cargo if the swing affected the handling of the chopper. He landed and asked if we were prepared to accept the risk. With visions of number 1,000 falling on houses in the nearby village, we asked him to go ahead, but we had an apprehensive time before the exercise was over.

Meanwhile, after days of bad weather, the sun shone and hundreds of Police officers arrived at the circuit, which was soon busy with cars and motorcycles. We were in radio contact with the helicopter and around noon I used the public address system to ask everyone to look eastwards for the arrival of delivery number 1,000. The chopper came into view with its cargo trailing behind at a steep angle, which then lessened steadily, and there was little pendulum as the pilot hovered and gently lowered to deliver the machine into the hands of the relieved reception committee. Miss Hampshire handed over the keys and number 1,000 was, as far as I know, the first Police motorcycle to be delivered by air. The day went well, many Police officers enjoyed their miles on the circuit, and there was a pleasant celebration that evening in the White Horse at Thruxton. I wondered whether I would be around for delivery number 2,000 and, if so, how I

The Chiswick Chapter

The arrival at Thruxton in 1978 of Police BMW delivery number 1,000. In the foreground is delivery number 1, with 90,000 miles on the speedometer, which was supplied to the Thames Valley Police. It was ridden to Thruxton by PC Phil Bingham, who had the machine from new.

Chapter Seventeen

With charming actress Susan Hampshire, who handed over the keys of BMW 1,000 to PC Brian Hill of the Hampshire Traffic Police. The interested onlooker is BMW Concessionaires' Sales Director Peter Beaumont. I have tried unsuccessfully to remember what I was saying to cause Susan to look so pensive.

would celebrate it. I was to find out in 1980.

Some weeks after the Thruxton affair, I had an interesting experience on the M3 motorway. I had loaned my R80 demonstrator to the Hampshire Police for a special assignment and when it was returned the rider mentioned an unusual noise at the front of the machine. I made a mental note to check it, and promptly forgot. A few nights later, I used the machine to ride home and left Chiswick at dusk. I heard the noise at once and suspected a loose fairing bracket or headlamp reflector. At Sunbury, before joining the motorway, I stopped to investigate, checking the fairing brackets and headlamp mounting, without result. I pressed on along the M3 and soon became aware of the curious behaviour of cars after I had overtaken them. There were not so many as it was late evening but each one seemed to pull over to the slow lane and their headlamps disappeared from my mirror. On Police machines I had always enjoyed special courtesy, but nothing like this. Towards the end of the M3, my homeward route took me off the motor-

The Chiswick Chapter

Introducing the new BMW R80RT at a Police Guest Day at Earls Court. Left to right: ex-Metro Police Officer Ted Clements, ISDT rider and racer Dave Minskip, Metro patrol motorcyclist PC Deidre Donohue, the Author and Commander Ken Fairbairn.

way on to the more bumpy A303 and, as the front end noise had become worse, I stopped on the hard shoulder at the A303 exit. As I put the machine on the stand I discovered the reason for the strange behaviour of the motorway traffic. The POLICE STOP sign had been flashing all the way from Sunbury, where I had accidentally knocked the switch when checking the fairing. I looked back down the M3 beyond Basingstoke and not a single vehicle was moving westwards. Back in Chiswick the next morning I telephoned my Chief Inspector friend who was head of Hampshire Police Northern Traffic Area at Basingstoke. Innocently, I asked him whether there had been any accident or unusual incident on the M3 westbound the previous evening. The reply was negative but he added 'Something curious must have happened as you are the seventh person to enquire'. I was tempted to confess, but decided to keep quiet.

Police business had grown to such proportions by 1978 that help was needed, particularly on the technical service side. It was my aim to have specialised BMW mechanics in every Police Force and there were something like one hundred workshops with provincial Forces. The training facilities at Brentford had given some help but one occasional course was inadequate. Surprisingly, I was given the services of Les Walker, a bright and competent young instructor from the service school, who was immediately successful. As each week went by, more and

Chapter Seventeen

more mechanics were comprehensively trained in their own workshops to factory certificate standard, and they were proud of the certificates we issued. Never before had Police motorcycle fleets been maintained so efficiently and, in my experience, never before had motorcycle mechanics ceased to agitate for a move to cars.

I was also authorised to appoint a deputy and I selected a man who was not only a keen motorcyclist but one who had just retired on the younger side of middle age as Commander of Metropolitan Police Traffic Division, Gordon Maggs QPM. He had come to my office to ask about buying a new BMW which, in fact, he did buy, but he joined the Company a month later. From its humble beginnings at Brentford in 1976, the Police Department had become important and towards the end of 1978 this was recognised. The Department was given Division status. I contemplated the possibilities of developing some car sales to Police forces and I saw as the first essential, a model produced by the factory to meet UK Police specification, and delivered ready for duty except for radio installation. Two forces already had a few BMW cars, but they had been supplied as standard models.

I flew to Munich and took with me a Senior Police Engineer who knew much more than I did about technical specifications. The result was a 2.5 litre car which not only incorporated Police equipment which was absent from those produced in the UK but was also price competitive with them. I commissioned the first one as a demonstration car and added a trailer. For the first time, a fully-equipped Police car towed a fully-equipped motorcycle of the same make. Several more Forces bought fleets of the 2.5 litre BMW but I was too well aware of political problems to start an active sales campaign. It had been difficult enough with motorcycles, even when Norton and Triumph were in trouble in 1976. To challenge the Rover and Ford Police business would have been interesting on a normal competitive basis but this was not possible for several reasons. Firstly, the Home Office Police Department sees fit to circularise all Chief Constables reminding them of cars which are manufactured in UK. Superfluous advice, one might think, but it is given in the context that there must be a good reason if any other make is purchased. More powerful, however, than any Home Office circular are the county council politicians and the civilian committees who supervise Police financial budgets. It is not unreasonable that they should wish to give support to Rovers and to those Ford models which are manufactured in Dagenham, even though they themselves may own Japanese or Continental cars. It will be an interesting situation if and when the Japanese association with Leyland becomes effective. As far as I was concerned, I continued to be too occupied with my motorcycle business to give much attention to cars. However, car fleet sales went into three figures.

As the months of 1979 went by and the deliveries of BMW Police motor-

The Chiswick Chapter

The Precision Display Team of the Metropolitan Police, whose polished performances thrill many thousands of spectators each year. On daily duty, they are part of the Metro Police Special Escort Group, which has earned a world-wide reputation. So impressed was the Emperor of Japan by his SEG escort on his visit to London that Japanese Police motorcyclists are sent each year to the Metro Driving School at Hendon, for special training.

Chapter Seventeen

The impressive formation of the Display Team at Wembley for the 150th Anniversary of the Metropolitan Police in 1979. Their superb performances were a highlight of the week. [Commissioner of Police of the Metropolis]

cycles increased beyond 1,500, my main concern was to ensure that manufacturing quality was maintained. The UK was quickly becoming the largest Police market and promised to overtake France, and even Germany. It was not easy, however, to convince the factory that certain modifications and improvements were necessary. The main problem was to get through to the man with sufficient authority to take action. Several of the problems I had encountered years before at Meriden and I knew the answers. For example, there was the case of what is known as full suppression of electrical equipment with which I had much experience with the Triumphs supplied to the Garde Republicaine of Paris. BMW had always insisted that full suppression was essential to prevent interference to the radio equipment. I did not agree and I objected to Police paying £46 extra for something which was not necessary. Also, I suspected that full suppression might be connected with the problems some forces had encountered with electrical equipment.

    The argument I put to Germany was simple and, in my view, convincing. Firstly, full suppression had never been used on the Triumphs and Nortons supplied to the UK Police forces. Secondly, the Pye Westminster radio equipment installed on their BMW machines was exactly the same type which had been used for more than ten years and, in fact, all the BMW radio sets had been taken from Nortons or Triumphs. Why then should it need full suppression? BMW electrics

The Chiswick Chapter

This photograph turns back the calendar several years, to recall the very long association between the Metro Police and Triumphs. The machines have changed but most of the Officers seen here are still in the team. The aircraft is, of course, the Concorde. [Commissioner of Police of the Metropolis]

261

Chapter Seventeen

The team in Concorde configuration. [*Commissioner of Police of the Metropolis*]

were essentially the same, and coils, condensors and contact breakers did the same work whether manufactured by Lucas of England or Bosch of Germany. My arguments were not answered and, strange as it may seem, it took the Liverpool football team to convince the factory that I was right.

The Merseyside Police had taken delivery of more than 30 machines a month or so before Liverpool F.C. returned triumphantly to the City with the F.A. Cup. Many thousands of people cheered them as their coach was escorted by the new BMW fleet. At walking pace the machines were in first gear, the condensers overheated and, as they ceased to function, the contact breaker points of five machines burnt out. Along the route of the parade were five BMWs waiting to be collected by a recovery truck. My telephone rang early next morning and a very distressed Transport Manager gave me the news. The Chief Constable had demanded a full report and it was more than likely that press publicity would result in severe damage to BMW. I considered this was inevitable, in fact. My first action was to telex Germany and the text of my message was not friendly. My second step was to 'phone Parts Division, Dover, to arrange express delivery

The Chiswick Chapter

Seated on Triumph Saint 478 AKD in this 1959 photograph is Acting Sergeant Cliff Halsall of the Liverpool City Police [now Merseyside]. In those days he could always be relied upon to secure a cabin on the Isle of Man boat for the Author.

Still enjoying motorcycling 22 years later, the same Cliff Halsall, but now Assistant Chief Constable of Cheshire. Surely the highest ranking Police Officer in Britain to ride a motorcycle regularly on duty. [Chief Constable of Cheshire]

Chapter Seventeen

to Chiswick of new condensers and contact breaker sets for the Merseyside fleet. On my own initiative I specified standard components to replace the suppressed type and it was essential that they were taken to Liverpool the next day. I had promised the Transport Manager that, within thirty hours of his call, we would have modified every machine and he could assure the Chief Constable of no further trouble. I should have known better than to make a promise which depended upon other people. Dover 'phoned to report no stock of the parts required and the situation suddenly went from the serious to the critical. My office telephones were busy for the next half hour calling BMW dealers in the London area and from three of them we were able to collect what we needed. The promise to Liverpool was kept. My telex to Germany had the desired effect and no more machines were supplied with full suppression. I would have appreciated a message from the factory acknowledging that they had been wrong but that would have been expecting too much. As always, it was left to the complacently generous warranty system to acknowledge responsibility.

I had always admired the design and quality of BMW and only rarely when I was developing Norton Interpol sales overseas, was I successful in taking over from a BMW fleet. However, the loyalty which I gave to the factory through my employers was all the stronger because of my responsibility to UK Police forces and consequently my efforts to eradicate technical problems were not exactly welcomed. It seemed evident to me that the traditionally high standard of BMW quality had tended to deteriorate since 1976. Faults were being found on Police machines at the Andover assembly line which ought to have been picked up by quality control checks in the Berlin factory. Having visited the factory I was well aware of the difficulties there of getting skilled labour. Many workers had to be recruited from countries outside Germany, and trained. Someone at high level had the idea of looking towards England for skilled men and in the spring of 1979 I was asked to attend a meeting in London with a Director of the German company to give my views on this project. I gave my opinion that, with acceptable conditions of employment and accommodation, there were men in the Coventry and Birmingham areas prepared to work in Berlin. They were men of skilled ability and experience in the British motorcycle industry which had failed them, and they would be highly valuable to BMW.

I was asked to take preliminary steps to go ahead with the project and arrange interview centres. Meanwhile, news of the recruitment appeared in the press, and applications began to arrive at the Chiswick offices. I arranged interview points at Coventry, Birmingham and Wolverhampton and awaited instructions as to the dates. No instructions came and my enquiries failed to get any information. After some weeks I had to conclude that the project had been abandoned, but I was never able to discover the reason. However, I had my suspicions and I have always believed they were well-founded. Undoubtedly the press publicity of

The Chiswick Chapter

BMW recruitment reflected badly upon the failure of the UK motorcycle industry and was considered particularly harmful to the serious situation at Triumph Meriden. With the Government so involved at Meriden it was reasonable to suspect that a political channel was used between London and Bonn to express concern about the project. My suspicions may have been wrong, but of two things I was certain. One was that a number of Midlands craftsmen were very disappointed, and the other was that BMW machines would have benefited from their skills.

As 1979 neared its end, so did the BMW Concessionaire franchise, and it became known that, as from January 1980, the Munich organisation would take over the UK market operation at new premises in Bracknell. During my visit to Munich in September I was invited to join the new company and I agreed. In discussions about UK Police business I estimated that by the end of 1980 I would have reached my self-imposed target of 2,000 motorcycle deliveries and would then consider that I could do no more. I would resign and it would be the responsibility of other people to preserve the business I had created.

Chapter Eighteen

A demonstration R75/5 model supplied to the Avon and Somerset Constabulary for evaluation purposes during 1974 [M. Haimes]

Chapter Eighteen

The Sussex Police Saga

A FEW days before Easter 1977 began a remarkable series of incidents with repercussions which went on for more than three years. The Sussex Police had a fleet of BMW R75 models delivered the previous year and were quite satisfied with them. In fact they had requested a quotation for another fleet for early delivery, and would replace the remainder of their Norton Interpols.

The Service Manager at Chiswick informed me that he had been to Police headquarters at Lewes to examine a machine on which a rider had crashed. He reported that the torque loading of the steering head bearings was slightly below the recommended figure, the tyre pressures were a couple of pounds low, and the rear suspension dampers were on the top load setting. His report had been given to the Police Transport Manager whose duty it was, in conjunction with the Traffic Chief Superintendent, to investigate the circumstances of any accident involving a Police vehicle. I was soon to learn that the circumstances in this particular case were unusual. I was also to learn that, shortly after this accident, a Sussex Police sergeant was sent to carry out high-speed testing on a wartime airfield in Wiltshire used by the Avon tyre company for testing. This rider had been injured when he crashed at high speed. We had not been made aware of this accident

Chapter Eighteen

when it happened just before the Easter holiday break.

The day before my office closed for the holiday, I telephoned the Transport Manager at Lewes to discuss the enquiry into the first accident, but he was not available. I was concerned because this was the first accident involving a Police BMW and from my experience of Police rider crashes on Triumphs and Nortons, I knew how important it was to establish the reason. When I was still unable to contact the Transport Manager in the late afternoon, I left a message asking that he should call me but I had heard nothing by the time I left the office at 7 pm. I returned on Tuesday after the holiday and during the morning he called and asked whether I had been trying to get in touch about the new order. I was shocked when he went on to say that his BMW fleet had been withdrawn from duty the day before the holiday. Immediately I told him to expect me to arrive at Lewes within two hours and I went straight to my boss to ask him to accompany me. Returning to my office minutes later, I found on my desk a telex from Sussex Police which had come from the Car Division at Brentford through the internal mail system. It had been sent from Lewes the day before the holiday closure and was lying there even whilst I was trying to contact the Transport Manager. Thus began the most extraordinary sequence of events I have ever known, and which became progressively more unpleasant. It was never explained why the telex was sent to Brentford instead of to the Police Department number at Chiswick, which was well-known at Lewes. However, in the absence of a prompt response, the Police assumed that it had been ignored. A remarkable assumption, for the telex informed BMW that in view of two accidents it was proposed to withdraw all machines from duty at once and to telex this information to all Police forces after Easter. It was significant to me that the decision to withdraw machines immediately was quite inconsistent with the intention to notify all forces after Easter.

I should explain here that when the Transport Manager of a Police force finds a defect in a Police vehicle, or has reason to believe that one exists, he is required by Home Office Police Department authority to notify all other forces at once. Most Transport Managers use their own discretion, having many times received telexes for trivial reasons. The Chief Constable of Sussex was at the time traffic affairs spokesman for the Association of Chief Police Officers and in this capacity he saw fit to circulate his own telex. It was regrettable that there had been little, if any, opportunity for BMW Chiswick to convince the Police there was no justification for withdrawing machines from duty,

On arrival at Lewes on Tuesday after an illegally fast journey, I was anxious to explain why there had been no immediate response to the Thursday telex, apart from the fact that it had been sent to the wrong number. It had been taken from the telex machine in the Brentford mail room by an elderly individual who should have known that any Police telex message was important and required immediate attention. He had phoned Chiswick and instead of asking for the Police Depart-

The Sussex Police Saga

ment he spoke to a junior girl in the General Office. In the subsequent investigation she claimed she was not told that the telex was important, which was why she told the caller to send it in the internal post. Whoever was to blame had caused a major problem. Whether or not the explanation was believed at Lewes I could never be sure, but I did not expect it to be.

The meeting was attended by the Traffic Chief Superintendent, his Deputy Superintendent and the Transport Manager, all of whom I had known well for a long time. Reports on the two accidents were produced and included rider statements. The first accident involved one of four riders on the A23 Brighton to London road, a few miles north of Brighton, and these were the facts. The riders were travelling towards London at high speed down a succession of left and right bends which have a statutory speed limit of 50 mph, prominently signed. Their admitted speed was around 80 mph, though the reason for this was not stated. One rider failed to negotiate the last bend, ran on to the grass in the centre and lost control. His colleague behind him made a statement describing how the rear end of the machine was weaving immediately before the crash. I was to upset a subsequent meeting by questioning the value of this statement. In similar circumstances, both on and off racing circuits, I have been far too occupied with my own preservation to pay attention to the rear behaviour of an out-of-control machine immediately in front of me. It seemed quite evident to me that, unlike his three partners, the rider entered the bend on too wide a line and, at his speed, he could not get round. A colleague and I each rode through these bends at 80 mph and confirmed somewhat unnecessarily that it was impossible to get round the last one unless the correct line had been followed on the previous ones. We emphasised this at the subsequent meetings.

Meanwhile, the point at issue as far as the Police were concerned was the stability of a fully-equipped BMW on high speed bends. We asked that observed tests should be carried out and this was done a day later on roads around Lewes. The results were entirely satisfactory and should have ended the case, with a verdict of rider error. It was, in fact, just the beginning and I have always believed that, but for the second accident, nothing more would have been heard about the first. There was no relationship between the two and we would have been entirely justified in declining to discuss the crash on the airfield, as the machine was fitted with tyres which were not one of the makes approved by the factory and listed in the machine handbook. This was known to the Police and why they were used, or why the Sergeant was sent to do high speed testing on an airfield, are questions which remained unanswered. There was no witness of this accident but it was revealed that just before the rider lost control on a curve at high speed, he was passed by an Avon company rider, also on a BMW.

At a third meeting at Lewes an impasse situation was reached. We insisted that no evidence had been produced to support the claim of machine instability:

Chapter Eighteen

the A23 accident pointed clearly to rider error and as to the airfield crash, there could have been several causes which exonerated the machine. Nevertheless, the Police officials were not prepared to put the fleet back on duty, although I emphasised that hundreds were being used by other forces, without complaint. Finally, I proposed that one of the Sussex machines should be subjected to test riding on an airfield circuit where maximum speeds could be reached. The results would surely be conclusive one way or the other. This was agreed and I telephoned at once to the Thruxton circuit and booked the track. Having ridden there many times I knew that any evidence of instability would be found out by the left and right hand sharp corners of Cobb, Campbell and Seagrave, the long sweeps of Village and Church, and the tight chicane before the finishing straight. Thruxton would put an end to the arguments.

On my return to the office the following day, I had a 'phone call from the Assistant Chief Constable of Cheshire Police, whom I had known since he was a motorcycling sergeant with the old Liverpool Force. In view of the Sussex affair, the Chief Constable had decided to have a full scale test day at the Oulton Park circuit by his BMW riders, and I was invited to attend. He wished to find out for himself if there was any high speed handling problems with fully-equipped machines. Each rider would do two fast laps, video camera recorded, and the Press would be present. The circuit had been booked and I learned it was for the same day as the Thruxton tests. I imagined the consequences if any rider made a mistake and crashed at Lodge Corner, Knicker Brook or any of the other notorious bends at Oulton where many expert riders had fallen. However, the stage had been set and, although the Thruxton testing was important enough, I would know when the curtain fell at the end of the Oulton Park performance whether I had major problems or could finally end the Sussex controversy. Adverse results at either circuit could well have a serious effect on BMW Police business. The Sussex authorities and the Home Office Police Department would see to that.

I decided it was more important for me to go to Oulton Park and rely upon my boss to attend Thruxton. He was joined there by the Sussex Transport Manager and, in addition to a Sussex rider, an expert tester had flown from Germany. He lapped the circuit much faster than I have ever been able to do and he swept through the corners with the confidence of a top class TT rider. Certainly no machine as heavy as the fully-equipped BMW had ever gone round the circuit as fast as this. It handled like a racer and, to leave no doubt about the inherent stability, the rider weaved from side to side with hands away from the bars and the machine straightened out of its own accord. The demonstration was entirely conclusive.

Meanwhile, away in Cheshire, machines and riders had assembled from various parts of the county, the Press boys were there, and with the senior Police Officers was the Traffic Superintendent from Sussex. Directing operations was the

The Sussex Police Saga

Assistant Chief Constable, Cliff Halsall, who continues to enjoy riding his machine on observation patrol. I know of no other Officer of his rank who does this. After a few practice laps, the serious business began and each rider in turn accelerated away to Knicker Brook where one of the video cameras was located. To Cliff Halsall I confessed my concern that his men were lapping at racing speeds but he knew their capabilities and was not perturbed. As the last rider finished, I borrowed his machine and rode a couple of laps to end the day and I am sure I was the slowest. The Cheshire boys were really good, as I was to see later on video. At the conference which followed, the Chief Constable began by announcing that unless he could be certain that his riders had every confidence in BMW, the fleet would be withdrawn from duty without hesitation. He then instructed each rider to give his views and judgement, not only on the Oulton rides but on his experience on daily patrol. Without exception every report commended the machine, and not one criticism was made. The video recording was then shown and was most impressive. One rider took Lodge Corner so fast and at such an angle that he grounded the fairing and the film showed a piece of fibreglass flying away. The Sussex Superintendent was then invited to comment on the demonstration, but he preferred to decline and left the meeting. The Chief Constable then issued a Press statement to the effect that he and his officers were entirely satisfied with the performance and safety of BMW machines. I returned to Chiswick quite confident that, after Oulton Park and Thruxton, we should hear no more from the Sussex authorities, but I was to be proved wrong.

A report of a third accident made another visit to Lewes necessary. It was of a minor nature but, as with the A23 case, a statement had been made by a following rider about the behaviour of the machine when the rider lost control. If the statement was, in fact, correct, then I had little doubt as to what really happened. After having previously ridden Nortons with the gear change on the opposite side, the rider had either tried to change gear with the brake pedal or had forgotton that the gears operated in the reverse direction of a Norton. Several times I had made both mistakes myself but the last one was on the Pyrenees circuit and that cured me permanently.

For some time after the last visit to Lewes, all had been quiet and the machines had been put back on duty. Then trouble began again. The *Police Review* published a statement by the Sussex Traffic Department that certain modifications had been made before the machines went back into use. This was contrary to the agreement we and the Police had originally made when we jointly prepared the text of a brief announcement to be made only if either were approached by the Press. Nothing more than this would be said. Our Managing Director was upset with what appeared to be a breach of agreement and, despite my strong objections, he insisted on 'phoning the Chief Constable. Late that afternoon I had a call from Lewes. The Chief was away, the Managing Director had left a message

Chapter Eighteen

to say he would 'phone again the next morning, and did I know why? I explained the reason and added that I intended to prevent the call. Then I was advised to get a copy of the AA magazine *Drive* which would certainly stop the Managing Director from 'phoning again. I obtained one quickly and found that it contained a detailed story of the Sussex accidents and was hardly complimentary to the Police. It was clear why they had given a statement to *Police Review*. To my dismay I discovered that the story had been given to *Drive* by the Press relations man at BMW Brentford and he had obtained it from the Motorcycle Division at Chiswick.

It was essential to stop the Managing Director from 'phoning Lewes and I called his office at once. He had left and I emphasised to his secretary that I had to see him immediately he arrived in the morning. He was normally there around 9.30 and I was waiting half an hour before, watching for his car to appear in his reserved parking space. This had to be the morning when he drove it round to the Service Department and went to his office the back way. By 9.45 I was apprehensive and went to check with his secretary. She was not there but not only had her boss arrived but he was on the telephone. To the Chief Constable of Sussex. Of all people, they were the two who ought never to meet or talk to each other, especially that morning. I went into his office, was waved away angrily but stood my ground and heard the end of an unpleasant conversation which was terminated abruptly by the Chief Constable. The angry gestures were followed by angry words and I was less than respectful as I told how I had been trying, since the previous evening, to prevent the call. There was an enquiry into the leak to *Drive* but the damage was done and a difficult situation had been made worse.

It was not long before a letter arrived from the Sussex Police Authoritity Solicitor, claiming that BMW Concessionaires were held responsible for the accidents, damage to the machines and injuries sustained by the riders. We had a meeting with the company insurers and reviewed the facts of the situation. Two Police riders were claiming compensation for injuries sustained whilst on duty and in accordance with the prescribed routine they were claiming against the Police Authority. In turn, the Authority was claiming against BMW Concessionaires. What were the grounds for the claims? As far as the Police officers were concerned, they were bound to obtain compensation from one party or the other unless it could be proved that they themselves were to blame. It is a first axiom in the Police service that a driver or rider is rarely to blame for an accident. There is a legendary animal known as the Driving School dog which runs across the road whenever he is needed, and he has caused many accidents. In the case of the A23 affair, the company took the firm view that the rider was at fault but the Police asserted that the machine was to blame and, in particular, wrong tyre pressure information. They had a point here, though a very slender one. On the underside of the saddle, the tyre pressure label was out of date and the figures were two

The Sussex Police Saga

pounds below the correct ones for a fully-equipped Police model. However, the claim inferred that the other three riders were on machines with the same pressures as their colleague, so why did they not crash also if this was a critical factor in causing the accident? In any case, all the Sussex mechanics had been given a comprehensive course at the Brentford training school and should have known the correct pressures. It was absurd, in my view, to suggest that a two pounds pressure difference determined whether the rider got round the last bend or not. Finally, it had to be remembered that the pressures, as checked by our technician a day or two after the accident, might well have been lowered by the impact forces when the wheels hit the centre division of the two lanes of the road. He had reported dirt and grass between the tyre and rim of the wheels.

So much for the tyre question and now to the other two items pointed out by our examiner. The torque loading of the steering head bearings was fractionally low. The margin was so small that it could not possibly have effected the steering, and the Police did not suggest the contrary. In any case the torque setting was a service responsibility of the Police mechanics who were quite familiar with the recommended figure. The third item was the setting of the rear suspension units. They were found to be in the maximum load position and this was quite wrong. The rider was below average weight and the machine handbook stated quite clearly the correct settings. For normal weight rider, the bottom position and, for a very heavy rider, the middle position. The top position to be used only for a rider with pillion passenger and heavy luggage. The company did not make an issue out of the wrong setting because, like the other two items, it did not in our opinion make the difference between negotiating the bend and crashing.

Turning now to the airfield accident, the company was clearly in no position to discuss circumstances of which they knew nothing except that unapproved tyres had been used. Whereas they had been used knowing that they were not approved by the factory as being suitable, we did not suggest or infer that they had been the cause of the rider losing control. Indeed, the Avon company test rider was going even faster on his BMW, with no problems. Only the Police Sergeant himself could know what really happened and all we were told from his report was that the machine went out of control at high speed on a bend. I was always curious not only about why the testing was done on an airfield with unapproved tyres, but why the rider was a Sergeant instead of a civilian mechanic whose job included testing. Once I asked a senior Metro Officer for his comment and he replied that he would not like to be the person responsible for instructing any Police Officer to carry out such testing, especially in those circumstances.

Now that the Legal Department of the Sussex Police had taken over, there could be no further discussions and our Insurers were instructed to follow their normal procedure but to disclaim responsibility. In due course we were advised that unless the claims were met, action would be taken in the courts. By this time

Chapter Eighteen

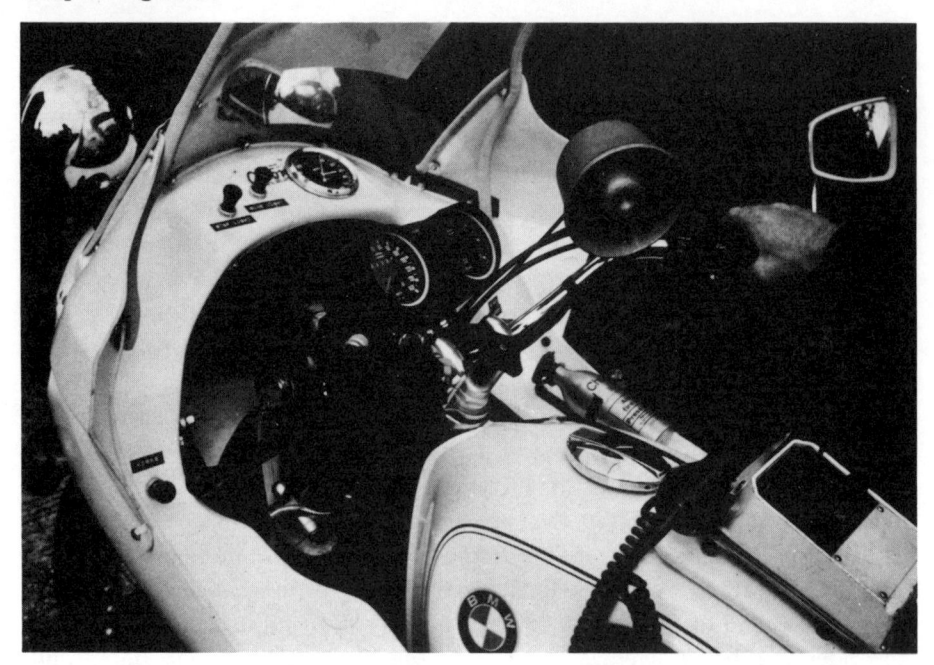

A close-up of the cockpit of an R75/6 model supplied fully equipped to the Avon and Somerset Constabulary. Note the specially-calibrated Smiths Chronometric speedometer mounted immediately behind the screen. The original equipment speedometer alongside the tachometer is disconnected. [M. Haimes]

the whole affair had dragged on well into 1979, more than two years after the accidents. I urged that the company should stand firm and I had complete confidence that a court action would be successfully defended. More time passed, we were informed that a date had been set for the court hearing but, as nothing happened by that time, I began to believe that no more would be heard.

At the end of 1979, the Concessionaire franchise for BMW ended its contractual term and the UK market was taken over by BMW (GB) Ltd. a direct subsidiary of the German company. This meant, as far as the Sussex affair was concerned, that the new company was not involved. Or should not be. Occasionally, I enquired whether there had been any further developments and the answer was always negative, until around the middle of 1980. The solicitors on either side had been going through the prescribed legal performances and neither wanted to go as far as court proceedings. I would have preferred that they did. As I had expected, the suggestion of adverse publicity for BMW emerged and the new company, or in other words the German parent organisaztion, was close to becoming involved. The solicitors for the ex-Concessionaires were prepared to recommend out-of-court settlement to avoid the expense of legal costs, but they wanted the German company to share the amount of settlement. The correspondence was passed to me and I submitted to Germany a report on the complete history of events with the strongest recommendation against making any contribution. It was quite clear to me that the ex-Concessionairs had no further interest in the affair and had left it to their insurers. It no longer mattered to them if BMW suffered adverse publicity and in any case they now had the franchise for an Italian competitor.

The Legal Department of BMW headquarters sent me a copy of the letter they had written to the ex-Concessionaire's solicitors and I was shocked to find that it did not disagree with the suggestion of a settlement contribution. With only a short time to go before I ended my service with BMW (GB) Ltd. I could have been excused for taking no further interest in this long drawn out affair. However, my personal principles were involved. I had maintained from the beginning that the machines were not to blame and for BMW Germany to make any contribution to a settlement would tacitly, if not directly, admit some product design or quality responsibility. I knew from my Norton and Triumph experiences how dangerous this could be.

I was due to fly to Munich with two Scotland Yard engineers and I telexed to make an appointment with the Legal Department Executive who was handling the case. My discussion with him was short and to the point. He had studied my report on the accident histories, there was clearly no evidence that the machines had any inherent fault and, if the ex-Concessionaire's insurers chose to make a settlement out-of-court, that was a decision which could not and must not involve the factory. He commented upon the publicity which would result from any court proceedings. I was adamant that the result of a court hearing could not possibly be adverse to BMW but on the other hand, there could well be unfortunate inferences if BMW contributed to settlement of the Sussex claims. He accepted my advice and sent me a copy of his letter to the solicitors stating that the BMW company found no reason to support the settlement made by the ex-Concessionaires.

My job was done and I closed my file of correspondence on an affair which had been unique in my experience of Police business. Over the years I had known Police riders killed on Triumph and Nortons but never before had I been involved in anything so controversial and yet so simple as the Sussex affair. I had spent many hours and days trying to bring it to a proper conclusion but, in the end, the solicitors had determined the outcome. They were paid their fees, the riders were paid their claims and I was not even thanked for preventing the factory from creating a precedent which could be used by any Police rider who crashed on a BMW in future. My major regret was that Sussex Police ultimately changed to Guzzi but, by that time, nearly 2,000 BMWs were in use with other forces. In late 1980 I was on my way back from Brighton on my BMW Police R80 after watching the

Chapter Eighteen

Veteran Car Run. Near Crawley I found a Sussex Police rider with a broken-down Guzzi. I was able to find the trouble and get the machine going, but I resisted the temptation to tell him who I was and send my compliments to his Superintendent.

Chapter Nineteen

The Last Lap

BEFORE THE seven million pounds premises opened at Bracknell on 2nd January 1980, all office accommodation was either already occupied or reserved. The staff was almost entirely new and in charge of the Motorcycle Division were three gentlemen from Volkswagen. My two assistants and I had been delayed in clearing up work at Chiswick and when we arrived at Bracknell it seemed that we had been forgotten. The whole office area of the proud Police Division at Chiswick was demoted to half an office at Bracknell and my assistants had to find a desk in the car sales section. I had a feeling that my department was intended to lose the specialised identity it had earned, and it was not long before my apprehension was justified. The title Police Division was to be dropped and the department absorbed into the general motorcycle operation. The new Sales Director, with no experience of motorcycle business, listened to the reasons for my objections, fully accepted my arguments but a day or two later went ahead with the change. It heralded the policies which the new company was to introduce and which followed the Munich pattern. BMW Bracknell was a computer-orientated marketing operation which discounted personal involvement with the product and customer. Market penetration, dealer promotions, corporate identity planning, and compu-

Chapter Nineteen

A test run on the Police R80 which I rode to Denmark and back, via north Germany.

ter operations, occupied most of the comfortable offices and the parking area for company staff cars was larger than the Brentford and Chiswick premises put together. It had to be, for the staff was twice the size it had been previously. I missed the modest office at Chiswick and its Police rider visitors, often sitting on a pile of panniers as they drank coffee. I missed the two tone horn salutes of the Special Escort Group as they rode by on their way to Windsor or Heathrow. The magnificent new premises had no room for the motorcycling atmosphere of Chiswick and it was not long before I was told to keep my riding gear out of sight.

As spring approached, the income of more orders indicated that the total of 2,000 would be reached even before the end of the year, but technical problems intensified the work of the Police Department. The increasing failures of centre stands finally demanded an expensive campaign change to prevent the distortion

The Last Lap

of frame lugs, which would then necessitate replacing the entire frame. We examined the first cases and saw what modification was required. The private rider, who used his centre stand once or twice a week, might never have any trouble, but the design was not good enough for a fully-equipped Police machine which used the stand many times each day. The bolts worked loose, allowing the stand to twist and frame damage was imminent. The situation was too urgent to wait for factory modification components so we went ahead with our own and had them manufactured quickly. The first 85 sets were fitted to the new fleet of machines awaited by Metro Police and within a few days the affected machines of other Forces were dealt with. There was a humorous sequel to the problem. A senior service engineer flew from Germany to inspect examples of stand failures and we took him to the Birmingham workshop of the West Midlands Police. I learned, incidentally, that in his travels around the world he had met people I knew well in countries like Jamaica, Kuwait and Dubai. After the workshops he was taken for lunch to Police headquarters in Queensway. In the dining room at the top of the very high building, he stood looking out over Birmingham and a senior Police Officer asked conversationally if he had seen Birmingham before. The answer, given quietly as he gazed across the rebuilt city, was somewhat unfortunate. 'Yes' said the German guest, 'many times from a Heinkel'.

A complex problem arose involving gearboxes and it first affected Metro Police machines. The early symptoms were increasingly fierce clutches, unpleasant and potentially dangerous. I was to have the same trouble with the R100 I rode in the International Circuit des Pyrenees in June. Helped by Metro engineers we found the cause and the cure. With constant use in congested traffic the gearbox casing was stretching laterally, causing excessive play of the input shaft. Excessive play meant only 40 thousandths of an inch but it was enough to destroy proper clutch operation. Shimming prevented any further trouble and closer quality control over gearbox manufacture was promised to eradicate the problem in future. Once again, UK Police had proved the most effective testers.

In my past years with Triumph and Norton I had the highest regard for the ability of Police engineers, workshop mechanics and riders. A Police motorcycle has to work very much harder than its civilian counterpart and technical improvements have often been the result of Police experience. I like to feel that BMW machines have benefited accordingly and this will continue if Munich have carried out all promises made when I took two Metro engineers there on my final visit in 1980. One of the items on the agenda was the alloy wheel, which is a good example of a specification change which was introduced without being subjected to the conditions likely to confront Police riders. The replacement of wire spoked wheels by alloy was a fashion set by the Japanese and was the natural outcome of racing practise. However, not all racing development is good for ordinary machines and, as far as wheels are concerned, there is a great difference between a

Chapter Nineteen

racing motorcycle designed to survive for a few hundred miles and a Police machine weighing nearly twice as much and expected to last for years.

When the first consignment of Police models arrived with alloy wheels, I did not like the change and considered it retrograde as far as the appearance was concerned. However, the machines were delivered to various Police forces, including Metropolitan. The immediate reaction was that whereas the average cost of repairing a buckled spoked wheel was not much more then ten pounds, a damaged alloy wheel would require a very expensive replacement. Insurance companies already had good reason to know this and to know also that fork and frame damage could result. The Metro riders soon discovered the limitations of the new wheels when controlling a large crowd of marching demonstrators, and having to ride up and down street kerbs. My telex to Germany ensured that all future Police machines were fitted with spoked wheels, and incidentally at an appreciable extra cost.

In May, when a new Police demonstrator was being prepared, I thought I would run it in and add a few more hundred miles to my log book. I rode it from Bracknell to Harwich and crossed overnight to Bremerhaven by the same ferry service which carries BMW cars and motorcycles to England. From there via Bremen to Hamburg over the north German plain, notorious for strong winds which frequently blow at gale force from the sea. I had experienced them before on Triumphs and Nortons and this time they were worse. Leaning the machine into the wind and keeping it straight on the two lane autobahn was often hectic and it was never upright all the way to Hamburg, except when passing under bridges. In the Hamburg area major road alterations and diversions were causing traffic confusion and, as I picked up the E4 route to Lubeck, a German Police car came alongside. The observer lowered his window, saluted and beckoned me to follow him. With two tone horns clearing a way through the traffic we soon left Hamburg behind and with a clear road ahead I was waved past and given a farewell salute. Then I remembered that on the left sleeve of my riding suit was the green and gold badge of the Bavarian Police, the Bayerischer Landespolizei, presented to me at Police headquarters, Munich. A useful decoration on this occasion but one which was to cause awkward questions a few weeks later on the E3 near Nurenberg.

Beyond Neustadt, where the autobahn ended and became a second class road, I stopped for petrol and chatted to a couple of young Danes who were making their way home from Italy on an elderly Triumph twin which was due to expire at any time. Laden with luggage and with no front or rear suspension left, it was struggling on with no help from one cylinder. Several cigarettes later I was able to get the motor running more happily on both. I hurried on to the end of the German E4 at Puttgarten and, as I came in sight of the harbour, my ferry was just leaving. However the Danes joined me on the next one and we talked motorcycles all the way across to Rodbyhavn in south Denmark. From there, another 120

The Last Lap

miles brought me to my destination north of Copenhagen, seven hours after leaving Bremerhaven. The BMW had 500 miles on the clock and would be able to use higher speeds on the return journey three days later. This proved unfortunate for a Mercedes driver west of Hamburg. I was overtaking a long line of heavy vehicles and the Merc made a nuisance of himself flashing his lights to get by when there was no room for me to pull over. I moved in between two trucks at the first possible gap and as he went past accelerating hard, I came out behind him. Suddenly from the Merc exhaust pipe came a large cloud of smoke and as he pulled across to the hard shoulder, I took a quick look at a very discomfited German. No doubt in his teutonic hurry to get away from a GB motorcycle, he had missed a gear, the revs had gone way beyond the red line, and a valve had holed a piston. I reached Bremerhaven in good time, leaning the opposite way this time against the still strong wind. From Harwich the next morning I rode to Norwich and handed the machine over to the Police, who were waiting to evaluate it against their Guzzis. They were one of only two forces using the Italian machines and by the time I resigned from BMW six months later it appeared that the evaluation results were bad news for Guzzi.

As June arrived I looked forward to what would surely be my last ride in the International Circuit des Pyrenees. I was anxious to use one of the several prototype GS80 models which, with its road and rough country capabilities, would have been ideal for the mountain tracks. The new machine was due to be announced a few weeks later and I thought some advance publicity would be welcomed by the factory. I telexed a personal appeal but received a negative reply and so I again used an R100, with the results described in another chapter. After returning from the event I began to consider plans for celebrating Police BMW delivery number 2,000. The first idea was a repeat of the 1,000 delivery at Thruxton but to take place more centrally at Donington. Cost quotations went far beyond my budget and so I checked with Mallory Park. This seemed a very appropriate venue, being at Earl Shilton, close to my home town, but the facilities were unsuitable to entertain several hundred Police Officers. Time was short as the 2,000 figure would be achieved in August and suddenly I thought of tying up the project with the Earls Court Show where I would, in any case, be having the traditional Police luncheon. Having been on duty at every post-war show, the 1980 one would not only be my last but also the last International Show to be held at Earls Court. The idea grew and, thinking back to November 1946 when I rode my Speed Twin from the Meriden factory to the show, I knew that I had to ride from Munich to my last one.

A new fleet of 50 R80 Police models was due to be despatched from the Berlin factory at the beginning of August and I telexed for one to be prepared for collection at Munich on Thursday 21st, the day before the Show Press review. This was in the middle of the German National holiday period and I could obtain no

Chapter Nineteen

My 1980 and last ride in the Circuit des Pyrenees. The photograph was taken on the long climb through the Issaux Forest, which leads to the top of the Houratate Mountain.

information as to where the machine would be located and whether it would be prepared or still in its crate. However, I went ahead with my plans, the press release was issued promising my arrival at Earls Court at 10 am on Friday 22nd and in due course my deputy and I drove to Dover, en route to Munich. The car boot was packed with Police equipment, panniers, two tone horns, radio cradle, Police signs, plus tools, oil and UK registration plates. We arrived at our Munich hotel in late evening, expecting to find a message telling us to 'phone someone or informing us where to find the machine the next day. There was nothing and my earlier impression that the factory had no interest in the project seemed to be correct.

The next day we went to the main office building and talked with a Security Officer, who did some telephoning and directed us to the export collection centre some distance away. There we found a very helpful girl who came from Penrith in Cumbria and who knew about us. The machine was there and we spent the rest of the day working on it, helped by Munich beer which Miss Penrith kindly fetched for us. On the following morning I was anxious to start the long journey quickly,

The Last Lap

especially as the French channel ports were strike bound and there were reports of long queues at Ostend where we were making for. Surprisingly, a publicity man and photographer arrived as I was getting into my riding gear and they were somewhat upset when I declined to ride into the centre of Munich for pictures. At around 11 am, with my companion following in the car, I joined the E6 autobahn, and began the 500 plus miles to Ostend via Nurenberg, Frankfurt, Cologne, Liege and Brussels. Keeping the rev counter needle at 3500 and easing back the throttle, to help the new engine, was irksome on the German autobahns which have no speed restrictions. Some distance beyond Nurenberg I slowed down approaching a petrol service area and a car came alongside, with the driver and passenger signalling me to stop. They rushed from the car, told me in German to stop the engine and get off the machine. They were distinctly unfriendly and I did not see why I should obey, especially as it was raining. I invited them to join me under the roof of the petrol station, which annoyed them and repeating their instructions they produced their Police identity cards and demanded my passport and driving license. This made things awkward, as they were in the car with my colleague and there was no sign of him. How does a motorcyclist explain to the German Criminal Police that his documents are in a car which is nowhere to be seen? I was about to be taken back to Nurenberg when I remembered that in one pannier I had put the export documents for the machine. I began to open the pannier and two hands reached for pistol holsters, so I handed over the keys and the document was examined. Then began the game of questions and answers. 'Where have you come from?' — 'I have come from Munich'. 'Then why is this document prepared at Berlin?' — 'Because, as you should know, the BMW motorcycle factory is in Berlin, but the export collection establishment is in Munich'. 'Where are you going and why?' — 'I am riding to the International Motorcycle Exhibition in London where this machine will be displayed as number 2,000 to be supplied to the UK Police'. 'Why do they use BMW instead of British?' I was getting wet and I gave only a brief answer. There was one final question. 'Why are you wearing a Bavarian Police badge?' — 'Because it was given to me by the Traffic Chief when I took Scotland Yard Officers to Munich headquarters last year and I rather like it'. I was permitted to go after they had explained unnecessarily that they had never before seen a motorcycle in Germany wearing British Police signs. I would think they will never see another.

As the kilometres and hours passed by I took the engine up to 4,000 and made good time to the German/Belgian customs control at Aachen, where the officials did not even want to see any document. I have been through there many times and only once, when I had a machine on a trailer, was I asked for papers. Riding with Police markings I was always waved straight through. Approaching Liege after dark the heavens opened and the storms continued until the glow of the Ostend lights appeared in the sky. I was grateful for the fairing on the BMW

Chapter Nineteen

UK Police BMW number 2,000 north of Nuremburg, en route to Earls Court. The Police signs had just been covered over with masking tape to avoid any more questions from the Politzei.

which kept me dry, except that the wash from the front wheel went through my riding boots. Behind me my companion could just see my tail lamp through rain so heavy that his wind screen wipers could not cope. My only problem was misted goggles and I have never been able to solve that. The delay at Ostend was a long one and we were glad to get on board and open a bottle in the cabin. I left Dover at 07.30 and by far the worst miles of the whole journey were those from the south of London in the morning traffic. As I pulled into the Warwick Road entrance to Earls Court, the clock on the BMW said 9.40 and the journey was over twenty minutes ahead of schedule. From the tube exit as I stopped came my old friend Bengt Bjorklund, the Editor of the Scandinavian motorcycle journal *MC Nytt,* and he took the first pictures which were used in his story 'The last ride to Earls Court'. Twelve years before he had done the pictures and story of my ride from Gothenburg to open the International Show at Stockholm. I waited outside

The Last Lap

The end of the ride from Munich to the 1980 Earls Court Show on Police BMW number 2,000.

The photographer insisted on having a pretty girl to brighten up the photograph.

Chapter Nineteen

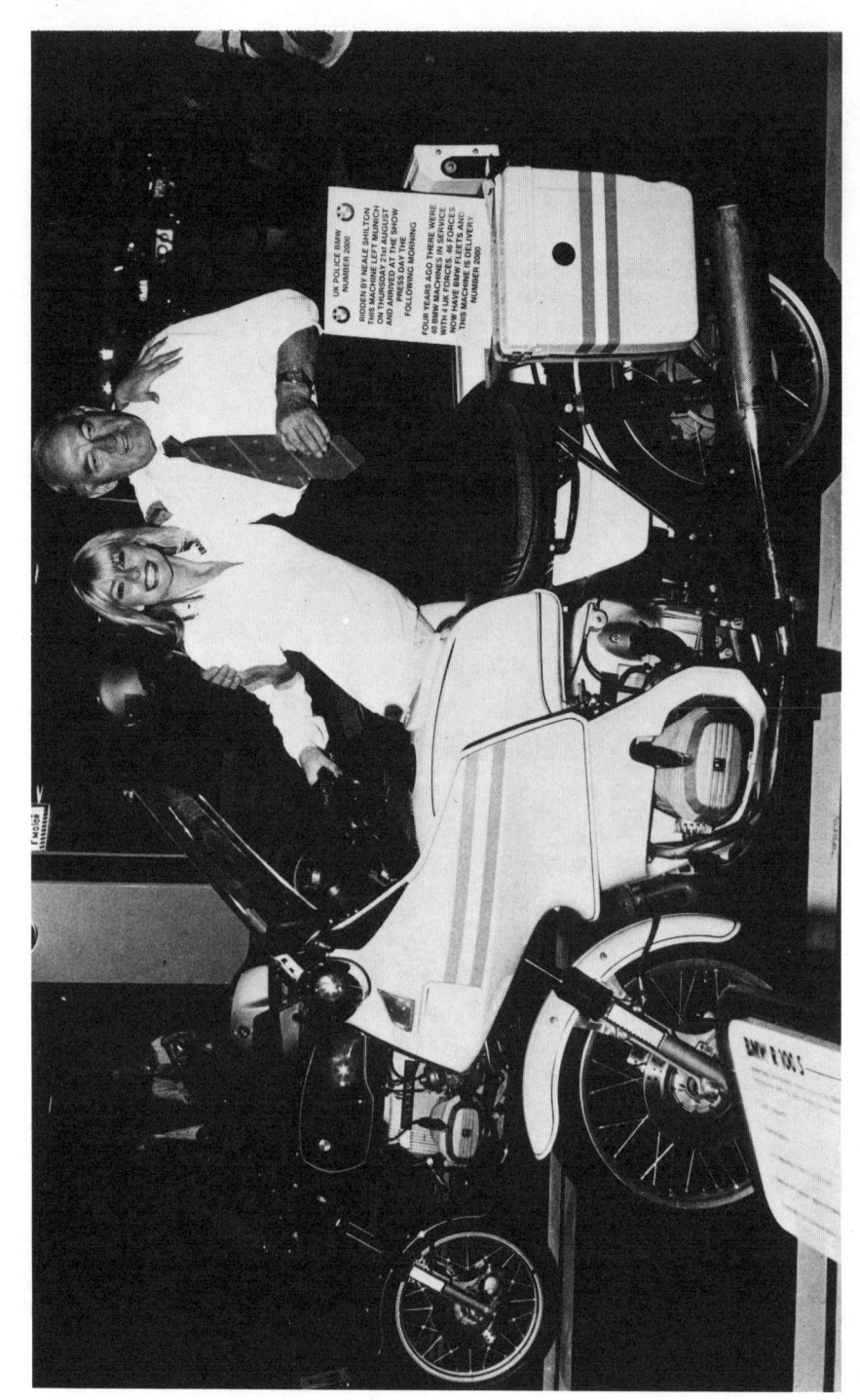

Inside Earls Court number 2,000 takes its place on the BMW stand, and I take my place to be photographed for the last time at my 35th and last Show.

The Last Lap

Earls Court whilst a dolly bird was brought out for other photographers. It seemed that pictures at the end of a high-speed ride from Munich had to feature a pretty model. The machine was displayed on the BMW stand and on the Thursday of show week I was host at the last of the many Police Guest Days I had organised over the years. In the Westminster Suite, crowded with Police friends from many forces and others, including John Surtees, I said a few words of farewell. It was in the same room that I had held my first Triumph Police function thirty years before, the same room where I had introduced my Triumph Saint and Norton Interpol. The room held many memories and as I talked I did not quite succeed in hiding feelings which were somewhat emotional.

There remained three months before I left BMW Bracknell and there was still plenty of work to be done. Some technical problems had not been cleared up by the factory and I made my last visit to Munich accompanied by two senior engineers of Metro Police. This time we had meetings at top level and I believed that at last the factory accepted that the requests and recommendations of the UK Police service would be of the most important benefit to BMW quality. On my return I prepared detailed minutes of the meetings and sent copies to Munich, with a request for progress reports on the various items. It was not until after I had left the Company that assurances were given that everything necessary was being done and that the UK Police market was of the highest importance. I would have welcomed this statement several years earlier. In November, several weeks before my departure, the first of the 1981 Police models arrived. I had insisted on testing this before confirming the first fleet order for the new season as I was apprehensive about the power output reduction from 55 to 50. I was also concerned because the R80 civilian version was being dropped from the 1981 range, which I considered a retrograde decision. The export price to Bracknell of the Police R80 was adjusted to make it the same as the R100 1000 cc Police model and, although Munich did not say so, it seemed to me that they would like to abandon the R80 and have all Police Forces buy the larger version. Undoubtedly both machines cost the same to manufacture as the only difference was the engine capacity. However, I knew that many Chief Constables and their Traffic Chief Superintendents would take the view that the 105 mph R80 was fast enough and anything quicker was undesirable. I could not see the Metro Police needing the 1000 cc model for use in the Metropolis and I anticipate a problem should the factory finally cease production of the R80. Although the smaller 650 cc R65 performance would probably be adequate for many Forces, there would be technical difficulties with battery capacity and the fairing, which has no provision for installing the air horn compressor nor the radio control box.

I test rode the 1981 R80 on varying types of roads, including the M3 motorway, and found it very interesting. Compared with its predecessor, the engine seemed more eager and I first suspected that lower gear ratios had been used to

Chapter Nineteen

compensate for the lower power output. However, Munich denied this and the reason for the livelier engine had to be ascribed to the lighter clutch. My apprehension about a lower maximum speed was dispelled when I saw the needle closing on the 100 mph mark with some throttle left. I had no time to test with a certified accurate speedometer but I was informed after I left the company that Metro Police had conducted satisfactory performance tests. Knowing their competent methods I had no doubt that the new model relected the efforts made by the factory to satisfy the demands of Metro and all other forces. So be it. My last ride on the machine was to fulfil a long standing engagement at Papplewick School, Ascot, a preparatory school of distinction, and I recalled memories of the evening when John Surtees visited my son's prep. school years before. I took along my 'motorcycle man' film and after it was shown I talked to the boys about all apsects of motorcycling and my million miles of riding. Question time went on to school bedtime and many questions could well have come from much older boys. One youngster of nine or so came up with a complex one when he asked 'Sir, after so many miles of serious motorcycling, demonstrating, testing, and selling machines for your factories, are you now going to ride for pleasure?' I answered truthfully that all my motorcycling had given me pleasure and although I was leaving the motorcycle business, I could not imagine saying goodbye to motorcycling. At the end of my film story I am asked why I still competed in the International Circuit des Pyrenees at more than twice the age of other competitors. I have ridden in a few more since I gave the answer quoted in the story of this event. I once told Percy Tait that I would stop riding when he did and now I learn that in the 1981 Island Classic, he lapped at 100 mph. Maybe he will emulate the great Stanley Woods, ten times a TT winner who had his first Island Race in 1922 and in June 1981 and 1982 was rushing around the Mallory Circuit.

  I said farewell to my colleagues at Bracknell at the end of November 1980, not quite five years after I joined BMW Concessionaires at Brentford and started work on their target of 100 Police machines. I left behind a UK fleet total of 2,000 and a potential annual order income of around 500 replacements. Whether the word potential should read reliable depends upon two factors. One of them is the essential need to maintain a high standard of quality and service. The other rests upon the survival and progress of Triumph, for if Meriden can again produce a machine of the Saint quality, then in time they could recover a lot of the Police business which was once all their own. Although the workshops of fifty UK Police Forces are tooled up for BMW, and mechanics have been BMW trained, many Police authorities are committed to take acceptable Triumph machines. Many times in the past, and indeed recently, those machines have been promised but are still awaited. Their emergence must in any case depend upon the ability of Meriden to rebuild the foundations of its once successful markets now dominated by the Japanese. The prospects look remote but when I left Bracknell and travel-

The Last Lap

led eastwards, I would have preferred to travel northwards to Meriden and offer some help. After the last Earls Court Show the Press printed a report that I would be doing that and rejoining my old company. A cynical friend said that I would be warmly welcomed provided I took along £5 million. He added that Government interest in Meriden was greater than it had ever been, but the problem was that the company could not pay it. I can only hope that by the time this book is published, the Meriden flag will be flying higher than its present half mast position but the reports which reach me as I near the end of my stories indicate that it is likely to be lowered further.

When I left England, I sailed from Harwich on the same ship which had taken me to Scandinavia, twice with a Saint and once with an Interpol. I looked back and watched the lights of the Essex and Suffolk coastline become fainter until they disappeared into the darkness of the North Sea. At the end of that half hour watch, an idea came to me and I went to my cabin to write down the theme of a book to be called 'A Million Miles Ago'.

Epilogue

THIS HAS been the chronicle of many experiences, of many miles, of many memories and especially of many friendships. It is good to know that I do not need to travel far in Britain, or indeed in most continental countries, before there is a welcome from someone whose friendship I owe to the years of my life with motorcycles. There are the more distant countries to which a cable will ensure a warm greeting at the airport and the invitation to stay at the home of someone I have known from my Triumph days. No other industry could produce such reward and I am fortunate to have enjoyed its happier years. Now as I look around the Japanese-dominated scene I am sure that those involved can never experience the pleasures and friendships which were once the very basis of the industry and trade. Of course that basis was not enough to sustain for ever the factories of Woolwich, Birmingham, Coventry, and Redditch, but it did so for some fifty years and the Japanese have a long way to go to beat that. With their present volume of production, Honyamuki are heading rapidly towards world market saturation and no brilliant new model can overcome that barrier. Ah so!

My log book of memories is separated under two headings, personal and commercial, or in other words motorcycling and motorcycle business. Some of

Epilogue

Looking back over the years and miles. The BMW motif is no longer on the helmet, but the other remains. It is the emblem of the Federation of British Police Motor Clubs, to which I was elected an Honorary Member in Marsh 1977 for services to Police motorcycling sport.

the million miles were difficult, most were enjoyable, but all gave a rewarding satisfaction. The airfield at St. Nazaire, the rides to and from Montlhéry, Cologne, Hanover, Geneva, Belgrade, The Hague, Copenhagen, Stockholm and the ten unforgettable experiences in the Circuit Des Pyrenees. When the Norton Villiers Triumph Company was liquidated I bought the cabinet which once displayed the many TT trophies won by Norton. It now contains my own, some from the Pyrenees years, Royal Signals, Royal Marines, the Federation of British Police Motor Clubs, Scotland Yard, the City of London and other Police Forces. I would have liked just one replica from the Isle of Man but my entry for the 1948 Manx was vetoed by Edward Turner. The commercial entries in my log book begin pleasantly when I joined Triumph but then recall unpleasant events, beginning at the day when Sangster announced the sale of Triumph to BSA which, as we know now, determined the fate of both. If only he had formed a public company instead, Meriden would have been a strong company today and my log book would not have had these sad entries. My resignation after my last battle with Lionel Jofeh to protect Triumph, the destruction of my Saint and Interpol, the failure of my efforts to keep the Wolverhampton factory open. The promise to General Aloufi which was not kept and which was my only failure to

Epilogue

I had to wait until now for a ride on a Triumph Tiger 90. This immaculate specimen was one of the first to be built in 1936 when the Triumph Engineering Company was formed by Jack Sangster. The machine is part of a Danish collection.

honour an undertaking. The bad Nortons which went to my friends in Kuwait. The last entry in my list of disappointments is comparatively unimportant except that it again illustrates the attitudes of those I have met in the Industry who were not motorcyclists and could not properly understand those who were. At BMW Bracknell now, the smallest office amongst the many others of spacious executive standard is occupied by one man, my ex-deputy. He is the Police Department, the only remaining evidence of the division which I built up from nothing at Brentford to become the proud supplier of motorcycles and cars to 50 UK Forces. I first appointed him because he was a practical motorcyclist but, as I was reminded in the early days of Bracknell, riding gear must not be allowed to disfigure the office.

Credit must go to BMW for giving to Triumph every opportunity to recover the UK Police business, but it seems that the opportunity will not be taken. The financial support given to the so-called Workers Co-Operative by the Government should have ensured their survival and progress but, whatever may be the merits and the ideals of a worker-controlled company, there has to be a capable and fully supported supremo. He was not allowed to exist by the shop floor Board of Directors and when my old colleague John Nelson, ex-Triumph Service Manager, came back from the Puch company as Managing Director Meriden, he was promptly told to stay in his office and not interfere. He soon returned to

Epilogue

Many of my miles were ridden on Triumphs and I now enjoy adding to them on this beautifully preserved 1939 Speed Twin, despite the girder forks and lack of rear springing. It brings back many memories of the happy days of the motorcycle industry, of friends too numerous to mention in this book, and with whom I enjoyed the pleasures that only motorcycling can give.

Puch. More recently some of the remaining good Meriden men left to join the Hesketh project at Daventry and those who remain may wonder how long it will be before one of the supplier creditors, or perhaps the Government, calls in the Official Receiver. After Sangster and Edward Turner he has been the next most successful figure in the British motorcycle industry.

    Recently, I had a letter from a past colleague written on paper carrying the old piled arms trademark of BSA, the Birmingham Small Arms Company, but with the modified name BSA Company Ltd. At the bottom, the Directors' names are headed by the Chairman and who else could it be but R.D.Poore, still retaining a slender interest in what remains of the industry which, in his own words, the Government invited him to rescue in 1972. The range of lightweights now marketed under the BSA name helps the Italians and the Japanese, who manufacture the engines. As to the Norton name, it is preserved on the tank of the long-delayed rotary model, and Mr.Poore would do well to note that even Suzuki abandoned this type of machine after a very short attempt at production which did severe damage to their finances. Perhaps Mr.Poore will donate his prototype to the British Motorcycle Museum being built near Meriden. I suggest that Mr.Poore is invited to open the Museum by lighting the eternal flame of a brazier to perpetuate the memory of the Meriden factory which he closed. With an escort of the 1973 pickets and perhaps the original brazier around which they stood for two winters.

INDEX

A

Aagesen, Jorgen 193
Adiseba, Colonel 195
Allen, Johnny 95, 99-102
Aloufi, General 229, 234, 291
Alves, Jim 66, 69, 86
Amal carburettors 97
AMC Group 137, 182
American Motorcycles Association 96
Amsterdam Show 122-4, 136
Anderson, Andy 26
Anderton, C.J. 188
Anthony Gibbs Ltd. 229, 231, 237, 246-7
Ariel Arrow 166
Ariel 3 145, 172
Ariel Pixie 145, 172
Aubury, Norman 116
Automobile Association 60
Avon Fairing 37, 80-1, 115, 157, 249
Avon Somerset Constabulary 266, 274

B

Bablake School 10
Bacon, Alice MP 159
Bailey, Graham 110
Baker, Edwin 238
Baker, Frank 59, 167
Baker, John 239
Banbury Run 123
Barker, Alf 152
Barnett, J. 92
Baumer, Hans 61
Bayliss, Len 63-5
Beaumont, Peter 256
Beckford Hotel 31
Bedfordshire Police 120
Beier, Mogens 177
Bell, Artie 43, 48, 168
Bennett, Alec 43
Bennett, Brigadier 18
Bennett, Cliff 23
Benton, Margaret 210
Bevan, Robert 28
Bijani, Sabeh 229
Bills, Ken 46, 48, 51
Bingham, Bing 20
Bingham, Phil 255
Bjorklund, Bengt 125, 176, 284
Blamire, Percy 11
Blandford Circuit 57
BMW Concessionaires Chapters 16-8
BMW GB Ltd. Chapters 18-9
Bonneville Salt Flats 99, 100
Boudin, George 43
Bourne, Arthur 26, 34
Bradley, Peter 26-7
Brandon Speedway 13
Briggs, Alf 182
British Communications Corporation 80, 84
British Motorcycle Museum 102, 293
British Motorcyclists Federation 228
Brittain, Vic 27
Brown, Lord George 174, 176, 191
Bryant, Tom 41
BSA B40 169, 171
BSA Beagle 145, 172
BSA Beeza 145, 172
BSA Dandy 145
Buckley, Wilf 13
Burney, Bob 21
Burton, Squib 13

Index

C

Californian Institute of Technology 97
Camfield, Tiny 37
Camwell, Alf 49, 60
Cave, Alistair 235
Central Office of Information 210, 213
Ceylon Police 129
Charteris, Leslie 110
Circuit des Pyrenees Chapter 14, 282
City of London Police 245
Clare, PC 158
Clarke, Barbara 49
Clarke, Freddie 45-6, 48-9, 59
Clarke, Jack 248
Clement, Ted 257
Coates, Rod 166
Colcombe, Archie 29
Coles, Bert 139, 151
Collier Brothers 183
Cologne Exhibition 111, 193
Colquhoun, W.B. 183, 189, 203, 207, 223-4, 227, 237
Cooper, John 74
Cope, Douglas 43
Cope, Frank 32, 43
Cope, Roy 43
Cossor Radio 107
Craig, Joe 59, 136
Crossley, Don 49
Currie, Bob 164

D

Daily Express 110
Daily Mail 112, 118
Daimler Cars 88
Dale, Dickie 43
Daniell, Harold 25, 27, 43, 48-9
Danish Army 169-71
Danish Triumph Importers 52
Davies, Dickie 31

Davies, Doreen 57
Davies, Howard 43
Davies, Ivor 46, 57, 84-5, 101, 135
Davison, Geoff 43, 48
Dixon, Freddie 43, 46
Docker, Sir Bernard 84
Donohue, Deirdre 257
Douglas Dirt Track 13
Draper, Major Chris 144
Duke, Geoff 66, 138
Duke of Kent 191-2
Dunlop Tyres 97, 99

E

Earls Court Show 55, 90, 281, 285, 286
Eddy, Jack 30
Ekins, Bud 125
Elder, Sprouts 13
Elson, John 28
Emmerson, Bill 203
Enfield Bullet 225
Enfield India 225, 227, 236
E.T. Developments 84
Evans, Wilmot 26, 27
Eyre, R.E. MP 232-3

F

Fairbairn, Ken 257
Fallon, Kay 240
Farmer, Len 112, 158
Farndon, Tommy 13
Fearon, Bob 148-9
Federation of British Police Motor Clubs 291
F.I.A. 97
Fiji Police 128
F.I.M. 96-7, 100, 103
Finlayson PC 113

295

Index

Foenss, Bo 209
Fosse Way 30
Foster, Bob 39, 40, 48, 168
Fowler, Rem 25, 40, 41, 61
Fox, C.P. 92
Frith, Freddie 47-9, 162, 168, 176, 178
Fry, Frank 43
FVRDE Chobham 80, 119

G

Garda Police 247
Garde Republicaine 126, 132, 201, 211, 231, 260
Gaymer, Bert 86
Goodby, Harry 41
Gott, John 155
Gough, Eddie 152
Goujon, Jean 231
Graham, Les 24, 40, 43
Grandfield, Charles 89
Great Rift Valley 19
Greek Gendarmerie 191
Griffiths, Thomas 28

H

Hack, George 11, 13
Hailwood, Mike 35-6, 43, 93, 94, 193
Hailwood, Stanley 24, 35-6, 43, 84, 93
Hallen, Les 121
Halsall, Cliff 263, 271
Hammond, Peter 86
Hampshire Police 254
Hampshire, Susan 254, 256
Handley, Walter 11, 43
Hargreaves, Bernard 87
Harley Davidson 17, 20
Harley Peashooter 13
Harris, 'Bomber' 131
Harrison, Jim 43, 181-2

Hartle, John 43
Hawkins, Ron 199
Heath, Phil 198
Hele, Doug 59, 135, 155
Hicks, Bill 34
Hicks, Freddie 46
Hickson, John 41
Higgins, Terence MP 188
High Waterguard Officer 121, 123
Hill, Brian 256
Hitchcock, Jock 72
Holland, Harry 79
Home Office Police Dept 258, 268
Homer Company 107, 185
Honda 50 181
Hopwood, Bert 135-6, 139, 148, 150-1, 154-6, 163-6, 172-3, 178, 180
Horsman, Victor 43
Huggett, Sam 26
Hunt, Len 30
Huxham, Joe 39
Huxham, Peter 40

I

International Police Exhibition 146, 156, 160
International Six Days Trial 66
Isle of Man 46, 59, 81, 84
Ivanisevio 190-1

J

Jackman, Roger 217
Jackson, Mike 194, 203, 206
Jackson, Syd 13
Jarman, Frank 30
Jefferies, Allan 26-7, 43, 66, 69, 70-2, 201

Index

Jefferies, Nick 75
Jefferies, Tony 73-4
Jensen, Sid 50, 62
Jofeh, Lionel 145, 163-5, 172-4, 178, 180
Johnson, Bill 103
Johnson Motors 96, 100
Jones, Alan 148
Jones, Brian 136, 166

K

Karam, Ali 227
Kavanagh, Ken 121
Kennedy, President 112
Kent Police 244
Kuwait Police 227

L

Laird, Henry 49
Lamb, Doug 11
Lancashire Police 178
Langhorn, Len 15
Lawton, Syd 46
Lees, 'Ginger' 13
Lewis, Jack 36
Lockett, Johnny 49, 168
Lodge Plugs 97
Longman, Frank 11
Loughborough, Tom 97, 100
Lowe, Maurice 59
Lucas Magnetos 97
Lynegaard, Jacob 170
Lyons, Ernie 44-9

M

Maggs, Gordon 240, 258
Majewski, Edmund 107
Mallory Park Circuit 88
Mangham, 'Stormy' 95, 99
Manio, Jack Di 112-4
Manns, Bob 65-6, 69
Mansell, Dennis 27
Manufacturer Liability 234
Manx Grand Prix 45
Marsh, Reg 37
Mason, Roy MP 124, 136
Matchless 350 G3L 17, 18
Mayne, Philip 97, 103
Mays, 'Spike' 122, 124
Mc Candless, Rex 46, 48
Mc Carthy, Pat 246
Mc Dermott, John 214
Mc Gregor, Bob 29, 33-4
Mc Intyre, Bob 43
Mc Kinsey Consultants 147-9, 153
Mc Queen, Steve 125
Merseyside Police 262
Metropolitan Police 80, 92, 107, 154, 158, 201, 248-9, 251, 253, 280, 287-8
Metro Police Special Escort Group 248, 259-62, 278
Mewis, Bill 27
Ministry of Defence 119, 169
Minskip, Dave 257
MIRA 154, 235
Mitchenall, Doug 80
Montlhery Circuit 57, 63
Moule, Albert 46, 47
Mussett, Frank 169

N

Nelson, John 292
Newdigate, Sir Francis 9, 10
New South Wales Police 166-7

Index

Nicholl, Leslie 110
Nielson, Cook 207, 211
Noe, Max 114
Norfolk Police 281
Nortier, Piet 97, 100, 103
Norton Atlas 184
Norton Interpol Chapter 13
Norton Isolastic 184
Norton Motors 136
Norton Villiers 182-3, 221
Norton Villiers Europe 223
Norton Villiers Triumph 227, 291
Nott, Ernie 10, 11, 27, 43, 63, 65, 85
NSU 96, 99
Nurdin, Frank 81, 84

221-2, 224, 237, 293
Poulo, Marcel 199, 213, 217
Pountney, George 9, 10
Price, Brenda 178-9
Prince Aziz 231
Princess Margaret 233
Pye Radio 157, 260

Q

Quantrill, Cyril 164
Queensland Police 167

O

Official Receiver 235
Osborne, Bernal 39, 130, 155, 164
Oulton Park Circuit 270

R

Radford, Norman 131
Ranch, Uno 67
Rawson, Bill 149, 169
Reinhardt, Carl 109
Reinhardt, Kim 209
Rickman Brothers 184
Robinson, Allan 212
Robinson, Geoffrey MP 241
Rogers, Charlie 27
Roussel, Ginette 197, 212-13
Roussel, Roland 197, 199, 206, 208, 217
Rowell, Bertie 46
Rowley, George 22
Royal Marines 157-8
Royal Netherlands Army 121
Royal Signals 126, 138, 140-43
Royal Ulster Constabulary 188
Rudge 350 Radial 12, 13
Rudge 500 Special 17
Rudge Whitworth 10, 11, 13
Ryerson, Barry 106, 134, 135

P

Palin, Hugh 178, 183, 184
Parker, Charles 24, 133, 137, 149, 164, 170-1, 174, 178-9
Parker, Jack 13
Parker, Norman 13
Parkhurst, Joseph 180
Pau University 216-17
Payne, Fred 76
Pechar, Art 13
Pedley, John 187, 232
Perrigo, Bert 27
Perry, Harry 27
Peterson, Axel 54
Plant, Nan 134
Police Review 186, 271
Poore, Dennis 137, 182, 186, 189,

Index

S

Sangster, Jack 24, 84-5, 88, 116, 133, 147, 154, 163
Saudi Arabian Defence Force 229, 247
Saunders, Bert 189
Saupe, Karl 159
Scobie, Alex 63-5, 69, 85
Scott, Sir Harold 91
Shearsmith, Joe 181
Shelsley Walsh 48
Shorey, Bert 153
Shorey, Dan 36, 93
Shortland, Jack 229
Simpson, Jimmy 15
Slocombe, Bill 39, 242
Small Heath 88
Smith, Alec 198
Smith, Gilbert 48, 136
Somen, Major 22
Spring, Nigel 48
Steel, Kenneth 188
Stephens, Eddie 28
Stockholm Show 174-5, 177
Stokvis Rotterdam 121, 158
Stratton, Harry 122
Sturgeon, Harry 148-56, 180
Styer, Richard 242
Surtees, John 40, 171-2, 193, 288
Sussex Police 186, Chapter 18
Suzuki 293
Swedish Army 125

T

Tait, Percy 85, 120-21, 138, 144, 155, 288
Tasmania Police 169
Taylor, Arthur 40
Taylor, Harold 65-6, 76
Taylor, Shaw 215
Texan Cigar 96, 100, 101
Thames Valley Police 254, 255
Thaw, John 245
Thom, Alex 28
Thomas, Clive 202
Thruxton Circuit 220, 254, 270
Tilley, Steve 85
Tomos Company 189
Tozer Kemsley & Milbourne 246
Trigg, Bob 186
Triumph Models:-
  Bonneville 94, 105, 139
  Grand Prix 45, 49
  Military 121, 124-5
  Saint 94, 104, 107-10, 114, 117, 166, 174
  Speed Twin 24, 68, 78, 80, 91, 293
  Terrier 93
  Thunderbird 57, 63, 67-8
  Tiger Cub 90, 292
  Tiger 90 292
  Tiger 100 24, 58, 68
  Tiger 110 82, 127
  Tigress Scooter 130
  Tina Scooter 144-5
  Trophy 68, 90
  TRW 80
  Twenty One 89
Triumph Owners Club 122, 176
Triumph Sprung Wheel 35, 68
Triumph Workers Co-Operative 228, 292
Triumph World Speed Record Chapter 7
Troberg, Picko 177
Truslove, Stan 59, 85
TT Marshals 81
Tubb, Syd 139
Turner, Edward 12, 23-4, 34-5, 41-2, 49, 50, 53, 56, 79, 87, 93, 96-7, 106, 116, 133, 134, 137, 147, 149, 163, 165, 237
Turner, Eric 88, 133
Tyrell Smith, H.G. 10, 11, 43, 63, 65

U

Umberslade Hall 166, 173

Index

V

Vanhouse, Norman 208
Varey, Frank 27, 66
Varley, Eric MP 232
Venables, Ralph 39
Vickers, Jonathan 217
Victoria Police 169

W

Walker, Graham 11, 25, 27, 43, 84
Walker, Leslie 240, 257
Warr, Fred 216
Warwickshire Police 184, 186
Watsonian Sidecars 23
West, Cyril 195
West Midlands Police 239, 279
Wheeler, Bob 131
Whistance, Ken 148
White, Bill 172
White, J.H. 27
Whitworth, David 43
Wickes, Jack 85
Williams, Alfred 27, 29, 36
Williams, Andrew 36
Williams, Eric 46
Williams, Jack 8, 12, 14, 16, 18, 27, 29, 36
Williams, Peter 220
Willis, Harold 59
Wilson, Jack 95, 99
Wood, 'Ginger' 27, 85
Woods, Stanley 25, 27, 46, 288
Wooldridge, A.J. 34
Wyatt, Wally 183-4

Y

Yamaha 172
Yapp, Sir Stanley 242